MW00527313

HERESY: SANDOR RADO AND THE PSYCHOANALYTIC MOVEMENT

PAUL ROAZEN, PH.D.
BLUMA SWERDLOFF, D.S.W.

JASON ARONSON INC.
Northvale, New Jersey
London

This book was set in 10 point Goudy by TechType of Upper Saddle River, New Jersey.

10 9 8 7 6 5 4 3 2 1

Library of Congress Cataloging-in-Publication Data

Rado, Sandor, 1890–1972
    Heresy : Sandor Rado and the psychoanalytic movement / Paul
Roazen, Bluma Swerdloff.
        p. cm.
    Oral history of Sandor Rado edited by Paul Roazen.
    Includes 36 letters written by Sigmund Freud to Rado.
    Includes bibliographical references and index.
    ISBN 1-56821-321-2
    1. Rado, Sandor, 1890–1972. 2. Psychoanalysts – Biography.
3. Psychoanalysis – History. 4. Freud, Sigmund, 1856–1939 –
Correspondence. 5. Rado, Sandor, 1890–1972 – Correspondence.
I. Roazen, Paul, 1936-   . II. Swerdloff, Bluma. III. Freud,
Sigmund, 1856–1939. IV. Title.
    [DNLM: 1. Rado, Sandor, 1890–1972. 2. Psychoanalysis – history –
personal narratives.   WZ 100 R131 1995]
    BF109.R33a3   1995
    150'.92 – dc20
    [B]
DNLM/DLC
for Library of Congress   94-21882

Manufactured in the United States of America. Jason Aronson Inc. offers books and cassettes. For information and catalog write to Jason Aronson Inc., 230 Livingston Street, Northvale, New Jersey 07647.

Contents

Preface

Oral history is as old as human civilization. People have always related personal experiences and events. Stories and myths are passed from one generation to the next, accumulating amendments and additions that reflect the life circumstances of each group. With the invention of tape recorders, collecting memoirs and living history of events gained popularity. In 1948, the first organized department of oral history was conceived by Pulitzer prize–winning Columbia University historian Allen Nevins.

The Oral History Office at Columbia never limits the lengths of interviews, so long as important information is gathered. The emphasis is on securing intimate material that generally would not be available in the public domain. Each interviewee has the option of keeping certain portions of the data from public view for a specific time period, usually 10 to 20 years.

Today many universities throughout the world have oral history archives. There is no longer any debate about the validity of oral history as history. It is readily recognized as a way of preserving vanishing, crucial source material that can be utilized by historians, scholars, researchers, and interested individuals. Recently, the present director of Columbia's Oral History Office, Ronald Grele, and the associate director, Mary Marshall Clark, reported that their collection now contains more than 6,000 taped memoirs and 600,000 pages of transcripts. Every year more than 2,500 scholars consult the materials, and 500 books have been written by a variety of professionals based on Columbia's oral history source material.

The philosophical approach to collecting oral history memoirs remains essentially the same as it was at the idea's inception. Below are excerpts from the most recent Oral History report, which are germane to understanding exactly what is being read when one begins to peruse an oral history memoir.

> Increasingly our work has focused on the life history or autobiographical approach to complement our more topical interviews. . . . Inclusive biographies offer us insights into the full life of the person and thereby provide a glimpse into the evolution of society, as well as the individual, in defining the context for later social and political actions. In many cases, these later actions can be understood as explained only by such subjective factors as belief systems, personal psychology, ideologies, visions and dreams. Life history interviewing is also resonant with recent developments in the historical profession and in other social science disciplines. In historical studies, most scholars now search for data about *motivation in order to gain a sense of either the interior life of social processes or an internal view of these processes. They seek information about the more complex processes of personality development,* the formation of political consciousness, and the intersection of action and belief. In the words of Jean-Paul Sartre, they are interested in what was "done to people but also in what people did with what was done to them." . . .
>
> Part of the action of cultural construction which allows people to create their own histories through their own activities has its origins in the attitudes and visions which motivate their actions. To understand their history, one must understand the processes by which such consciousness emerged, and the effects of consciousness on cultural construction. In oral history, that can best be done through the collection of biographical histories in which social, political and cultural history is illuminated through the telling of a life story. . . .
>
> Oral history is, in this sense, the quintessential historical text. Involving, as it does, historians and public figures in the creation of their own documents, oral history merges past and present in the dialectical transformation of text into cultural artifact. [italics mine] [p. 2]

This segment of the Oral History report has been included because it synchronizes well with Rado's insistence that his "adaptational framework for behavioral inquiry is interaction of the human organism and its cultural environment. Its immediate purpose is to discern the past shaped by the societal as well as the organismic mechanisms of motivation and control" (Rado 1960, p. 8). In his emphasis on motivation, Rado upheld one of Freud's original postulates as described in *The Interpretation of Dreams* and the early period of writings from 1890 to 1905. Of the six postulates of Freud's that Rado thought were the most enduring—motivation, pleasure seeking and pain avoidance, repression, mental mechanisms, mental apparatus, and evolutionary and individual history—the first, motivation, was considered by Rado to be the most important. Rado (1960) adds, "For centuries, men have used the point of view of motivation to understand, predict, and control human behavior. As Freud mentioned, he observed this point of view from the psychology of daily life. Motivation became the basis of his dynamic theory of mental activity" (p. 4).

I (BS) have reviewed some current biographies and books about the history of psychoanalysis, especially those that deal with the Berlin period, 1922–1931, to see how Rado's contributions were recorded. I found that Rado was most effectively written out of psychoanalytic history. A striking example is Peter Gay's 1988 biography of Freud. In the sections entitled "Vitality of the Berlin Spirit" and "Revisions 1915–1939" (pp. 460, 463, and 467), he discusses the popularity of the Berlin school in considerable detail. There are four brief references to Rado, which state that he was among the talented analysts who migrated to Berlin from Hungary, he was an analysand of Karl Abraham, he was among the analysts who left Berlin for the United States, and also a reference from a quote of Alix Strachey's amusing letter to her husband, James, in defense of "die Klein"—her reference to Melanie Klein. The letter states that Drs. Franz Alexander and Rado were the opposition, but that "speaker after speaker" rushed to "defend die Klein" and attack the "swarthy Hungarians." The truth was that Rado was loyally allying himself with Freud, who disapproved of the Kleinian theories, and was backing Anna Freud's version of child analysis.

Professor Gay taught at Columbia in the 1960s and discussed with me the four initial oral histories I had completed for the Psychoanalytic Movement Project. Yet Gay and other biographers, even with these materials at hand, discuss in detail figures lesser known than Rado; Rado essentially ceases to exist in their texts.

In Elisabeth Young-Bruehl's 1988 biography of Anna Freud,[1] the

1. See pp. 142, 149, 124–125. Cf. Reuben Fine, *The Development of Freud's Thought*, 1973, pp. 195, 255, 279. Rado is mentioned although merely as a "deviant." See p. 257. Phyllis Grosskurth, *The Secret Ring: Freud's Inner Circle and*

only mention of Rado is that he migrated to Berlin and that he was appointed editor of Freud's major journals when Otto Rank's relationship with Freud deteriorated after the publication of Rank's book, *The Trauma of Birth*. Anna Freud chose to say nothing about Rado's contributions.

From the same period, October 1929, there is also extant a short letter from Freud to an American psychoanalyst, Smith Ely Jelliffe. Answering Jelliffe's request that Freud see a friend of his, Freud wrote that poor health would prevent this and added:

> Alexander, as you know is most popular with American Doctors, he is excellent no doubt, but I can not see why he should have the privilege of instructing American doctors and why accomplished analysts like [Max] Eitingon, [Hanns] Sachs, Rado at Berlin or [Hermann] Nunberg or [Paul] Federn at Vienna should be left aside. [Burnham 1983, p. 229]

This book is an effort to place Rado in the history of psychoanalysis—the man and the evolution of his ideas.

The Oral History memoir reflects only some aspects of Rado's personality. The reader must remember that the dialogue of an interview is very different from a written document or formal debate. Rado's memoir, in particular, is a unique example of the difference between the written paper and verbal discourse. Rado was famous for his quick temper. As is evident in the memoir, these outbursts brought with them distortions and exaggerations. In addition, as he described his early activities in Budapest and Berlin, and later as educational director at the New York Psychoanalytic Institute, he often attributed his current views to descriptions of past events. As a result, his view of some events is sometimes distorted.

It is essential to remind the reader that this volume is not a biography of Rado, nor an exposition of his significant contributions to psychoanalytic theory and practice. It is also not a carefully researched tract. It is Rado's story as he perceived his work and includes only what he wished to reveal in our 300-page dialogue.

I have filled in some gaps to expand and clarify his story. This data has been gathered from other writers' books and articles, comments about

---

the Politics of Psychoanalysis, 1991, pp. 98, 126, 162, 164, 175n, 188, 204n. Grosskurth quotes from the Rado oral history but out of context, misrepresenting Rado's relationship with Ferenczi. They were not "old enemies" as she has it.

him by people who knew him personally, and some personal observations from my long contact with him.

I have also included as an appendix (see Appendix 1) Rado's own summation of his critique of Freudian theories. It is included because it acts, as Rado wrote it, as a succinct summary running parallel, at times, to some of the discussions in his oral history.

In my mind, Rado will be remembered as one whose passionate concern for his chosen field dominated his entire life. The hope is that this book will locate him in his rightful place in the history of the psychoanalytic movement.

Acknowledgments

My thanks go first to Louis M. Starr, director of the Oral History Office at Columbia University in the 1960s, who agreed to my starting the Psychoanalytic Movement Project, and who arranged funding for the first four oral histories. Sandor Rado was one of the first four psychoanalysts I interviewed. My gratitude also goes to Kurt Eissler, who directed me to the New Land Foundation, which made a generous grant to the Oral History Office that enables me to continue interviewing analysts in the United States and Europe.

Paul Roazen is no stranger to the techniques of oral history, having interviewed psychoanalysts for his many books. His remarking that the Sandor Rado memoir "cried out to be published" was the start of our collaboration. Roazen, a historian, is particularly sensitive to the fact that many contemporary historians and other writers respond to mainstream assessments, ignoring so-called heretics as though they never existed. His interest in writing about such individuals and recording their contributions has, at times, been erroneously characterized, especially by orthodox psychoanalysts, as being anti-Freud. In Roazen's books and articles, the dissidents' contributions to psychoanalysis are substantiated with carefully researched historical evidence. His own critical assessments have been subject to controversy, but his opinions are frankly expressed as his personal judgment. In no way does he belong to the current wave of Freud-bashers, who in the last decade have received undeserved notoriety. Rado is one of those who have been effectively written out of psychoanalytic history.

Roazen's find of thirty-six letters written by Freud to Rado, translated by Tom Taylor, gives ample proof of Freud's own appreciation of Rado's contributions in the first successful phase of Rado's psychoanalytic career. Prior to starting this book, I listened to several lectures delivered by Jacob Arlow at the Columbia University Psychoanalytic Center and at a seminar in Cape Cod. I became aware of the changes in his thinking about psychoanalytic concepts and treatment. As a result, I decided to interview him. These interviews were of value to me in writing my chapter on the future of psychoanalysis.

To Roger A. MacKinnon, the present director of the Columbia University Psychoanalytic Center since 1991, I want to express my thanks for a series of interviews in which he shared his thinking about the current status of psychoanalysis and his plans for research, which continue in the Rado tradition of subjecting psychoanalysis to acceptable scientific methodology.

Above all, I am indebted to Rado, not only for the time, during the mid-1960s, that we spent working together and taping his memoir but also for having had the privilege of auditing his lectures and seminars. I maintained contact with him from 1947, when I first became a member of the staff at the Columbia University Psychoanalytic Clinic for Training and Research, until his illness and death in 1972. I had hoped to interview him further and fill in the gaps in the recorded memoir. Although this never came about, my memory is replete with many images of Rado–his vitality, his capacity for pleasure, his ability to transform everything he talked about into an exciting experience, and the contrapuntal quality of the amazing contradictions that made up his personality.

In retrospect, I am impressed by the profundity of his ideas and his ability to predict thirty years ago both the problems and the potentials of psychoanalysis in the future.

It was difficult sometimes to get Rado to answer questions about his personal life. He effectively evaded certain queries by simply pretending not to hear them at all or by conversing about whatever came to mind. I am therefore grateful to his sons, Peter and George Rado, for providing some personal history that would have otherwise been unpreserved.

I would also like to thank Eric Elshtain for his help in transcribing the material and proofreading the text, and especially Joy Hornick for reading the manuscript with a fresh eye and editing it and pointing out unclear concepts and grammatical errors.

                                                                       –Bluma Swerdloff
                                                                       March 1995

PART I

INTRODUCTION

by Bluma Swerdloff

Two words, *controversy* and *ambivalence*, generally characterized discussions of either Sandor Rado's contributions to psychoanalysis or the nature of his personality. Controversy arose because many of his ideas and concepts were ahead of their time. They did not fit in with the historical development of psychoanalysis, which was then still very much under the firm leadership of Freud himself. Some of Rado's theoretical ideas have now been substantiated by new data and are beginning to be accepted. Others are still being debated, but these discussions generate less heat and vituperation.[1]

Controversy arose because of Rado's complex and contradictory personality. He was passionately and stubbornly committed to what he

1. See Bluma Swerdloff, "A Historical Portrait of Sandor Rado," *Bulletin of the Association for Psychoanalytic Medicine*, 1986, 25(3/4): 118–126. Cf. Franz Alexander, "Sandor Rado: The Adaptational Theory," in *Psychoanalytic Pioneers*, Franz Alexander, Samuel Eisenstein and Martin Grotjahn, eds. 1966, pp. 240–248. Good discussions on Rank and Ferenczi are also in this book. See also Howard Davidman, "The Contributions of Sandor Rado to Psychodynamic Science," in *Science and Psychoanalysis*, J. H. Masserman, ed. 1964, pp. 17–38. See discussion by Harold Lief, p. 35. Other articles that contain discussions about the evolution of the Columbia University Psychoanalytic Center, along with other books and articles by and about Rado, are included in the bibliography.

believed in but was impatient and pugnacious if his ideas were not quickly understood or accepted. These qualities of his engendered hostility and led to opposition to his concepts as well. He aroused ambivalence because it was difficult to refute his logical, concise, lucid, and brilliantly organized exposition. Yet accepting many of his ideas required restructuring previously held dictums and some basic, long-held, cherished concepts as well. Specialists and catalysts for change know how painful and slow a process change can be – how resistant and defensive one can become. Though Rado himself railed against closed systems, stressing that scientific growth required a flow of ideas and free discussion to lead to a modification or change, he tended to be dictatorial and authoritarian. Some see Rado as a major figure in the psychoanalytic movement. Many more would see him in this light had he been better able to put into practice what he so keenly believed – that authoritarianism is a poor bedfellow for scientific inquiry. At the core of his wish to reform and change psychoanalysis was his constant, urgent desire to transform it into a scientific discipline under the aegis of medicine.

In the classroom he was a spellbinder. It was difficult not to believe every word he said, so convincing were his lectures. Only away from his presence was it possible to rethink and evaluate his expositions. He would occasionally stun his students by quoting Freud verbatim, adding the page number from which he cited. He was a formidable adversary. At a memorial meeting honoring Rado, held in February 1973, Willard Gaylin, one of Rado's students who continues to acknowledge Rado's influence on him and his career, described "Rado the Teacher":

> He was exhilarating but exhausting. He was intimidating but inspiring. He was evangelical and irreverent. He was impatient, intolerant, exacting, explosive, insatiable, acerbic, exasperating, contentious, and Hungarian. He was, however, never patronizing. He was never pompous. He was never pedestrian, and thank God, he was never a bore. [p. 10]

Another of his grateful students recollected years later that he never imagined that his first class as a psychoanalytic candidate would begin with Descartes.

Even the students who found Rado's new ideas inimical to their classical orientation recognized that his interests were broad and important in scope. In addition to concentrating on psychoanalysis, he kept up with the literature of neuroscience and biological, medical, and genetic findings as well as developments in scientific methodology.

At professional meetings he is best described by Franz Alexander, a contemporary of his at the Berlin Institute and a long-time friend in The United States. In his 1966 book *Psychoanalytic Pioneers*, he wrote:

> From the first Rado demonstrated his unusual organizational talent and leadership qualities – persuasiveness in debate, determination, and that amount of stubbornness that leadership requires . . . [H]e became a formidable debater – usually succeeding in rapidly ferreting out the weak spots in his opponent's argument. In polemics, he was terse, to the point, logical to the utmost, and often devastating. Although this did not contribute to universal popularity, even his enemies respected his brilliant cognitive abilities. [p. 241]

Rado's writing is similarly terse, his papers rarely exceeding twenty pages. Every few sentences a new idea was elucidated, sometimes in a startlingly different fashion. The result was sometimes difficult to absorb, requiring rereading and considerable thought.

In social situations Rado's presence generated excitement and he always became the focus of attention. He amused his colleagues and students with anecdotes and witticisms, often laughing merrily at stories he considered to be psychoanalytic absurdities. At these gatherings it was obvious that he appreciated good food and enjoyed it with gusto.

Whatever his shortcomings, Rado was a man capable of enjoying life on his own terms. It has often been said that among the early generation of psychoanalysts were some flawed giants. Rado belongs to their camp. But it is an error to see him as an eccentric caught up in the malaise of his emotional states. His many accomplishments prove the contrary.

The best source for Rado's theoretical contributions is his collected papers, compiled in two volumes and entitled *Psychoanalysis and Behavior* (Rado 1956).[2]

Rado's career can be divided into two phases. The first, from roughly 1913 to the early 1940s, represents his contribution to classical psychoanalysis. When he graduated medical school in Budapest in 1915, he was already deeply involved in his psychoanalytic career. Under the mentorship of Sandor Ferenczi, he met Freud and became one of the founders of

---

2. Rado's *Adaptational Psychodynamics: Motivation and Control* (1969) is a volume based on transcripts of his lectures available to the editors. Rado wrote brief introductions prior to his illness; the rest was written without his aid.

the Budapest Psychoanalytic Society. In 1922 he moved to Berlin, where he achieved his greatest success.

In the Berlin Psychoanalytic Institute, Rado was considered one of the most brilliant theoreticians expounding Freud's theories. A teacher who easily engaged his students' adherence, Rado was also sought after as a psychoanalyst. Some of his analysands later became well known in their own right, among them Heinz Hartmann, Rene Spitz, George Gero, Otto Fenichel, and Wilhelm Reich (whom Rado diagnosed as being psychotic and saw only briefly). Many of his analysands later disassociated themselves from Rado when he was considered a heretic. Gero, however, at the 1973 memorial to Rado paid homage to him even though he found it hard to agree with all of his new formulations. He stated that Rado "had the ability to clarify complex concepts with great lucidity" and that "my [analysis] with Sandor enabled me to make fundamental discoveries about myself which later helped me understand my patients. . . . For this aid to me in this regard, I shall always remember Sandor with gratitude and affection" (p. 4).

During this period Rado (1956) also wrote a number of classic papers that are still quoted by both psychiatrists and psychoanalysts: "The Psychic Effects of Intoxicants," an attempt to evolve a psychoanalytic theory of morbid cravings (drug addiction), and "The Problem of Melancholia," a paper on depression. The subject matter of these two significant papers illustrates Rado's keen ability to discern what would become focal issues in the future and to tailor psychoanalysis to meet these challenges. Even during his early orthodox period he never departed from his determination to follow and absorb medical and biological findings. From the first, he had a sophisticated view of evolution in relation to psychoanalytic theory. His thinking was rooted in the concept that the complexity of humans evolved through the emergence of integrative levels of organization in which the whole was more than its parts. Although this formulation became clearer to Rado later on, his biological orientation and consistent interest in brain and mind were the early tenets for his later concepts, which seemed so revolutionary to his more orthodox colleagues.

It is reasonable to conjecture that some of his discontents with what he thought was the "mythology" of psychoanalysis would have emerged sooner had he not been highly gratified by Freud's choosing him as editor of the *Internationale Zeitschrift für Psychoanalyse* and, later, *Imago*. This indicated to Rado Freud's trust in him, although it aroused jealousies from others, particularly from the Vienna group. It also generated in Rado an even greater sense of loyalty to Freud and increased his emotional tie to him. The trait Rado regarded most highly was creativity, and Freud and his discoveries embodied this ideal.

The vitality of the Berlin school and Rado's astute political aware-ness were also contributing factors to his success from 1922 to 1931. Rado came to Berlin when the Austro-Hungarian Empire was in the throes of the disintegration that ended in the fascist regime of Horthy in Hungary. Rado chose Germany as his new homeland because during the Weimar Republic Germany was, in the words of Gero (1973), "a place of great intellectual stimulation and vigor. The Psychoanalytic Institute in Berlin became one of the leading institutes in psychoanalytic training" (p. 5). This atmosphere of creativity and the leadership role he played in the shaping of the Berlin Institute were great boosts for an already flourishing Rado, who thrived there.

Rado describes this early and happy period in the oral history. Though at times he exaggerates his role, nonetheless he accurately illumi-nates the ambience of the era.

Rado arrived in the United States in 1931 to become educational director of the New York Psychoanalytic Institute on the invitation of A.A. Brill, then president of the Institute. A number of calm and unified years ensued. Simultaneously, other honored European psychoanalysts emigrated to escape Hitler's growing power in Germany and Austria. They became the controlling group. Jacob Arlow (1991) has written an amusing paper, read at the eightieth anniversary of the New York Psychoanalytic Society, describing how the American students perceived the newcomers: they were seen as living embodiments of Freud himself, and their teachings and analyses were unquestioned. Brill selected Rado because he wanted Rado to organize the institute along the lines of the Berlin model. Some of the Europeans also imported a Germanic, authoritarian view of the "professor." This suited Rado and he maintained his orthodox views up to 1935, when he had his rift with Freud. After the rift, Rado decided that he no longer needed to keep his early discontents to himself and began to introduce his own ideas into his lectures and into his supervising activities. This presaged the end of the first phase of his career as a revered, orthodox psychoanalyst. He retained his title as educational director until his dismissal in 1941. Subsequently, he was also dismissed as a training analyst. He did retain his membership in the New York Society, though he stopped attending meetings. Later on, he submitted his resignation. He remained a member of the International Psychoanalytic Association.

The general theory is that the catalyst for Rado's criticisms of Freudian theory and the development of his own theoretical system was his break with Freud. This, of course, neglects other contributing factors, such as his keen intelligence, his broad cultural interests, and his ability to absorb knowledge from other disciplines available to him during his lifetime. His wish to have psychoanalysis become part of medicine was known by both Ferenczi and Freud from the very beginning. Rado's belief was that this would ensure the scientific basis of Freud's discoveries and would allow for changes in theory when new scientific data were available from the adjacent sciences. Although he learned much about psychoanalysis from Ferenczi, Rado never felt that there was any merit in his abstract evolutionary hypotheses. He does credit Ferenczi with introducing the biological concept of adaptation through his distinctions between autoplastic and alloplastic processes.

Currently, there is much interest in Ferenczi and also Otto Rank, especially in a monograph that they wrote together. Many psychoanalysts accept their view that the analyst's personality, experience, and human responses to a patient's realistic sorrows are an important part of the analytic process. Rank's emphasis on trauma later became valuable to analytic theory, but his birth trauma theory was, for Rado as well as others, a scientific absurdity.

Ferenczi's co-authorship with Rank, after Freud's criticism of Rank and some of Ferenczi's differences regarding the therapeutic stance of the analyst, cast the first shadow on Ferenczi's reputation and close friendship with Freud. The book written with Rank emphasized analysis as an emotional experience in contrast to Freud's more intellectual approach (Ferenczi and Rank 1986). Ferenczi, whom Rado described as a warm, intuitive person, was also subject to enthusiasms that, for Rado and others, tended to undermine common sense and reason.

Ferenczi died a few years later, in 1933, from pernicious anemia. Rado gave a laudatory obituary speech at the American Psychiatric Association and later published it. Rado maintained that Freud, under the influence of his daughter Anna, found exception to his kind words about Ferenczi and wrote his own, less warm, obituary notice. Anna Freud, Rado believed, was more and more resolved to be the protector of Freudian psychoanalysis and resented the dissidents with more fervor than her father.

Throughout his life, Rado never resolved his strong emotional tie to Freud. Prior to the break in their personal relationship, Rado visited Freud every summer and out of loyalty to him kept whatever criticisms he had to himself. Even after the rift, when he altered or abandoned some of Freud's theories, he always tried to find excuses for what he considered Freud's errors. Perhaps Rado's silence was also a way of remaining in Freud's favor—a desire shared by most of Freud's loyal followers. Rado was also keenly aware of the disappearance of Carl Jung, Alfred Adler, Rank, and Wilhelm Stekel from the psychoanalytic movement when theoretical differences arose between them and Freud.

Even though in his oral history Rado confuses his past and present discontents, his teaching in Berlin followed Freud's theories as gospel. It was not possible to be an important member of so influential an organization and not succumb to its emotional hold.

Another contributing factor to the break was the sense of isolation and hostility that Freud felt toward the large number of his followers, including Rado, who migrated to the United States. Freud seemed to deny the growing danger of anti-Semitism and believed that the exodus of important followers was premature, while Rado and his wife Emmy helped many colleagues to migrate to the United States. It is well known that Freud's visit to the United States left him with considerable disdain and the conviction that the European culture was more receptive to his ideas and to his desire to maintain a strong cohesive psychoanalytic movement.

The cause for the complete rift between Freud and Rado was the critical review of Rado's article "The Fear of Castration in Women" by Jeanne Lampl-de Groot, an analysand of Freud. Rado was convinced that Freud shared her critical opinion. He believed that the enormous amount of work he had put into his editorship of Freud's major journals was now inconsequential to his mentor. Rado's degree of anguish, sense of betrayal, and regret that he had kept his own disagreements and discontents unexpressed are verified by Helene Deutsch's description of this episode, which is reported in Roazen's comprehensive biography. In 1935, Deutsch wrote to her husband, Felix, afraid that Rado was "in a beginning phase of a psychosis." He was

> obsessed with Lampl's report—in fury-filled hatred against everything and everyone connected with it. So far one would think only of an excessive reaction of someone severely narcissistically offended. But this hatred extends in a paranoid manner to the rest of the surrounding world: the society, the city of Vienna, all of Europe. All cultural values that are "European," and which in him were so pronounced, are met with furious disdain, and are contrasted, in ridiculous chauvinism, with America. . . . Professor [Freud] becomes an evil old man who wants to destroy him with his hatred. All of us around him are either crooks, or mental cases under Professor's spell and in his service, etc. [Roazen 1992a, p. 282]

She implored her husband, Felix, who was in Vienna at the time, to talk with Anna Freud in order to forestall "the outbreak" and ask her to keep the review from being published. Felix replied that he had done so, "but since he [Rado] is in the wrong there is no mercy. . . . It's hard against hard and Rado will come out the loser" (p. 283).

Obviously, the Deutsches were not aware of the volatility of Rado's outbursts of anger. In the spirit of oral history's philosophy that anecdotal material often sheds light on important aspects of an individual's traits, I will describe an occasion when I witnessed Rado's short fuse.

I offered to deliver some written material to Rado from the Columbia University Psychoanalytic Clinic to his home. We chatted for a short time and as I got ready to leave Rado looked at the pages I had brought him. To my astonishment his face turned reddish purple. He paced rapidly the length of the room shouting invectives. I heard myself say meekly, "Dr. Rado, I'm afraid you'll get a heart attack." He stopped short, a benign expression on his face, walked over to me, kissed my forehead and told me not to be frightened. He then returned to his outburst. I left quite sure that after a while he would calm down, sit at his desk and edit objectively and effectively the pages that annoyed him so much.

Rado was neither paranoid nor psychotic, but he was prone to outbursts, which he would gain control over sooner or later. His vitality, ambition, and energy counteracted his rage. His oral history reveals many moments of anger and severe criticism of those who disagreed with him. It needs to be added that the attacks on Rado by his early colleagues and other orthodox psychoanalysts were equally vicious. His decision to dispense with libido theory and the structural hypothesis and to amend the use of transference was, indeed, a bombshell. No psychoanalytic journal would dream of publishing such heresy.

The most persistent attack, however, focused on the erroneous conclusion that Rado did not believe in transference as an integral part of psychoanalytic technique. Rado believed that interpreting all of a patient's current life events as transference was a form of overkill. It tended to infantilize adult patients and encourage their fantasies that the analyst and analysis would somehow solve their problems without any effort on their own part.

Like other dissidents, Rado believed that he was a true Freudian saving Freud's extraordinary contributions to the understanding of human behavior by separating his seminal contributions from later methodological errors. Rado feared that dogma and the unquestioned acceptance of all Freud's theories would nullify Freud's early reputation as a scientist and turn psychoanalysis into a cult.

A brief description of what has been referred to as *The Civil War* in American psychoanalysis in the 1940s may serve as a confirmation of Rado's and other analysts' views that psychoanalytic theory needed to be reassessed and revised.

As we examine the many papers in this time period that recollect the whole series of splits and splits within splits, two questions can be raised. What were the precipitating factors? In addition, if many similar ideological discontents were shared by each group, why did they not unite? Instead they formed separate schools of training, ignoring their similarities and focusing on their differences.

Although Rado and his group of colleagues and followers were not the first to leave the New York Psychoanalytic Institute, for a number of reasons Rado was treated as one of the most heretical and dangerous defectors. The classicists focused their sharpest and most vicious attack on him. The status he had previously enjoyed in Berlin and the United States as one of the most influential orthodox psychoanalysts probably added to their anger.

The discontents and, finally, the rebellion are carefully documented by some faculty and students of psychoanalysis who were active in the early 1940s. From all the articles written and papers presented at psychoanalytic conferences, I (BS) have found three reports to be most revealing and/or objective. John Frosch's (1991) article, "The New York Psychoanalytic Civil War," Marianna Horney Eckardt's (1978) thoughtful article, "Organizational Schisms in American Psychoanalysis," and George Daniels' (1971) detailed, calm description of both the break and the maneuvers that, after four years, won the change in the American Psychoanalytic Association's bylaws to permit the organization of other training institutes under their aegis. Previously, only one training institute was permitted to function in any given city. It is Daniels who is the unsung hero of the lengthy negotiations. He was able to control Rado's impatience and anger.

There were schisms not only in America but in Europe as well, with each group maintaining that they were not abandoning Freud's concepts but clarifying them. Each group defined Freud's language and writings to suit cultural variations. This is substantiated in *The Freudians: A Contemporary Perspective* (1989), by sociologist Edith Kurzweil. Differences in conceptualization, technique, and language were the major causes of the emergence of dissidents, who either added new ideas or, as Rado maintained, separated Freud's scientific theories from Freud's "poetic imagination."

In the New York area, rumblings of discontent by both faculty and students began in the mid-1930s. The first defection by the Karen Horney group in 1941 was followed by others, all of whom resented the dogmatism and authoritarianism of the mainstream organizations. The leading, controlling group found any deviation a threat to psychoanalysis as they conceived it. The result was infighting, dismissal of faculty members, and discrimination against the analysands and supervisees of the dissidents.

The disaffected members organized into a variety of different groups and began planning their various strategies. In Rado's group were the major founders of the Columbia Psychoanalytic Clinic: Abram Kardiner, Daniels, and David Levy. All three resented what they considered was the *closed system*, which did not permit them to develop their own ideas and interests. Soon after Nathan Ackerman, George S. Goldman also joined them. Viola Bernard had been working with Daniels at the Columbia-Presbyterian Hospital prior to the formation of the clinic. She joined the faculty, as did Henriette Klein, who had been working in the Department of Psychiatry since the 1930s.

The 1940s seemed ripe for the schisms. The original reverence for the European psychoanalysts, who tried to maintain their control over the New York Institute, had subsided. Some of the younger psychoanalysts had their own ambitions and a desire to participate more fully in the inner workings of the institute. The men who interrupted their training because of the war and returned to complete their studies were more mature and less intimidated by their teachers. A fair proportion of students followed the dissidents because they shared their discontents. The very nature of psychoanalytic training also creates strong adherence from students to their analysts and supervisors.

It is difficult to pinpoint exactly why the various groups did not make efforts to unite. Each one had its specific leader who seemed unable to find enough common ground to unite with any one of the others. Personality differences seemed to be a major reason for the disunity. Each leader preferred to define psychoanalysis according to his or her own concepts.

Of the hostile attacks against Rado, the most devastating and influential was a 1957 scholarly review of Rado's collected papers by Edward Glover. An excellent writer and a man of integrity who was highly regarded in Great Britain and Europe, Glover contended that Rado's drastic changes in psychoanalytic language and his disagreement with some basic Freudian concepts precluded his being considered a psychoanalyst. This was quickly picked up by other Rado detractors. As a result, Rado, his colleagues, and even Columbia Clinic graduates found analytic journals closed to their papers and the psychoanalytic congresses and meetings unamenable to their participation.

Early in 1941 Rado started plans for a new home in which to expound his ideas without obstacles. His dream was that this should take place under medical auspices, and Columbia gave him that opportunity. It was facilitated by the fact that Daniels was already part of the Columbia-Presbyterian faculty and was especially interested in psychosomatic medicine. Daniels was highly respected in the field of psychiatry and psychoanalysis and was modest, patient, and well liked. He had been supervised by Rado in Berlin while simultaneously being analyzed by Franz Alexander. Rado's ideas were not well known to Daniels or the other founders of the Columbia Psychoanalytic Clinic because of Rado's scant publications. Daniels, as well as the other co-founders, disliked the authoritarianism of the New York Institute. Daniels' role seemed to be the glue that kept the "mavericks" in line.

The founding group began to plan their strategies. It was Daniels who envisioned the advantage of remaining part of the American Psychoanalytic Association. This would ensure that the future graduates of the new institute would not be totally isolated from the mainstream.

Prior to the establishment of the Columbia University Clinic, the founders decided to start an independent forum for free discussion open to other interested psychoanalysts and qualified mental health professionals. It was to be a separate entity, friendly with but not subject to the Clinic's authority. This later became the Association for Psychoanalytic Medicine and is still in existence. The formation of this separate but friendly association attracted adherents to the Clinic. It became the facility where clinic graduates as well as other interested professionals could introduce new ideas without retribution.

Nolan Lewis, an analyst and director of the Psychiatric Institute and also a faculty member of the medical school—Physicians & Surgeons— aided the establishment of the Clinic by giving it a home at the Psychiatric Institute. Both the dean of the medical school of Physicians & Surgeons and the influential chairman of the Department of Internal Medicine were actually in opposition to psychoanalysis. But a patient of Rado's knew the provost and some members of the board of Columbia-Presbyterian. She was willing to use her influence on behalf of the new clinic. Rado did not mention in his memoir that $100,000 was also donated to Columbia-

Presbyterian at this time. The identity of the mystery donor was recently uncovered by Craig Tomlinson, a candidate at the Center, who has an interest in history. In looking over some old files left by Daniels, he found a clipping from *The New York Sun* dated May 2, 1944. The clipping reported that a young Air Force lieutenant, accidentally killed in India, left two million dollars to be contributed to medical and educational institutions. His name was Lester N. Hofheimer. How this information became available to Daniels is unknown. However, this foundation allocated a 3-year budget for the new clinic. The total amount granted came to $100,000.

Rado related a parallel story in his oral history, though ironically he seemed quite unaware of its relationship to this financial bonanza. He recalled that Freud's professorship was aided by a patient who had university contacts. She donated a valuable painting to the state, which in return gave Freud his desired professorship.

The Columbia Clinic was organized along medical school lines. There were four services: the children's, the psychosomatic, the psychotherapeutic, and the analytic. Rado called the latter two *reparative* and *reconstructive*, respectively. His faculty consisted of psychoanalysts, often of Hungarian origin, who taught classical analysis. He had no choice because no one was cognizant of his innovative theories. Rado taught those himself. His plan was to replace the classicists when he had more graduates who were trained in Radovian theory—and he did exactly that. There were some discontented students, and a few of them withdrew from the Clinic. Others met in secret groups to air their dissatisfactions, but on the whole there were no serious schisms. Even the dissatisfied students remained until graduation and then pursued more classical careers.

In addition to including other disciplines in the curriculum, such as genetics, biology, neurology, animal experimental studies, and research psychology, Rado also presented selected patients before his classes, as is done in medical schools. Because the Clinic's fees were so low, the patients readily agreed to this requirement for their acceptance for treatment. Few presentations had any adverse effects. Rado was extremely sensitive in his interviews. Gaylin (1973) wrote that "he was gentle, he was kind, he was a model of the way we would have wanted to be treated had we been the patient" (p. 10).

Rado periodically brought in nonclinic patients to illustrate specific diagnostic categories or specific issues he wanted to elucidate. These striking and divergent demonstrations illustrated Rado's teaching innovations and his concept of what a clinic under medical aegis should and could do.

No one could deny that his leadership created excitement, even though his personality also tended to provoke antagonisms. His years at the clinic were, by his own admission, the happiest period in his career.

Simultaneously he started to expand his theoretical framework. He began to write papers on his theory of adaptational psychodynamics, which were published in nonpsychoanalytic journals. Rado's desire to stimulate research was, to some degree, thwarted by the fact that he himself was not trained in research. The students who came to the clinic from medical school had also little training in research methodology. Only a few students were interested in actually pursuing a career in research. As a result, the Columbia Clinic of Training and Research remained, mainly, a training institute for the practice of psychoanalysis and psychotherapy.

During Rado's leadership of the Columbia Clinic and after his retirement in 1955, attacks on him continued. What differentiated Rado from other theoreticians and contributors to Freud's theories was his tailoring of his concepts of adaptational psychodynamics and treatment to new findings from brain research. He believed that this new data would add to or detract from analytic theories, and therefore his adaptational psychodynamics was geared to include such new data. The brain, he argued, was the matrix for the mind, awareness, and the unconscious. In Radovian language, the last two terms become the *reporting* and *nonreporting* activities of the brain. Motivation, the desire for survival and pleasure, enhanced an individual's capacity to make efforts to improve and deal with life's exigencies, a capacity Rado called the *action self*.

One advantage that the other dissidents had over Rado was that their written material was not only understandable to psychoanalysts but also to the general public. Rado, a talented writer, stubbornly refused to subject his concepts to journalistic language. He geared his investigations toward other scientific disciplines, and often his writings were difficult to comprehend. Rado seemed to keep himself poised in a waiting stance, fearful that his ideas might need to be altered to better reflect whatever new knowledge became available. He constantly edited and modified his collected papers, never writing a definitive opus that clearly defined his divergent ideas.

Rado's detractors were also encouraged by the awareness that their techniques produced improvements in their patients. Rado contended, as did a number of writers in their articles—including George Klein's (1973) "Two Theories or One?"—that theory remained separate from the actual practice of psychoanalysis. Undoubtedly, the more sensitive analysts would respond to the needs of their patients, even if it necessitated disregard for their own published theoretical views.

Just as Rado, early in his career, wanted to be part of the mainstream, some members of the Columbia group pulled away from Rado's camp. At the same time, classical institutes became less dogmatic. The creation of more than one institute allowed for the free movement of faculty and graduate students among different institutes. As time went on, psychoanalysis ceased to be a cause. Students wanted analytic institutes to teach them to be practicing analysts. Rado's and the other founders' contributions were gradually erased from the curriculum as "new" ideas took the fore.

In 1955, Rado reached 65, Columbia University's mandatory retirement age, and was obliged to leave the Clinic. However, he had great plans for a similar center, which he established and which opened shortly thereafter as the New York School of Psychiatry at Ward's Island. His objective was to train psychiatrists in psychoanalytic methods. A number of loyal followers left Columbia to work with him. He procured grants from governors Averill Harriman and Nelson Rockefeller. Rado also served for several years on the New York Mental Hygiene Council. He lectured at various universities that were interested in a clinical addition to their psychiatric training. Rado's friendship with and influence on Adolf Meyer of Johns Hopkins is described in detail in the oral history.[3]

The project on Ward's Island, however, never achieved what Rado had intended. He suffered several small strokes, which exacerbated his irritability and impatience, making him difficult to work with. Finally he suffered the major stroke that ended his career. It was so sad to see the man with the photographic memory remember nothing.

For the psychoanalysts who were able to overlook Rado's flaws, his influence persists. His extraordinary, broad knowledge, his unusual talent as a teacher, his ability to expound his views, and his unswerving dedication to transform psychoanalysis into a scientific discipline left an indelible effect. Rado's career and life, as described by him in his memoir, posits the necessary ingredients for growth: an open mind to new ideas along with the courage to assess and question not only Freud's contributions but Rado's and others' as well.

---

3. See Nathan G. Hale, Jr., *Freud amid the Americans*, 1971, for more information on Adolf Meyer.

PART II

ORAL HISTORY OF SANDOR RADO

Edited by Paul Roazen

1

GROWING UP IN HUNGARY

Features of my own biography had an influence on my psychoanalytic work and indirectly, therefore, on the development of psychoanalysis. I was born (1890) in northeastern Hungary, in a small provincial town of about 10,000, which had and still retains the name of Kisvarda; it is 360 kilometers away from Budapest. When I was last there in 1934 the population had remained about the same; but anybody who was capable of doing anything left. The village itself is today a part of Hungary, but to the north is now the boundary toward Czechoslovakia and a succession of

Editor's note: I have cut redundancies, reorganized everything into individual chapters, and smoothed out the grammar. Repetitions were meaningful to me in underlining what Rado thought was most important, but they had to go. Sometimes Rado made flip or polemical judgments which I do not think he would want to stand the test of time, so I have exercised my own editorial prerogative in omitting what I thought did not deserve to be preserved in public. I recommend that specialists might want to consult for themselves the original transcripts, now available for inspection. Originally Rado had asked that certain portions of these interviews be closed for varying periods of years, but now everything he had to say can be freely examined. I wish I could be clearer about my own standards of selection from the whole manuscript, which runs to some 317 typed pages. I have tried to include everything that I believe will be permanently interesting in what Rado had to say. (PR) other countries. This was not the case at the time of my birth, when the Hungarian border was considerably further away.

What I know about my family's past concerns chiefly the history of my mother. My father's father died when he was 5 or 6, and he was brought up by a stepfather. So that he knew little about his father, and I learned virtually nothing. My parents were well-to-do, middle-class people. My mother's family lived in the place where I spent my early years and they remained there, while my father came from a much larger city — Novarad. When I was born, my mother's parents were still alive. I was told that my maternal grandfather carried me in his arms. I was the first grandchild, and my mother was their first child. They had another daughter, about two years younger, who married away from that part of the country. My mother adored her father, and throughout my early life I heard of no one else as much as I was told by her about my grandfather. His father, so my mother reported, was some sort of Jewish scholar, not a rabbi. My mother's grandfather made wise remarks, told them to my grandfather, and he repeated them to my mother, who reported them to me. My mother's father, a businessman like my other grandfather, died of appendicitis when I was about 1 year old; he was 50 or 51. My mother's mother remained alive, was a member of our family, and died sometime during World War I. I remember coming home to her funeral wearing a military uniform.

My mother was a brilliant woman. Her memory was phenomenal; my own capacities for recall, remarkable enough as we shall see in the early days of the history of psychoanalysis, were nothing compared to hers. She would sit and talk, saying: "On February so-and-so, 1886, I remember it was a gray Wednesday morning, around ten, and Uncle such-and-such arrived." Everybody was struck by that characteristic trait of hers. She had what I can call retrospectively an unemployed intelligence. She went to all the facilities that were open to a woman, which meant that after grammar school there were four-to-six years of finishing school for her. That any girl then should go to the places which existed for boys was inconceivable.

Within the household she had plenty of domestic servants, so she had little to do. She must have read six to eight hours a day. She ate up books — one or two novels a day were nothing for her. That reading went on steadily with the exception of the summer and fall, when supplies had to be conserved for the winter. If you wanted to eat anything beyond what you could get in the winter, you had to preserve it yourself. So we had hundreds of bottles of every kind of fruit. As soon as the fruit was ripe, preserving began on a large scale; from then on it was no longer a home but a production unit. And since we had four children, two parents, a governess, and my grandmother, it defies my description to know how many bottles of each thing were prepared. The food had to be cooked, then cooled, and I watched this as a child.

My mother was an excellent housewife, and the central domestic activity she was concerned with at that time was the preparation of food for the winter. When the fall came, and the problem was only to watch out to see nothing happened to the preserves, she settled down again and read. She consumed every newspaper and book she could get her hands on.

There was a club in Kisvarda, and it had a library. I imagined that there was not a page in that library she had not read; I myself examined the whole little library there, most of it in German, for the simple reason that not so many Hungarian books existed. My mother also bought books; she read Hungarian and German, though not much French that I can recall. But this was on her part a cultivation of romanticism. These works were all fiction, short stories, and novels. She had a remote respect for science and scientists, but I am unable to conjecture what she thought science was. The newspapers then did not have science writers, and the magazines we read were wholly literary. The basis of her knowledge of science must have been the multiplication table, what doctors can do, buildings, and new engines—that sort of thing. I do not remember ever seeing one volume in that house that would have been in the neighborhood of a scientific subject. At school the same thing was true; it was all belles lettres, Hungarian and German, but my mother did talk of scientific discoveries.

My mother could discuss Tolstoy and Dostoevsky, although she did not tell me much about her reading. The historical knowledge she had was chiefly derived from having read histories of a modern sort, going back to the Enlightenment. From her I first heard the name of Voltaire, about the French Revolution, and the various upheavals in Germany and Hungary. But she was on uneven ground, without a systematic school knowledge.

To me the nicest thing was that by the time my grandmother died I was already a doctor. When the change took place from my being at first a social scientist, my mother was unhappy with me. She did not understand the alteration in my career plans. She would tell me: "You know, I am ashamed. People ask me what you are going to be, and although I always thought a lawyer, now I have to say 'a doctor.' What sort of man is that who changes his mind? Will anyone ever give you his daughter as a wife?" She was worried that I appeared too unstable, but by World War I, when everyone, including myself, was a soldier, everything had already come out all right for me.

In reality I never wanted to be a lawyer; it was my father who had wanted that professionally for me. In my private evaluation, my mother was the source of my brains and my father the mother of kindness. He was unspeakably gentle but did not have a fraction of my mother's intelligence. Not that he was stupid, but he could not compare with her in education; to him education meant reality—money, et cetera.

Actually my father was to me an abstract entity. In the morning he went to work in another part of the house, and from then on I did not see him. He came back to lunch, and then we were together, and again in the evening, but I was quickly put to bed. I must have been an overactive child. The story I many times heard from my mother was that my character was unchanged from the beginning. I was running around all day long. Many times by the time supper came (the meal at noon or one o'clock was our dinner), I was often falling asleep by the end and they had to undress me to put me to bed. This apparently was characteristic of my early childhood.

My father had a variety of businesses. First of all, he had a wholesale place in town and sold to merchants; for awhile he also had an oil refinery, because Poland was not far away and they imported crude oil from there. One refinery was in town and another about 40 kilometers away; he did not own these alone, for there was a small group of which he was a part. And then he was involved in a bank. This was typical in those days; people who had money participated in many different enterprises. He was a member of a business community, with a pretty large surrounding set of farmers and landowners. Everyone was dependent on the village itself and whatever commerce it had or was able to produce.

My father participated in none of my mother's interests. He read the economic parts of the newspapers. I do not remember ever seeing him settling down to read fiction. He had a mild contempt for it as having nothing to do with the world around him. My father was a high-strung man. He could go into a rage in a moment, shouting, and be angry. These attacks of anger lasted from ten minutes to an hour, and then he was transformed into a sweet lamb. That trait went all the way through him. He was an exceptionally warmhearted person, beloved by people for that. Nobody took his quick temper seriously. All you had to do was escape the next half hour, and then it would be over; that characteristic I got from him.

However much my father earned of his own, my mother had had a lot of money from her father. How much money my father brought to the marriage I never knew or asked; I had no idea that that sort of problem existed. My calculated guess afterwards was that when he started out with my mother he could not have had any sizeable amount of money, for the simple reason that his stepfather had four or five children of his own and, by the time I looked around, they were all in an established position. They must have gotten money from my father's stepfather, who had only two stepchildren—my father and a brother of his. My hunch is that the natural children must have gotten more than the stepchildren.

At home my grandmother preferred to speak German and did so fluently, as she did Hungarian. Anyhow, in such a small country everybody had to know several foreign languages, otherwise they would be licked. So I grew up bilingual. Even before the first governess arrived, and I do not know how old I was then, maybe 2 years old, my grandmother talked German to me.

I know from stories I was told that I had had a wet nurse. She had a baby of her own and, after she was almost through with the breast-feeding of her own child, she was hired to feed me until I finished the ninth month. And then, overnight, I was taken on to ordinary food. What formula existed, if any, at that time I would not know. But according to my mother this weaning, which was more a ritual than a medical procedure, was received by me with the utmost indignation; eventually I gave in.

From an early age there was an unbroken succession of governesses—for a long time Germans and then French. The series of such help was—at that level of society, a normal thing. The house was always littered with servants, who got nothing. It was like in Mexico today; they received what they needed to survive, but monetary wages were negligible.

I have some isolated remembrances of these early years, which were later subjected to psychoanalytic exploration that led nowhere. Typical, routine types of interpretive tacks were taken. One trait emerged: I was a very stubborn, insistent child who had to have his own way, rain or shine. The amount of fighting and arguments with everyone that resulted from this creed of mine can be only indirectly conjectured.

There were no nursery schools at that time. I had two sisters and one brother; my first sister was born about two years after me, my next sister came three years later, and my brother was nine years younger than myself. So the nursery school was at home. I remember the first day, at the age of about 5½, that I went to a state school. In those days, in the smaller places in Hungary, usually there was one kind of school; and whatever that school happened to be, you went there. Most of the grammar schools were maintained all over the country by the state, except that the religions sometimes had small schools. There was a Catholic school, a Jewish school, and perhaps a third one. I had nothing to do with these. At the state school, the majority of students were the sons of farmers from the neighborhood whom we called "peasant children."

The intellectual life of the town consisted in some of the women sharing my mother's own interests, at least to some extent. And when the theater was in town, they could talk about the new plays they saw. There was no trace of anything else to be concerned with. The men talked wholly about business, whatever it happened to be. From grammar school I remember no teacher who had interest in anything but what was printed in the textbooks. I saw them occasionally and talked to them; they were all kind. You can imagine what their salary was, as they all tried to get some other marginal employment – in the bank bookkeeping, that sort of thing. It cannot be said I was a good student.

There was a secondary school, but of a lower type, not a humanistic *gymnasium*. So when I was 9 ½, I had to go to another village, which had 40,000 inhabitants. It was exactly 40 kilometers, about 24 miles, away. I had to live there because of what transportation was like in those days. In the village itself we had cobblestone roads, but only to go to one of the next small villages, which might have had 100 to 400 people. When I left Kisvarda, I remember my family had a French governess. And from then on I saw these governesses and the family only on vacations.

An intellectual atmosphere did exist within my family, although where my tremendous evaluation of learned people came from I was unable to find out; I absorbed the Eastern European Jewish value system, that knowledge is the number-one thing, a heritage from Maimonides. Kisvarda had its own weekly newspaper of about four pages, of which two and a half were advertisements. Every afternoon the morning papers from Budapest arrived. Budapest then had about twenty-five such daily papers, which caught the early trains and arrived in our village later, being rapidly distributed. I remember how the whole family tried to read these papers before, during, and after supper. In addition, we had I do not know how many magazines, which all came from Budapest. And every year a traveling theater presented a five- or six-week season. That was naturally a very important part of my life, because it is how I became acquainted with theater.

The motion picture was not in existence, but when I was young I was taken to hear a speaking machine. That was the first primitive gramophone, with a horn, and I was astounded that, without participation of any human being, by purely mechanical means, you could reproduce the human voice. But there was no opportunity to carry out my investigative inquiries which had ruined all my sisters' toys – the dolls that closed their eyes or which had a voice. It was a steady despair of my mother that the minute a new toy came, I would break it to pieces. They could not keep a toy which had any mechanical part, nor even an alarm clock. Naturally, when I was brought to see the gramophone I was amazed. And this man made a livelihood out of owning this machine and wandering around with it. I was unhappy that he would not let me look at how it was made.

Then I went to that larger town to enter secondary school, the *gymnasium*, which lasted eight years; added to the earlier four years in Kisvarda, that meant twelve years of formal education, and after that you got the *certificate of maturity* that opened the doors to anything in a university. If you had Latin and Greek, which I did, you could go into medicine, law, architecture, and all the physical sciences, too. There was no branch of the university which was not open to you.

When still in my first year at the *gymnasium*, I lived at my aunt's house. From the second year on I was placed with a family. I stayed with families; there was nothing then like dormitories. I was in the same place for four years when, for reasons which are not clear to me, I went to a more northern town called Kassa, where I was again in a *gymnasium*. It was an excellent school. In one town you had a state school, in another a Catholic one. Naturally, all the boys in the town went to the one school and got the same education, with the exception that they did not have to go to the Catholic church except on one or two holidays. Always I was placed with Jewish families. But in Kassa all the teachers were ordained priests. I was there for two years, and then I came back to the other school, where I had started, and got my certificate.

Aside from studying I was involved in other activities; there were groups of boys who went around together. I remember, and it was confirmed by stories of my mother, that from the second year in Kisvarda grammar school already I was a leader; the boys came around me. We had a huge garden and a utility yard, so that there was abundant room. The boys came and we played ball. At 4:30 the governess came down and counted heads, and then servants came with gigantic trays of bread and butter about an inch high and huge glasses of milk. This lavish arrangement must have been a considerable attraction to the other boys. When we were a little older we began to play soccer, which was the national sport of Hungary. It was the only big, well-known ball game. I was involved in a lot of physical activity all day long and on holidays with my brother and my family.

When I got to the *gymnasium* the situation changed. I was living with a family that did not have a large yard with empty space or a garden in which to lie down and eat grapes. I was in no position to throw a party every afternoon; nonetheless, we got together. In the spring and fall our meetings took place in the playground. In my birthtown there was no such thing, but where there was a *gymnasium* the school had a playground. So we went there and took along something to eat, or bought food for a few pennies, and played. There was no longer a feudal system of entertainment, and everybody took care of himself.

As a student we lived with families as a matter of course; we paid for it. I became completely part of the homes; I had a room, ate meals with them, and was disciplined. That was the national way of getting a secondary education; the same system existed in Austria, Germany, and France. I liked the families I lived with. For example, a widow had two daughters approximately my age, one was a few years older and the other younger; but I spent little time with them. The city had a much higher cultural level. There were societies which gave concerts and artists who came down on tour.

It was in these first years of my formal education that I began to discover what science is. I had heard in grammar school about zoology, mechanics, geography, history, and naturally mathematics. We were occasionally taken to a farm, and an old peasant who liked children might explain to us how a cow lives, what one must give the cow in order to take care of her, what has to be done for the poultry or the dogs, et cetera. And "if I do this, then the cow will do that," or "if I do this then the dog will do that." Out of what one should do and what one should not do, without having any classwork, I learned the elements of biological behavior of the domestic animals. Also I learned about dogs going wild and the dangerous biting of hydrophobic animals. By the time that I arrived at the *gymnasium*, I already possessed the elements of what later became in my mind science.

And then came an experience which decided my life. It was after this indoctrination into the care of animals given me by one of the farmers— never by a landowner, though I visited more of them than farmers. The landowners did not know much, while the farmers had perfect knowledge. I remember that I began to think, "How funny. A rabbit behaves so differently from a dog." And I went over in my mind the different reactions of individual kinds of animals. "But, my God! My grandmother behaves so differently from my father. Why is that?"

I asked people a hundred questions, but not one of them had the remotest inkling of what I was talking about. In the early years of the *gymnasium* I had become interested in the observation that in similar situations, people behaved very differently. I tried to ask my mother and others "How is that?" And I got answers which never went in substance beyond the statement that "different people have different dispositions." That was all the explanation I ever could get. I read books; I found there the same thing. Understanding was nowhere to be found.

So I went to the only encyclopedia, which happened to be owned by an uncle, that existed in the first years of the century—1901, '02, '03. I looked up the word *mind*. The Hungarian language, in contradistinction to the German, has—like English—a different word for mind and soul. When I looked up *mind* I found only quotations from one philosopher or another, what I later discovered to be philosophical formulations, and I did not understand a word.

The encyclopedia was a huge one, multi-volumed. After reading about *mind* I went to the word *soul*. The same thing happened, except the references were not philosophical but theological; still it was incomprehensible to me. Then I looked up the word *brain*, and that was the greatest disappointment of all. What I found under *brain* was an abstract of the then known anatomy of the brain; and while I was a student of Latin, still I had no idea what all these Latin technical terms meant. So my whole project of clarifying my outlook by consulting the encyclopedia had failed.

I do not know how I brought the question of the behavior of men and animals into any connection with the brain. My aunt did have a neurotic tic in her eyelids. She was a good-looking woman, more so than my mother, and her husband took her to the great professor to see if anything could be done for her. Needless to say, her symptom was never treated. But I heard it was a *nerve pulsator*. What is a nerve pulsator? What is a nerve? They tried to explain to me that there are nerves and that there is a brain. That was the first I had heard that something exists which regulates and directs activities. But that behavior should belong under the same agency was not suggested. There was no word for behavior, that was all called *nature*. Good disposition, bad disposition—but that that should have something to do with the motor centers in the brain I could not have known. Nobody could have told me that then.

In the course of several months I consulted the encyclopedia a hundred times in addition to that. It was a favorite activity of mine. And I used it effectively, because once I started reading I kept on, provided I could understand. By some miracle I had all the three words which I knew were somehow related to each other and to something in the human being, but I could understand nothing of what these entries said. And the question I was tracing was, "How is it that while all the cows behave the same way, all the dogs behave the same way, according to my observations and the instructions I had got from the farmers, human beings behave so differently?" That was one of the first scientific problems that entered my mind.

And the result was zero. The teacher who might have explained it to me did not exist. I could not even formulate my question; I had to use a lot of stories to explain what I was interested in. These were the years when I was 10, 11, 12, perhaps 13. Possibly in Kassa someone could have explained it, I am not sure. The whole concept of behavior did not exist. I did not look for religion; so I gradually buried that curiosity.

Then, after I graduated, came the central issue: What now? I was 17½. My answer was "I want to go to the University of Berlin," skipping Budapest, taking advantage of my command of the German language. My father suggested, in line with the time when the most honored profession was the law, that I should study it. And I should also pursue economics; there was no financial problem. Then I could eventually go into a big bank and pursue what we would call a profession in finance. I could study economics or whatever in Berlin and then come home for the next year to catch up with Hungarian law.

I had only one central thought, which was to get out of going to Budapest. I had been taken there several times. There was an academy of science at Berlin, and I had made some investigation of what science was, too. I had learned at school about physics and chemistry, for example; I was not as completely separated from scientific knowledge as my mother. My big idea was to see Berlin.

So I was very happy when I enrolled at the University of Berlin in 1907. I registered in a few courses on philosophy and art history and took courses that came near sociology. In Hungary the study of law was combined with sociology, and you could emphasize the law, the political sciences, or economics. That was how I started out. I lived in Berlin as a grown-up; we all rented furnished rooms and ate in restaurants. We were no longer accepted by families because we were too old for that.

I had to run around to the various schools, because these different courses were separated. In the Hungarian restaurant I met other boys, all of whom were medical students. I asked them if I could see what they were working on. They said, "Sure, you can come along." If a boy took someone else, the authorities never checked. So I got to attend various clinical subjects.

I was fascinated by obstetrics. None of the students happened to have any courses in psychiatry that year. So what I saw was operating medicine. I was fascinated to learn all about the nine-month intrauterine development, but still I learned nothing about behavior, or that the brain relates to everything else. But I began to be attracted by medicine, much more than by social sciences and the law, and became increasingly unhappy about what was then called political science. It seemed wild speculation to me. On the side, then, I had gotten more and more information about medicine. Until then I only understood what I had observed in myself as a patient of our family physician. I did have a maternal great-uncle, the younger brother of my grandfather, who was a doctor who lived nearby, and I knew him.

After I had tasted medicine in Berlin, I also went to Bonn. Then I studied philosophy for a year in Vienna; I began to go to lecture courses in Budapest and to get acquainted with the younger generation. Those boys I knew in Berlin were, by chance, a few years older than myself. I became more and more interested in medicine. I bought books about chemistry, but stuck to my guns. I had to finish this damn political science business anyhow.

2

SANDOR FERENCZI
AND THE
HUNGARIAN
RENAISSANCE

In the late fall of 1910, when I was already an avid reader, a Hungarian pamphlet came into my hands. It was written by a man named Sandor Ferenczi, whom I had never heard of before. The essay had a provocative title: "Analysis of the Soul." And I was shocked: how come this is a doctor and not a theologian? Why was he writing about the soul instead of the mind? It was only later that I discovered that he had mistranslated the word *psychoanalysis*. His pamphlet should have been called Analysis of the Mind or Mental Analysis. It was a collection of Ferenczi's writings, which originally were published in German and which he then had translated into Hungarian. If you wanted the world to take any cognizance of what you are doing, you had to publish in German because nobody reads Hungarian.

In this pamphlet he introduced me to someone I had never heard of before: Sigmund Freud. I saw that Ferenczi was presenting motivational analysis, just precisely the answer to the questions which I had been carrying along in my mind for about ten years. I read Ferenczi with tremendous enthusiasm. It opened up the world of studies whose existence had been unknown to me. Unhappy with my own work, I became excited and ordered from the bookstore everything Freud had written. In Budapest there was a wonderfully organized system of getting books, not like here where it can take a month.

I still have some of the books I bought then. I began to read Freud from cover to cover beginning with the *Studies on Hysteria* up to the last publication that was available in the fall of 1910. I had an almost photographic memory in those days and retained most of that material, re-reading some things; I was enchanted. I realized that this was a method for the study of the brain, because what people think, dream, and say, as well as how they behave, comes from the brain.

I decided overnight that this is what I wanted to do. To hell with the law and the social sciences; there were too many empty words which everybody interpreted differently. I was not interested in that. Hurriedly, I took my last examination to get my political science degree in 1911. On commencement day my father inquired, "And where will you go now?" And I replied, "You will be surprised. I will attend medical school." He thought I was joking and laughed, but I explained to him that there were subjects I had been interested in for a long time and that nobody had ever understood what I had been talking about, and that that was what I would like to study.

I was 20 or 21. I told him I was skeptical about the Austro-Hungarian Empire. One did not need to be a historical genius to make such a forecast, because we had eight nationalities which were constantly fighting each other. This whole chaotic business could not survive. The Hapsburg policy had long been to exterminate the Hungarian language and make everything German. The Hungarians, in turn, pursued the same tack toward the other nationalities within their own borders to make everything Hungarian. I thought this set-up had no future, and that anyone could see it. If the whole system collapsed, and I were a lawyer, then I would be a nobody elsewhere. The range of effectiveness of a legal training was artificial. But a Hungarian doctor could be a physician anywhere. My father recognized the point I made but felt I was too politically pessimistic.

I had already telephoned Ferenczi, once I had finished my readings of Freud. I had asked Ferenczi for an appointment. I went to see him to announce that I would like to give up my political science studies in order to become a medical man and specialize in psychiatry and psychoanalysis. This first conversation was soon followed by a number of others. I thought Freud had found a new method, and that it was sheer science. Ferenczi was excited to find a youngster who felt that way about Freud. But I did not want to give my father the feeling that I was running away from the final examinations, and so I finished my previous studies. While I was still working for my first degree I was already enrolled as a medical student. I found I adored physics.

Ferenczi was the first man who recognized my abilities. My initial interview with him may have lasted over two hours because he got increasingly excited; I seemed to know everything, including the page numbers. At that time he already had a small group of people around him interested in psychoanalysis. There were a couple of medical students among them. I joined, too, as a first-year medical student. (My final degree came from the University of Budapest in 1915.) Ferenczi used me as a sort of traveling encyclopedia. He himself did not have a good memory, and if he needed an item in Freud he just turned to me: "Page what?" he would ask, and I knew the answer.

Ferenczi's immediate circle included one or two well-known writers, such as Hugo Ignotus. There was an older doctor, Lajos Levy, who was the editor of a Hungarian magazine [Therapy] for general medicine; he was an admirer of the British journal the Lancet, which he tended to copy. We assembled about once every two or three weeks in the office of Ferenczi and had informal meetings. On these occasions Ferenczi talked to us about what Freud was writing. He was at that time already in the habit, which he kept up for a long time, of sending every manuscript to Ferenczi before publication. And Ferenczi quickly told us what was going to be the latest news to be published.

This group got together almost like the early Christians in the catacombs. Only a handful of people in the whole city of Budapest knew what psychoanalysis was. Ferenczi's pamphlet was written to be read by the general public; but I never met a doctor who saw any sight of it. Early in 1913, about three years after I had met him, Ferenczi surprised us with the statement that he had permission from Freud that this group of people be transformed into an official psychoanalytic society and thereby auto-matically become a member of the International Psychoanalytic Associa-tion. This momentous event took place on May 19, 1913.

The International Journal for Medical Psychoanalysis (the Zeitschrift) was the official organ of the International Psychoanalytic Association, directed by Freud and edited by Ferenczi, Otto Rank, and Ernest Jones. The Budapest group was headed by Ferenczi as president; I became secretary. We also had Dr. Stefan Hollos, who was a physician in the state hospital service. One of these men was also treasurer. There was great amusement about this group which had only five charter members, three of whom were officers. This was the way I entered the International Psychoanalytic Association. The name of our group became, if I remember correctly, the Hungarian Psychoanalytic Association.

Although Ferenczi was twice my age when I first introduced myself to him, he was still a young, unmarried doctor. He liked younger men and

I admired older ones. Ferenczi had been thrown from one residency into others and could not really find himself. He became a psychiatrist for the Hungarian court; according to Hungarian law, the courts appointed their own experts. The contending parties may have chosen psychiatrists for themselves, but the important one was the court's. That was then Ferenczi's chief connection with psychiatry.

The problem was chiefly to establish the difference between competence and incompetence, sanity and insanity—strictly legal issues. Is someone fully responsible or is his capacity limited by psychiatric illness? Ferenczi accepted that court job because probably few people were interested in it. Not many were concerned with psychiatry at all. The word *psychiatry* covered only insanity. The neurotics, to the extent that anybody knew something about them, were in a separate sphere; doctors who specialized in psychoanalysis called themselves *neurologists*. When I got my certificate as a specialist, it was in psychoneurology. I knew little, if anything, about organic neurology. It was much later that it was discovered that anything which has to do with the psyche belongs to psychiatry; there was then total chaos and professional confusion in this respect.

Ferenczi had become acquainted with Freud's writings, rapidly turned into a friend favored by Freud, went every few months to Vienna, and participated in what were already regular meetings of an established Vienna Psychoanalytic Society. Ferenczi had written the first statutes for the International Psychoanalytic Society, founded in 1910, when Carl G. Jung was elected the initial president. Vienna, of course, was a branch society, and Karl Abraham had established one in Berlin as well.

Ferenczi was an intuitively very gifted man. At the same time, he had little idea about scientific method. This point should be borne in mind because it will be important for the development of Freud himself: theories of knowledge, epistemology, were in those days practically nonexistent. There was no natural scientist who paid the slightest attention to such writings. That was buried as part of philosophical studies. The only exception to this generalization was an amateur theorist of knowledge, the physicist Ernst Mach at the University of Vienna.

In those days Budapest was a culturally flourishing city. A German philosopher-journalist, Count Hermann Keyserling, wrote a semipopular book at the time, *The Scepter of Europe*, in which he has a chapter on Hungary; he was amazed at what Hungary had produced, being on the road from East to West, constantly influenced by the East, at the same time trying to seek orientation in the West.

Hungary was unique; this was not just a personal impression of

Keyserling's, as has been established since. Over a long period, so many Hungarians migrated to the United States; and in whatever branch of activity you look, there will always be a number of Hungarians among the front rank. This was true in a science like physics, in psychoanalysis, in motion pictures, in music, in playwriting. There are various theories about the sources of this unusual creativity. Perhaps it was a biological mixture of previously remote types of men—in particular, Mediterraneans and north Germans.

While going to the university we had an intellectually flourishing life. In private groups we studied, for example, the epistemological ideas of Mach, of which Ferenczi knew a little. We were questioning how science got made. I had become familiar with this whole approach at an early date, before meeting Freud. Naturally, methodology was appealing to the upsurging youth. And someone older like Ferenczi liked to hear from me what was going on and what it meant. He remained a man of brilliant, ill-controlled intuition. As far as testing or careful validation went, he had no idea. He did not understand that it was necessary to do such a thing. The beauty, and persuasive character of an idea, carried with it, for him, the conviction that it must be true. That also was a Jewish heritage, and behind that a Greek inheritance.

I do remember that decades later I heard, from one of Bertrand Russell's lectures that I attended, how funny it is that Aristotle expressed the idea that women had fewer teeth than men. How is it that it never occurred to him to ask his wife to open her mouth? When I listened to Russell I thought, "I can understand that very well. The greatest discovery of the Greek philosophers was that nature can be understood by human intellectual effort, and with the aid of reasoning we can penetrate and learn how the world about us is constructed." All of them had no inkling of investigative work; Aristotle was centuries prior to Galileo and Bacon, and if you single out these two men to mark the beginnings of modern science, then he came long before them. Under those circumstances, the ancient Greeks had a grandiose overestimation of reason as self-evident.

It is a favorite idea of my own that it would not occur to Aristotle to make an observation because he may have had contempt toward anything that would have undermined his faith in the power of reasoning. This ancient Greek tradition, the overevaluation of cognition, was to influence later the development of theology in the Jewish tradition by Maimonides, and in the Christian direction St. Thomas Aquinas did the same thing. The value system announced by Maimonides is almost verbatim taken over from Aristotle, with the exception that the number-one place was to be taken by the Jewish sciences, by the study of the law of God according to the Jewish tradition. This was the ancient admiration of the power of reasoning that had a renaissance in Hungary at the early part of this century.

The difference between an intellectual and an ordinary person in Hungary then was greater than any gap among human beings that I have ever seen, including all the racial problems. There were people who went to the theater, enjoyed the arts, liked to listen to music, read books, and cultivated the subject matters they learned in the humanistic *gymnasium*; a dividing line operated in such a manner that, so far as the intellectuals were concerned, the other part of the population did not exist. Not that they had disdain for them; they just did not care to take notice of the existence of this separate group. A few economists were perhaps the exception, since they were forced in an agricultural country to take a look at what the peasants did and how agriculture ran. Sociology was still to come; there were one or two writers. This whole intellectual and scientific climate of the country was unique. It was a humanistic culture as compared with a scientific one, to use C. P. Snow's classification.

I was a member of a group of accomplished writers and painters. I religiously went to the various exhibitions of my friends. I remember one who is now listed in the Hungarian literature as one of the great figures of the past. That was the time when the Oedipus complex was the pinnacle of theoretical understanding and knowledge. When my friend painted something new and it was shown, Ferenczi was usually there and he would say, "This is the father, that is the mother, and so on." He reduced psychoanalytic knowledge almost to a vocabulary, like the ancient Egyptian interpretation of dreams where such-and-such means so-and-so. Later, when I looked back with amusement on this period, I concluded that now and then, although it appeared to be incorrect, he was perceptive. But the shortcoming was the absence of any dynamic thinking.

Ferenczi was finding universal symbols, and that was always a difference in his thinking and my own. I was already in medical school, and dynamic thinking, "What does what, how?" was ingrained in me. Ferenczi made no distinction between dynamic and decorative thought, as I jokingly called it then; he decorated everything with poetry. Sometimes it was just name-calling. He had a wonderful dynamic feeling, but it did not often find expression in his formulations.

I had a number of older friends, and they would ask me what was new in psychoanalysis. I used to say, "Please, we need so much time to confirm what Freud found while he was working in 'splendid isolation.' "

"Splendid isolation" was his own expression in print. Accumulation of observations is a slow process. It was eclipsed then by the more urgent task of identifying the theoretical concepts in the material of actual observation.

There were a small number of scientists in Hungary, among them my professor of physics who was internationally recognized – Baron Roland Detracz. The rest were all artists or humanists. Ferenczi was in this mainstream of Hungarian thought. It would not have occurred to Ferenczi to make systematic observations to find out something about a psychological statement any more than if somebody had come saying, "Here is a beautiful poem written by a great writer; let us investigate what he says." It would have been to Ferenczi a monstrosity, naturally, and he would have thought that anyone like that did not know what it was really all about. This was his attitude: a brilliant idea which made his eyes light up, leaving him happy, settled all matters.

From this followed an admiration of leaders in the humanities – great writers and artists. A similar orientation existed in Vienna, with one big difference. The language in Vienna was German; a large percentage of the people thereby had access to the German literature. Most of these Hungarians also spoke German. My grandmother chiefly taught me German. But at Vienna, in the whole running of the university, the outstanding empirical scientists – Hermann Helmholtz, for instance – had a tremendous respect, a much greater understanding, but still that was separated by iron curtains from the humanities.

So in Vienna and Austria, while there was a similar admiration for the great men in the humanities, notably writers, that was not completely dominant. A few people knew about science, and Austria also had its great physicians. In the 1890s, for instance, the Vienna medical faculty was supposed to be the best in the world, and I think it truly was. No such thing existed in Hungary. The wonderful Hungarian renaissance was almost wholly in the humanities and not science.

Nobody should be surprised by the lack of interest and grasp of what scientific procedure and methodology was in Budapest. Ferenczi could not carve a road for others to establish this purpose because it was completely beyond his whole youth.

In my own experience as a young man, my social life was centered on colleagues, first on classmate friends and then on the psychoanalytic group. To me psychoanalysis was a method to investigate the brain. The first paper I ever gave at the psychoanalytic society in 1914 was on "The Application of Psychoanalytic View-points to Problems of Biology."

(The title was not correctly translated; Ferenczi wrote it from memory at the time. What I actually had in mind was the *contribution* psychoanalysis makes to medicine.) I pointed out that anybody who finds an investigative method to study the mind actually also studies the brain, and that this was the great discovery of Freud's. Then, a few months later, the war came, and anyhow I did not have an interest in publishing that article because I thought everybody knew what was in it. And then it turned out that fifty years later it is only a small number of people who appreciate the point. I was the first analyst in Budapest to remain in the scientific tradition, which for me became biology.

There was another Hungarian who, years later, became a scientist, and that is Imré Hermann. He was an M.D., but his interest was entirely in clinical and experimental psychology. In the beginning he was sound, but that was before he went into analysis with Freud, which killed that whole interesting line of thought.

Life in the Hungarian Psychoanalytic Society was inspiring, dominated altogether by the interests of Ferenczi, which went miles away from clinical problems. He shifted from the humanities to biology. I do not mean he was concerned with the science of biology, as its many branches were taught at the university or found in textbooks, but he was chiefly guided by the extensive popular biological literature of the nineteenth century.

Months, if not years, passed by without anybody ever mentioning any case or a therapeutic task, not to mention the issue of proper technique. What we were talking about were questions of evolutionary biology viewed from the psychoanalytic angle. Ferenczi, by the end of World War I, had in manuscript his book *Thalassa*, and the most recent event on which we focused was the coming out of the oceans of our remote ancestors, the start of land animals. Ferenczi tried to trace the expression of human emotions to the geological and paleobiological events that have taken place.

Ferenczi was fascinated by a story which was elaborated to the lay public by Ernst Haeckel, a zoologist who became a popular science writer. He was, I believe, the first one who voiced or propagated the idea that the embryo repeats the whole evolutionary history of man in the intrauterine phase of development. While that later proved in a certain sense to be true, he went to extremes in speculative details. Haeckel was one of the deepest influences on Ferenczi. He put in *Thalassa* an apology that he wrote the book during the war when he was on some riot station and had little to do otherwise.

The significance of *Thalassa* was that even before its publication around Christmas 1923, these paleobiological speculations had been made at meetings of the Hungarian Psychoanalytic Society. We had unending discussions about how the human species had emerged from the ocean and how in particular the genital apparatus and the uterus, as well as the baby, developed. We had spent hours trying to figure out how the well-known emotional expressions which we can see in higher animals – in particular, man – develop. The overall hypothesis was that in some way or other they could be traced to man's emergence from the ocean.

For instance, what is crying? That is a question to which, twenty-five years later, I said this is an adversive reflex. I do not remember what Ferenczi had argued, but it had something to do with coming out of the ocean. All the conceivable items connected with this question stimulated every member of that society to wrack his brain, trying to find a speculative answer. The discussions can be found in the reports I sent in, as secretary, to the *Zeitschrift*. Geza Roheim excelled in this area. He connected the emergence from the oceans with certain cultural traits which he himself had studied in "primitive" people, so he had a link between them and contemporary society.

To give an idea of the spirit of the Hungarian Society, look at the 1921 report of the proceedings. The abstracts indicate that on October 3, Roheim gave a paper on "Ethnologic Comments on Totemisms and Cultural Strata in Australia." That is several pages. I see my own discussion reported: "How One Can Use Anthropological Material to Reconstruct the Cultural Evolution of Mankind." At that time we thought that the cultural growth of man was one process that reached separate stages of development in different places and times. And then came the paper "Problems of Psychology of Music in the Light of Psychoanalysis" by Sigmund Pfeifer. The first sentence of my discussion says that I have methodological doubts concerning this lecture, which moved within the framework of phylogenetic biological speculations. This statement of mine characterizes that whole period, which consisted in conjectures about what might have happened a hundred or more million years ago. And then comes my comment: "It is true that Freud himself used phylogenetic material in his speculative tenets, but at any rate he supplemented that with clinical observations. He did not substitute those conjectures for clinical observations." That was my comment, which meant that looking at contemporary mankind cannot possibly be eliminated.

Ferenczi did have poetic insights, but his brilliance could be undisciplined and reckless. He was capable of being too speculative. There is in a famous children's book a line in the story where a man is strolling on the meadow with a field glass and says, "Why shouldn't I while walking look into the distance? It is beautiful elsewhere too, and here I am anyhow." Among more down-to-earth clinicians there was great unhappiness about Ferenczi's theories concerning the sexual nature of male and female. The gist of his theory was that once upon a time, sexual intercourse took place between two equally formed animals until one, the stronger, specialized in strength, and that the vagina and the whole female apparatus is a consequence of the defeat of the weaker. This sounds vague, but I assure you it is not more so than the speculation itself; Ferenczi was suggesting something like the idea that the female originated by being forced by the male to submit to intercourse. Freud promptly quoted Ferenczi's words in one of Freud's papers. I thought that Ferenczi's running away from clinical observations and his operating in the evolutionary field was bothersome.

Freud's original system could be totally corrupted. Wild speculations can have a devastating influence; I think C. G. Jung threatened psychoanalysis as a clinical discipline. There is something wrong with promising people treatment and then talking about what happened years ago in the evolution of the species. But this was the spirit then of the Hungarian Society, as it became more and more abstract. It did not develop in the cultural direction as, for instance, Karen Horney and Erich Fromm tried to work things out later, because in those days there was no sociology in existence. Sociology was just a fight about first principles, not over the description of what already exists and can be verified.

3

CONTACT WITH FREUD

After the Hungarian Psychoanalytic Society had been first launched in 1913, in the fall of that same year Ferenczi had suggested that I should go to Vienna, present myself to Freud, and listen to one of his lectures. At that time he was in the habit of giving weekly talks on late Saturday afternoons at the university department of psychiatry, which was a part of the Vienna general hospital. Ferenczi wrote ahead to tell Freud that I was a member and the secretary of the Budapest group.

I had to wait outside in the corridor and could not go into the lecture room because only those could enter who had enrolled ahead of time or who were permitted by Freud to attend as special guests. Naturally, I arrived early; at that time I was exactly 23 years old. And I waited at the front door for Freud to turn up.

That was to be my first meeting with Freud, at a time when all my ideas about what a psychoanalyst is had been modeled on Ferenczi himself. Ferenczi was a rather sloppy dresser, careless in his outside appearance; and I expected to find in Freud a professorial type of man. Suddenly, looking along an endless-seeming corridor, in one of those big buildings that are still in existence, the factotum who was standing at the door said, "You see, this is the professor coming down."

Then I heard the noise of an automobile, in those days in Vienna a rarity. I was stunned that Freud would have one. It turned out later that he did not; somebody had given him a lift. The door opened and there stepped out a man taller than Ferenczi, wearing a fur-lined, fur-collared European type of great coat, a silk hat, and holding a walking cane with an ivory handle. He looked like a privy counselor; I expected nothing like it.

Freud brought along with him a young, poorly dressed boy who seemed agitated, fidgety, talked to him all the time; and this I later found out was Otto Rank. Freud arrived at the door, and I introduced myself to him. He said, "Oh yes, I know your name. You are most welcome, come in." He let me into the class he was giving, and that was the first time I heard Freud speak. He gave a two-hour lecture the topic of which, it just so happened, was the interpretation of dreams. At the same time he went through the whole subject of psychoanalysis.

My first impressions come back as if it had happened yesterday. First of all I was amazed at his abilities as a speaker. I never in my life had heard a man lecture the way he did, with the maximum emotional appeal. His sentences were each dictated for the typesetter. You could have printed his entire lecture without changing a word. I never saw that either. All the lecturers and teachers I had known corrected themselves all the time: "Oh I forgot this or that," or "I have to take this back," etcetera. Nothing of the kind happened with Freud.

But also he did something which struck me right away. You must remember that those were the days when the attention of psychoanalysis was in large measure concentrated on the interpretation of symptomatic actions—forgetting, slips of the tongue, bungling, parapraxes, and the like. The reason for focusing on this particular subject was that little about clinical facts was known. So we were turning to that which was understood.

Suddenly I discovered that after a few minutes Freud began to play with one of his rings. He wore two of them. Later I found out that one was his wedding band and the other was a ring which he shared with the so-called Committee, the close group of intimate friends about which Ernest Jones writes so much in his *The Life and Work of Freud*. I could see that he constantly played with his ring, hardly a minute passing before he again did so. I said to myself, "Now, why is that? Is that ring too tight and does it disturb him?" I did not know what to make of it.

He went through this whole two-hour lecture with no interruption. In the course of the presentation that I heard, he also made three individual slips of the tongue, as a result of which I made an observation which stood me well even up to the present time. For I thought: "Obviously the knowledge of mental mechanisms does not protect the man who discovered them from being victimized by the same processes."

He was very nice. After the lecture we again talked a few words to each other, and he introduced me to Rank. Freud said goodbye, and I went home to Budapest; I reported to Ferenczi in great detail about what I had seen and experienced, including Freud's playing with the ring and his three slips of the tongue. Obviously the personal attitude of Ferenczi to Freud was bound to have a great influence on the relationship between the informal Hungarian group and Freud himself. The picture translated by Ferenczi, who regularly brought back news from Vienna, continued to have a tremendous impact on us.

Freud's whole school was made up of a group of people emotionally tied together. He was like an old-fashioned father surrounded by a large number of children, each one of whom had only a single goal: becoming his favorite child. That psychoanalysis was a science, a part of medicine, and that other people elsewhere in the world were doing things that may be important to the field and have bearings on it was completely ignored.

I remember that when I came to my private meetings with Ferenczi or later to the official sessions of the Society while I was still a medical student, Ferenczi's first words always were, "What is new in medicine?" He had to ask because he had stopped reading medical journals. And I came to tell him the latest theories in chemistry, physics, biology; he listened and was sufficiently curious, but not enough to read anything. Occasionally I brought him magazine articles and books. In two minutes he was back to psychoanalysis. Later I did the same thing with Freud; I brought him items to read. And then I found out that he never touched any of them. This describes the whole ethos: psychoanalysis had become a cult, a group in which emotionality prevailed within the context of Freud's undisputed leadership.

The most important feature of such an organization is its intolerance toward anything in the outside world. The attitude was "Everything can be found within psychoanalysis. We can expect that others outside the magic circle will have no inkling of what we geniuses are doing here." So developments within science in general were annulled from the beginning. I was both troubled at the time and also enamored of what was happening within the movement itself. In retrospect I have analyzed my own early attitude. Although I never stopped being bothered by what was going on, I was carried away by the group sentiment. You cannot be an important member of an organization and deny its emotional orientation. I did not even begin to do that. Only on certain occasions had I a dialogue with myself and said, "This will lead to bad consequences." On the whole I was sharing in the fanaticism of the whole cause. As a result I was considered one of the most conservative of the orthodox people.

Much of that which I knew about Freud came from what he had

written about himself up to that time, and it was little, chiefly introductions to some of his papers. He could apologize that with his peculiar case histories and the particular kinds of dreams reported, he had not been able to transgress the limits of legitimate neuropsychiatric interest. His reports had to be fragmentary. Beyond that, I knew about this distant man Freud only by hearsay, what Ferenczi was able to tell us.

I learned, because Ferenczi told me so, that Freud was in the habit of sending him every manuscript he wrote. From the time that I got together with Ferenczi, which was around December 1910, every single paper Freud wrote was put into an envelope and next day mailed to Ferenczi. He read the paper and, half an hour later, telephoned me that there was a new piece by Freud. So Freud's essays, after he finished writing them, were read by Ferenczi and, secondly, by myself. Freud may have had no inkling that Ferenczi shared them with me.

I read all these papers and can tell now what the manuscripts looked like. First of all Freud did not use either letter-size or so-called legal-size paper but the double of it, which was not broken in the middle; he wrote on these large white sheets.[1] And everything was composed in his own illegible Gothic handwritten script. It went so far that the publishers had to train one or two typesetters who were capable of reading his manuscripts. It required special study to read him, in which I achieved mastery. That he had no copy of anything he wrote is self-evident; nobody then had a typewriter.

Freud proceeded as follows: let us say that this is a sheet of paper. Here he wrote the title about four square fingers from the top. The first line started toward the righthand corner. Every other line moved from left to right, always upward; that was retained in every manuscript. I do not know whether that had anything to do with the way he held the paper. But you can identify a Freud manuscript as far away as your eyesight permits.

What impressed me inordinately, after reading one after the other of these gigantic pages, was that there were no corrections. They were original manuscripts, not second drafts. That was the way he wrote. Once on every other page he corrected a bit of grammar; he might finish a sentence with a plural where there had been a singular noun, or vice versa,

---

1. On being asked about the large sheets of paper he used, Freud remarked: "When I have to restrict myself in so many directions in life, I want to have space and freedom at least when I am writing" (Theodor Reik, *The Search Within*. New York, Grove Press, 1956, p. 22).

that sort of thing. But practically nowhere did he cross out a phrase or a word and put in another. I cannot tell, but it is most unlikely, whether he changed his mind, which led to extensive corrections that resulted in his rewriting that page. As far as I know he wrote these huge manuscripts without any alterations. It was breathtaking. The original itself wound up at the printer.

Ferenczi early had developed the habit of reading the papers together with me. Then we had discussions. I have to tell you that these did not start out as critical examinations. The first job was to find out what Freud wanted to say and understand that which he proposed. And neither Ferenczi nor I always comprehended what he was driving at. But most of the time we understood. Once in awhile doubts were expressed: "Is this what he means? Is that really so?" But these were intimate conversations and nobody has heard about them until now.

Years went by with this same system, and we gradually began to ask, "Now how is that? Could that be right? Is there not another possibility?" But these critical discussions really played a negligible part. The main thing was to read his handwriting, and which signs meant what word; next, to understand his meaning; and now and then a critical attitude, but that was a minor part. Then Ferenczi returned the manuscript to Freud, accompanied by a letter which naturally I never saw. So what he wrote Freud I do not know.

The greatest excitement we experienced in those days was in 1912, when Freud wrote the four articles which later were put together, not combined, as four chapters in a book *Totem and Taboo*. The four articles appeared separately in Freud's journal *Imago*; the title of the book did not exist yet, only the individual headings of the papers. He did not throw out a word or reformulate even a sentence.

Studying these manuscripts was an aspect of the warm relationship between Freud and Ferenczi. In retrospect, the peculiarities are clearer to me than they were at that time, when I never got beyond suspecting some of the unusualness of such things. I did not allow myself to be fully conscious of what was going on. If Ferenczi was completely under the domination of Freud and emotionally dependent on him, even more did that also apply to me in relation to Freud. He was a demigod. The attitude behind this system went on surely until World War I. I think some manuscripts continued to arrive in Budapest the same way after the war.

In Vienna itself the psychoanalytic group was not made up of physicians who went through the then-customary medical training and became outstanding in anatomy, physiology, ophthalmology, internal medicine, or anything else. These were all humanists, full of a desire to know something about human beings. They might complete medical school and pass the examinations, having chosen their lifetime profession. But they did not dream of getting positions at universities and hospitals, because these jobs were taken by people who had much better marks in these subjects than they did.

Also, the Jewish question has to be taken into account even though there was not the kind of anti-Semitism as later on under Hitler. In Freud's lifetime political anti-Semitism existed in Austria. I happened to be a student in Austria when Karl Lueger, the popular mayor of Vienna, died. His whole career was based on anti-Semitic propaganda; it was from Lueger that Hitler got the idea of anti-Semitism. As compared with what happened later, this was never to be taken seriously, as is seen from the following well-known story. Lueger, who always delivered these anti-Semitic speeches prior to election, was reprimanded that on the one hand he was hostile to the Jews, and on the other hand all his friends were Jews. He had a Jewish doctor, a Jewish lawyer, a Jewish architect, and so on. To which Lueger's answer was, "It is I who decides who is a Jew and who is not." That was the nature of his anti-Semitism, but not in Freud's mind. His fear of anti-Semitism was strong and never for a moment left him.

It had been self-evident while Freud was growing up that if the Jewish boy who, in addition to appearing in the eyes of other people as being eager to make money, also tried to be appointed to a theoretical, medical institution, people would shake their heads. This Viennese climate naturally affected Freud himself. Ernst Brücke, a revered teacher, told him one day, "You want to get married, and have money to support a wife and children. But you earn now 600 crowns a year." That was not enough to starve on. Five crowns made a dollar, but you cannot ever state it in dollars, for the crown only came in January 1, 1900. Freud's annual salary came to around $250. All of the university positions paid little. David Bakan asks a question which Jones raised but never answered; When did Brücke make his statement to Freud? Bakan traces it to the flare-up of anti-Semitism that took place a few years earlier in Austria and Hungary. While this was true, I assure you it was not the answer. The whole system meant that a Jewish boy who was considered to be greedy, hungry for money, should not even dare to go into a laboratory where research work was being done. What is commonplace today in the United States and elsewhere would have seemed then a monstrous idea.

Nor were people in those days so bashful. Brücke would have, and probably did, deliver a similar speech to Gentile boys who did not attract his attention by the brilliance of their work. It is obvious that Freud did not perform outstandingly under Brücke. Freud tried to do a routine type of investigation, every step of which was explained to him; that was hardly a remarkable accomplishment. He was one of the bricklayers who helped to build the wall; but he probably did not even know what the wall was going to be.

So Brücke delivered Freud a warning which he could have, and no doubt did, also give to Gentiles who failed to become conspicuous by outstanding research. "What in heaven's name are you going to do here? In thirty years you will be an assistant professor and have a salary which will correspond to perhaps $1,500 per annum and no private practice." The assumption was that those people who stayed in the universities came from families with means of their own, just as you could not become a diplomat unless your family could afford it, or else it was a misery. This was the social assumption and also the financial fact. One should not breathe any particular anti-Semitic mood into the general situation.

University life represented science for Freud. To him, science was identical with lining up with the great medical investigators. And he had at that time the ambition to be a professor investigating natural sciences. That was all he knew—science as distinguished from the humanities. He had done a good deal of general reading already, but his settled aim was elsewhere. At that time when I first met him, he still wanted to be a scientist and have a clinical staff. He sought to be the head of an organization or school like all the other big professors had.

And he did not fully understand the fights and jealousies that had already broken out in the Vienna Psychoanalytic Society. His few peers there were not people who wanted, like himself, to be scientists; they were those who, in one way or another, got their medical diploma, did enough work to pass the examination, knew for sure that there was no place for them in the university system, and were elated to find that within psychoanalysis they were on the periphery of psychoneurology or neuropsychiatry. They could now let loose all their desire to work in the humanities.

Within humanistic studies there is no scale or agreed-upon set of instruments. In contrast, when you have said that the caloric content of a compound is such and such, it is simple to verify; or you can burn a substance and state with any desirable degree of accuracy how much that is. The Viennese analysts had no interest in any of that; they were trying to produce a particular kind of literature.

One man of this early group is still alive in New York City, and I should like to use this opportunity to ask you to have the courage to invite him to participate in the Columbia Oral History: Theodor Reik. He came to my mind because I got a letter from him recently. His people bought the quarterly which was originally owned by Smith Ely Jelliffe; *The Psychoanalytic Review* now belongs to Reik's school. The editor wrote me that in a few days they will have an advance copy of a new book of Reik's, and I was asked if I would be good enough to review it.

Reik was an acknowledged writer before he joined psychoanalysis. He had a Ph.D. and wrote a book about Arthur Schnitzler. Reik is a gifted man; there is no question about it, despite all his hundred difficulties. He is a master of uncontrolled intuition, pretty much a lone survivor of the spirit that existed in that early time in Vienna. Reik was working in a field in which methodology did not exist because Freud paid no attention to it. In one paper written during World War I he began to write one-and-a-half pages that touched on methodological issues. Freud's own somewhat controlled intuition was always miles ahead of the whole group around him. In such a situation, out of insecurity, people had to turn from genuine investigation to the admiration of Freud as the master who is everything.

The assumption was that Freud was a magician and in knowledge stood way ahead of everybody by centuries; whatever he said became the law. That spirit, the organized expression of which became what was to be called the psychoanalytic movement, was already present in Vienna. And that was accepted by Freud inchwise, and he worked further away from his ambition to be a great investigative scientist. Applying the needs that were brought to him on a silver platter, he, without perhaps fully realizing it, accepted the role to be, he said late in life, the leader of a great psychoanalytic movement, in sharp contradistinction to what at the universities was called an empirical science, such as medicine. At that point he stepped into the Jewish mystical tradition.

Except that he may have had no idea that there was such a tradition. But his embracing it is revealed by the fact that he stubbornly stuck to emphasizing his Jewish origin, which nobody did in that time. Even those who failed to get formally baptized did not boast of the fact of being Jewish; he did. He became a member of B'nai B'rith and wrote them articles presenting his scientific papers. I have not the remotest inkling how much Freud knew about this Jewish mystical tradition. I never talked to him about it; I did not know about it myself. And whenever I had a chance to speak with him, I had more important things to discuss, I thought, than his ideas about Jewishness. I do not know whether he ever talked about it to Ferenczi. Ferenczi was also Jewish-born but knew nothing about this mystical tradition and that according to it there were pseudo-Messiahs.

From then on Freud gradually began to feel that his role was to be the leader of a movement. And that messianic orientation, away from science, was toward a cult which he would not have recognized under that rubric; he would have indignantly rejected the word *cult* as an affront. Despite how he would have objected, in actual fact and according to his real feelings, for the description of which he did not have the right words, it was a full-fledged cult that he led.

He made one concession to this effect. It was done in a place where nobody would look for it, and possibly no one has recognized it. When Freud wrote *Moses and Monotheism*, he held the manuscript back because he was afraid to offend the Catholic church, which at that time was extending some protection over the Jews. But this measure, such as it was, amounted to everything because nobody else was doing anything, so that the little help the Church offered was important.

There is written evidence, in one of his notes he wrote explaining the publication of his Moses book, that naturally he was shocked. By then he saw that he was one of the leaders to whom the nation lends its ears. He does not come anywhere near expressing the idea that he was one of the respected scientists of this nation. But he identifies with *nation*. Like Hitler, but without knowing it, Freud puts together Austria and Germany because they are all Germans using the same language. So *nation* meant to him people who talk German, the countries where the basic language was the same.

I just want to identify this note, about which I am talking, which explains to his readers why the publication of this precious work of his was delayed. In that same introduction, he also mentions his bitterness because he had thought he belonged to the leaders of the German nation, and look here what had happened. These two thoughts are related only by the fact that they appear in the same place.

Here is, to my knowledge, the only recognition on his part from which you can see that this man viewed himself as a leader of the nation and secretly as one of the leaders of mankind. But not in terms like Albert Einstein, who discovered a great natural law. Freud's opinions, his words, were what counted for him then. So by that time the personal transformation of Freud into a mystical or romantic leader, as distinguished from a natural scientist, was recognized by himself. I do not believe that anybody knows this, or at any rate has not talked about it, because the people who wrote freely about Freud were Americans, Canadians, and British—but they do not understand about these European aspects.

Freud, more or less without clear awareness, moved away from his early ideas to become a laboratory scientist, a university professor, and began to cultivate the idea of a movement, which of necessity made him a leader. All subsequent developments of psychoanalysis, so far as an organization is concerned, took place under these auspices, which reached a climax much later when he finally said these words in *Moses and Monotheism*.

This whole development, the much later end of which no trace existed at the time I am now talking about, before the First World War, was much intensified by the hostility of the outside world. Freud realized that none of his pupils succeeded in constituting a real clinical staff. What he achieved in creating has to be understood like the title of *bishop*, which was strictly honorary because the Pope had appointed them to countries which they had lost, and then each was a bishop in *partibus infidelium*. Freud had a clinical staff without a clinic. The essential item in this association of his, in terms of its local societies, like the ones in Vienna and Budapest, was chiefly determined by the exclusion from academic science in the universities.

So there was no alternative for Freud. It was in his blood and past history to go in this humanistic direction, and it got reinforced by the opposition of the outside world, so far as sticking to his first, naive idea of becoming a scientist was concerned. Nobody among Freud's followers could have dreamt of any appointment at one of the universities. In those days, still before World War I, no psychoanalyst could have imagined an academic career that would have led to anything. All he himself ever got was not the position but the mere title of being a professor.

So that was the spirit of the beginning movement, and Ferenczi brought it over from Vienna and, unbeknown to himself, transmitted to us and inculcated into the Hungarian group. For him this was all self-evident and natural. He had no idea of trying to "place" Freud; that was not a well-known idea anyhow, since the sociologist Max Weber, who talked about the sociology of science, was some years later.

Ferenczi had neither any great interest or knowledge of all these things. To what extent he tried, in his mind, to straighten out the figure of Freud concerned whatever ideas appeared in Freud's dreams, which he himself analyzed in *The Interpretation of Dreams*. You will find Freud identifying there with all political heroes—Cromwell, for example, as well as one of the Roman war leaders. Already you can see in these dreams and in the choice of thoughts that by real feeling he was attracted to the humanities and that this whole concept of becoming a natural scientist was forced upon him through his studies in a European *gymnasium*. These were the university subjects; and he saw that recognition and admiration went to the people who pursued scientific investigation. He adopted and, for a while, continued along this line, until Brücke kicked him out.

And then, one by one through fortunate circumstances, thanks to his acquaintance with Josef Breuer and by means of his seeing from Jean-Martin Charcot's demonstrations of the clinical use of hypnosis, he suddenly discovered the humanistic aspect of psychiatry and gradually went into psychology—what he called, at that time, *dynamic psychology.*

Then World War I broke out, and we all went into it. The private group in Budapest had already been transformed into an official society, becoming a member of the big international organization founded by Ferenczi. But it did not have a chance to operate for much time, because in Europe the First World War started in 1914, years earlier than here. By the time we returned from the war, the Budapest group was really getting into its activities, still under the same officers. Ferenczi was an eternal president, I continued as secretary, and so it went.

By that time, not long after the war, the psychoanalytic movement became an officially recognized matter, and we had a journal that was called *Psychoanalytic Movement.* And Freud became more and more proud of this "cause." Somehow he had the conviction that though he was excluded from the academic hierarchy, he still would triumph. He told the story of how he got the professorial title, through the intervention of one of his patients who was a friend of the secretary of state. This official said to that lady, "If you donate a picture to the state gallery, I will appoint your professor." Whereupon the lady said, "The picture is yours." That is how Freud became professor. It was the end of his academic career right up until his last days, by which time he was world-famous anyway.

To repeat: this development from the, for Freud, artificial idea of becoming a natural scientific investigator and professor led away from what had been grafted on him from the German academic atmosphere. His human response was enthusiastic when, via Breuer and Charcot and the rest of them, he discovered the psychological approach to human behavior. And from then on he more and more, with increasing rapidity, shifted from the ideal of the scientist, in the sense of Galileo and Bacon, to becoming a great leader. That change was facilitated by the hostile attitude of academic medicine toward psychoanalysis. And it was augmented by the fact that his pupils—for instance, in Hungary, Austria, and also Germany — were also people who, for some reason or another, had no hope of getting anywhere at the university. And then there were people like myself, who took his existing body of writings, which I viewed as a new procedure, which I thought would constitute a fresh development in science.

4

CONTROVERSIES IN FREUD'S SCHOOL

In Freud's *On the History of the Psychoanalytic Movement* he described his conflicts with Alfred Adler, Jung, and Wilhelm Stekel. All these controversies took place before I entered international psychoanalysis, and I have nothing to add except a comment on one of the statements Freud made in that historical paper of his, to the effect that he hoped that people who are working on a promising line of inquiry will be aware of the importance of their task and therefore avoid personal clashes. That, however, was not the case in what had happened with himself.

Also, he felt that some of his leading pupils had gone too far in sticking to their individual opinions which, according to Freud, were in head-on collision with his own views. All of that trouble eventually resulted in the withdrawal of these three people from his following. Yet what I saw and heard later makes it likely to me that Freud's own rigid attitude toward these three men was not so much his own choice as the decision made by him under the pressure of the Vienna psychoanalytic group itself. The picture of the faithful trying to find traitors in their midst was already at work in the early days. There was intense jealousy of the relative prominence of these three men, and the most devout wanted to be rewarded by getting rid of unpleasant competition. The first psychoanalysts were just as human as anybody else.

Especially Adler did not truly present his views in opposition to Freud's theories. In those days Freud was almost completely concentrated on the exploration of the new realm he had discovered, which he called *the unconscious*. That a conscious personality existed, which as yet had no name, was taken by him for granted. Adler went ahead and began to describe the conscious activities of the individual, the realm of the conscious mind, and became thereby the forerunner of what later came to be called, within Freud's own psychoanalysis, *ego psychology*. With a little goodwill and scientific fairness, the legitimacy of Adler's work could have been acknowledged, and without a rupture like that which took place.

But the boys were agitating against Adler's ideas because they misinterpreted the fact that Adler wrote about something else than the latest publications of Freud; they took Adler's direction to be oppositional and as incompatible with what Freud had previously written. In those days the members of the Vienna Society were not a group that had been assembled in a manner anywhere resembling the system which has now been in operation for several decades. No kind of real training existed then. At bottom Freud remained opposed to what came to be called didactic or training analysis. He said, "I still cling to my idea that a healthy person, reading my writings and analyzing his own dreams, can acquire complete understanding of psychoanalysis." That was what he believed to be a training process. The future will show how much truth, or error, there was in this view of his.

At any rate, one mistake was that he so easily assumed the normality of people. In view of what I have already said and the actual facts as they happened, it is clear that this prerequisite was rarely, if ever, fulfilled. Psychoanalysts, from the point of view of academic science – in particular, medicine – with chairs at universities, hospitals, and their staffs, have had a viciously hostile attitude toward them. The men who came to Freud were searching for a special opportunity. Some of them were genuinely impressed by the greatness of Freud's discoveries. Others simply wanted to find a place for themselves and recognized that by joining this group, they were then pariahs; they seemed to have made the devil's pact, which would cost them the opportunity of ever joining any academic institution.

Now this situation did not have to exclude healthy people. But it invited the abnormal. Accordingly, the first members of the private society with which the Vienna psychoanalytic group started around 1902 to 1906 was composed of former patients of Freud's – doctors with personal problems who had gone into analysis with him. Such analysis was, of necessity, therapy too. No other kind of treatment existed, nor was it even envisaged. After such an analysis ended, Freud invited these doctors to join him professionally, and this formed the kernel of the future psychoanalytic groups.

But the movement was not limited to doctors. Scientists, or people in high positions elsewhere, and intellectuals or university-trained people in the humanities, also were invited by Freud if they showed interest in his work. Freud early realized that knowledge of the mind must find an application everywhere that mental work plays a part, therefore in our entire civilization. So that was the means by which the early group around Freud got composed.

Two people in particular I already found when I first got to Vienna, and more and more they assumed leading positions—Otto Rank and Hanns Sachs. Rank was Freud's personal discovery. He was preparing at a technical school of some kind and wrote a book, I think on the artist. Freud read the manuscript, liked it, and then made that book the basis on which to sponsor Rank. He was a sort of adopted son. Freud's own children paid no attention to what he was doing.

In this connection I remember a story of Hans Lampl, who was later an analyst but also had happened to be a schoolmate of one of the Freud boys. Lampl told me much later that for some time his friend thought his father had "something to do with the feet," or perhaps even with the removal of corns. Where this idea came from I would not know, but you can imagine how much idea this Freud family had about what the father was doing. And that is not surprising either, because he was completely separated from it; he saw the children for five or ten minutes, for days, weeks, months, years, and decades.

At any rate, before World War I it was welcome for Freud to find so bright a boy as Rank, who was also a good writer. He persuaded Rank to finish up the *gymnasium*, which corresponds to high school and college here, and then Freud encouraged him to choose psychoanalysis for a lifetime job. And he advised Rank not to study medicine but to pursue the humanities and to dedicate himself to the application of psychoanalysis there. By the humanities he meant mythology, literature, and related activities. That was the goal he prescribed for Rank, and in turn Rank was elated to find in Freud a patron like this. Rank followed Freud's prescriptions.

How Hanns Sachs got to the Vienna group I do not know. He was an accredited lawyer in Vienna and went through the whole legal training, becoming an established and certified practitioner. But first of all he could not make a living as a lawyer, and secondly he had some ambitions as a writer. Sachs began to go to Freud's lectures. At that time Freud already lectured at the department of psychiatry as an outsider, or in some minor academic role. And Sachs also was admitted as a psychoanalyst. Whether he ever was analyzed by anybody, I never knew, nor was I interested.

In those days it was a peculiar-sounding set-up. We had still a Victorian background. An analysis was considered the private affair of a person, and it would not have occurred to anybody, or at least to me, to ask such a question. Sachs was an important member of Freud's early Viennese group and stood out as a converted lawyer.

In talking before, I almost said that Freud "wrote" a manuscript of Rank's. There was a reason for my slip. In one series of lectures Freud talked about the application of psychoanalysis to the humanities. He did write an early paper about some problems of law, to which he tried to apply psychoanalysis, and Freud made the beginnings of analytic studies in mythology and literature in order to analyze fictional characters. Then, probably before World War I, Rank and Sachs wrote together a pamphlet *The Application of Psychoanalysis to the Humanities.* Years later, in a weak moment at a coffeehouse, Sachs, who was then a close personal friend of mine, divulged to me the origins of that book. He and Rank, especially Rank, were excellent stenographers. They just wrote down what Freud said, and that became the book.

So those were Freud's original lectures which these two students copied. They did something which much later happened to me at the Columbia Psychoanalytic Clinic, where many people took shorthand notes and a few years later, forgetting the mention of my name, wrote papers and books about my lectures. So you see, a constant human nature goes through, like a red thread, this whole business. And I was so used to that that I did not pay any particular attention to it. Here in New York the same thing had happened as in Vienna. There, Sachs told me that he and Rank had got together; they needed transitions and little inserts. They had to try to follow up certain topics which Freud merely referred to or mentioned. And Sachs told me how they put in a little padding to fill out what Freud actually had said.

This anecdote gives an idea about the nature of the early Vienna group. In coming back to Freud's own references to that period, he acknowledged that it was difficult to achieve agreement in psychoanalysis. But he did not draw the conclusion that therefore it is vitally important to develop methods of validation and testing and to construct scientific points of view which would convince people and silence those who come forward with wrong opinions. As you can read in *On the History of the Psychoanalytic Movement*, Freud's answer to the question of how one achieves a degree of agreement on certain propositions was one single word. I do not know if this word explicitly appears in the paper, but the text leaves no doubt: *authority*.

If there is a sufficiently strong authority that says, "This is green," then everybody will accept that this is green. Freud never came into the neighborhood of the idea that you can eventually take a look and develop some methods of testing. By that time he had discovered that there was an approach to inner experiences through the psychoanalytic method, that he himself was a writer, that his interests were along these lines, and then he had already left behind the methodology of natural science, which he learned in the histological laboratory while dissecting the spinal cords of fish.

In addition, I have the strong feeling, which was confirmed over decades of contact with Freud, that somehow in his mind his approach still remained the methodology of histological investigation. A key extra step would have meant going from the study of histology, therefore asking, "What is the method of pursuing science in general when you do not have a microscope and there are other kinds of observations?" I do not want to do injustice to his memory, but to the best of my judgment he never did pursue such an inquiry. He had been behaving on the basis of a typical activity which had been imposed on him. He wanted to become somebody, the professor of physiology said, "Dissect this fish," so he sat down and learned the technique of how to do something like that.

But there is such a thing as scientific methodology in investigative science, which has principles that apply to any one branch. That idea never entered his head. So for him it was simply that he had left the histological laboratory, goodbye to all that he learned there; and he was already in the process of developing psychoanalysis as part of the humanities, and himself as a leader. The beginning of that is beautifully described in *On the History of the Psychoanalytic Movement*.

The early Vienna group had a few people from other countries, who gradually went back to their homes and became the heads of local societies. The first of them, and closest to me, was Ferenczi, who was also a direct member of the Vienna Society. *Member* meant that Freud announced at the meeting that he would like to have someone like Ferenczi join. It would not have dawned on anybody to vote against that choice or to ask any questions. In effect, people became members by appointment.

In short order Ferenczi became Freud's darling, second only to Rank. Rank did a lot of work for Freud, helping him in all sorts of things, and was always around. After all, Rank lived in Vienna, so it was natural that nobody could compete with Rank. He was also a younger man than Ferenczi. The consequences of the friendship between Freud and Ferenczi were momentous; I do not think I am being unfair to anybody if I say that for a long time Ferenczi was Freud's only real friend. Rank was an ersatz son and not a friend in the sense Ferenczi was. Freud showered recognition on Ferenczi, quoting and recommending him every time there was an opportunity. Much later, on some birthday, Freud sent him the *Encyclopaedia Britannica*, the famous edition of 1911, which was the current one of that time, and Ferenczi was ecstatic. In our sphere that was an expensive set of books. The price had to be paid in English currency; this was one sign of many pointing to Ferenczi's special standing.

The most important element in all this, which played a little part in my own later development, was that Freud desperately needed the admiring criticism of a scientific man. He could not exist without that. This particular role was fulfilled first by Wilhelm Fliess, a confused, grandiose numerologist. Fliess actually was, by training, a nose and throat specialist. He claimed to have discovered some correspondence between spots in the nose and the genitals. He advocated a numerological system in which certain numbers, like seven, were supposed to play a special part, based on some biological theories to which no one ever paid any attention. As you can see from Freud's correspondence with Fliess, when he sent those ideas to Freud in exchange for Freud's own papers, Freud always evasively answered that he was not an expert in Fliess's field. Freud said he liked Fliess's work and enjoyed reading it, but Freud has actually no criticism of Fliess to offer.

There was nobody in Vienna to whom Freud could turn for this kind of relationship, obviously no one who was scientifically trained. The scientists were at the university, an institution full of hostility toward Freud. He was totally isolated. That was the ten years of splendid solitude he writes about in his autobiography; he was still alone and to him Fliess represented a great man. Yet he was a swindler. If I am not mistaken, that was discovered later. In Jones's books on Freud's life, Jones tells the truth about that. In this respect, in spite of all else in Jones, he gave an accurate description. Fliess's son Robert has come to the States and probably is still a member of the New York Psychoanalytic Society. In the early days I had some contact with Robert Fliess, but that has petered out.

At any rate, Freud and Fliess got into a fight. Freud thought that the idea of bisexuality was invented by Fliess; Freud wrote that. Here you see not only Freud's gullibility but his lack of knowledge of the literature. All that was in the early part of the twentieth century. Freud somehow committed the indiscretion of telling Fliess's idea of bisexuality to a man named Otto Weininger, who was a highly neurotic writer. Weininger wrote a book about bisexuality, in which the name of Fliess naturally was not mentioned.

Then Fliess got mad at Freud, and Freud angry with Fliess. Freud began to read the literature and found out that this idea of bisexuality had been advocated ten or fifteen years earlier by American and other psychiatrists. So that the notion that this was a product of the brain of Fliess was an absurdity. And twenty years later it was discovered who used the word for the first time in the 1850s; this later scientist was a histologist who found in the gonads of both the male and the female cells of each sex. Instead of saying what he found, he declared, "This is bisexuality." That there may be some differences between one cell in the developing embryo and the mature individual in his functioning never dawned on anybody. But the psychiatrists were always in desperate need to find a biological foundation for homosexuality; in their fight against barbaric, medieval laws, naturally they picked upon inherited homosexuality. And the concept of bisexuality played a special role for them.

5

WORLD WAR I, THE BUDAPEST CONGRESS, AND FREUD'S FAME

When the war came I was still finishing up my medical studies. As soon as I got the degree I went into the army as a medical officer. Ferenczi also joined; everyone served militarily. Psychoanalysis itself was impossible. I had to work at the hospitals, mainly in the army facility and in my free time for the university's. During the war there was only a little time to speak about psychoanalysis. Sometimes I did not see Ferenczi for long stretches.

I was at the number-one hospital in Budapest, part of the army, but because of the shortage of personnel I continued working at the university, too. It was self-evident for us to work about fourteen or fifteen hours a day. So in the morning I went into the military hospital and then in the afternoon I went to the university psychiatric hospital. There was no private practice of any kind; I spent almost the entire war in the military hospital in Budapest. The reason for this was that we had a lot of war neurotics. Various people experimented with different methods of treatment; I was sent out to learn the new techniques and I became indispensable in the hospital. I stayed alive by my curing the war neurotics. I got about half a dozen orders to go to the battlefield here or there, and the commanding officer of the hospital always interceded: there were thousands of people at the hospital, and if they sent me away the work would stop. So these orders were always changed, and I remained there.

We had gotten these huge numbers of war neurotics, *shell-shock* cases in the American literature but called *traumatic neurosis* by the Central Powers. At first nobody had known what to do with them. Then one German came out with an electric treatment which is difficult to understand today. It had nothing to do with later electric shock and also bore no resemblance to the mild galvanizing of the nerves customary in the older days. That was the electrotherapy of the time when Freud was still a student. In World War I you gave the patient a very mild shock. There was never any idea of his losing consciousness, or having any clamp, or breaking bones, et cetera.

This method had been tried out in Hungary by another neurologist. I read about it and asked the commanding officer of the hospital to let me go to that place and learn how to perform this new procedure. The device was supposed to succeed in bringing the person out of his shell shock.

I arrived there and watched what this guy was doing. This was the whole technique: he collected all these fellows in one big yard. Then a man who could not stand or walk, and was trembling, was brought on a stretcher (or came with crutches) into the doctor's office. The electrical treatment followed. Afterwards the man walked out into a courtyard where hundreds, if not thousands, of similarly afflicted soldiers were watching.

I would not know what this man's theoretical explanation was for the recoveries he achieved. I did not bother much with following up on that side of things. But it was clear to me that this was a successful suggestive treatment. Without having an inkling of what he was doing, he built up their fantasies, or something that remotely resembled an illusion. I went home and I got a staff to produce the same current. It was important that it should not be too strong. It had to be a certain kind of current, which I have forgotten now.

Before I started to use the procedure, one of the sergeants was instructed to spread the rumor that there was a discovery and that I had brought it back to be used. So curiosity was aroused. And I deliberately and knowingly built up a rumor, which was easy, that all the boys suffering from the same illness would assemble in a huge courtyard. All this took place in the barracks, where there was abundant room. The men were then brought in on a stretcher or on their crutches.

I put each of them on a couch, giving them a mild electric shock – the word *shock* is too strong. Afterwards I said firmly and kindly, "Now stand up." And he would stand up. "Now, walk." And he walked. Then I opened the door and he left.

There was a funny episode connected to this treatment procedure.

When the war had broken out, a former professional career officer of the Hungarian military corps was reactivated. He had been retired with the rank of major and then got made the commanding officer of the neuropsychiatric department of the division. He was not a stupid man. As a Jew he had been baptized; in the old days, if you wanted to go into an army career, that was what had to be done. In addition, he was related to the minister of defense, or war as it was called then. As a matter of course he came in to watch me many times. One day he said that he and I should go to the equivalent of the Academy of Medicine to report this cure. Long before that happened newspapermen had begun to talk about it, and I gave orders that none of them could attend: it was "a secret." Such an order could not be violated because of the penalty of jail.

My commanding officer wanted us to read a medical paper to the effect that my dramatic cures were the consequence of molecular changes brought about by dislocations in the spine and brain; this electric current supposedly changed everything back into the natural order, and that was why the symptoms disappeared. Now I had the problem of what to do with this idiotic idea; and handling this became one of my successful maneuvers. I said to him, "Fine, we will start to collect material." I had a red bulb on this machine from which the electric current was extracted; there was a special attachment, so that you could light this red bulb even if the apparatus itself was not connected. Every time the electric current went on, the red light did so too; when the electric current ceased, the red light went off. I did this for several weeks, until everybody knew that this red light had something to do with it.

Then I began to omit the electric charge and manipulate only the red light. The result was exactly the same; the red light went on for a few seconds, and then the man got up. There was another trick. Everybody who got cured had a three-month furlough coming to them, after which they had to go back to their own military unit. Needless to say, when the boys went back to their units, they relapsed either during the trip or on arrival; at the latest, they fell ill at the moment they were supposed to go back to the front. So that was the end of the cure.

After I was through with my experimental studies, I showed the commanding officer that here was this red light that I could turn on and off even when the apparatus itself was not connected; my claim was that the red light can produce the same cure. He naturally asked how it could do so. I said, "Please, I do not know how but it does." Naturally, I kept my mouth shut about suggestion and that sort of thing. I just said, "Now we have to work on finding out how the red light cures." He was intelligent enough to see what was going on. From time to time he asked me how I was getting along in disclosing the secret. I told him that there was a lot of literature to read, and that it was connected with all sorts of phenomena. The war ended and so did my inquiries into the red light. That was the funniest experience of my military work.

We knew at the time about the relapsing. We got these patients back again; a certain percentage even returned to the same hospital. It was printed in the papers, and the military doctors realized it. You could cure them, send them home, but the minute they had to come back they relapsed. There was no doubt about that; the facts were known. And thousands returned. As the soldiers arrived, our first question was, "Have you been at the hospital before?" And then the record was looked up.

Otherwise we did not know what to do with such patients at that time. The most conspicuous and flagrant problem were the guys with a large tremble. Also, they screamed at night. They had nightmares in which they repeated the so-called traumatic experience, which was obviously mostly the product of what Freud called dramatization in dreams. By such an illness they could get out of the war effort and still be a hero. Aside from being a coward or a traitor, they had sacrificed their health for their country. So this was a constellation that nobody could treat.

In addition, at the hospital I saw I do not know how many soldiers, who were collected and sent from the rest of the troops, who claimed to be or were suspected of being epileptics. Our job was to decide whether the fits they threw were epileptic, hystero-epileptic, hysteric, or simulated. That was a pleasant assignment. One of the most difficult scientific questions concerned what was unconscious elaboration as opposed to a conscious thought process.

In the fall of 1918 it was decided to hold an international psychoanalytic convention in Budapest, inviting the Central Powers. That meant that the analysts from Hungary, Austria, and Germany attended, and neutrals like the Dutch. In those days, with the war still going on, the British, French, and Americans remained our enemies. The Budapest Congress was a memorable event. Since I was the secretary of the local Budapest group of analysts, I also served as secretary of this whole convention. That was the occasion when I met for the first time Karl Abraham, who arrived in uniform, and Ernst Simmel, who likewise was an officer. Everybody was in uniform except for Freud.

By that time it was clear that we were going to lose the war. I knew that at the beginning of the fighting. I said that it would be a miracle if we won because the Austro-Hungarian Empire was composed of eight different languages; since each nationality was fighting the other, this empire was doomed to fall apart. Some weeks after the Budapest Congress the military front collapsed, and we went through a period of various revolutions. Throughout everything we worked diligently; the Budapest Society had meetings at least twice a month.

For the sake of his being present at the Budapest Congress, Freud had spent a few weeks in Hungary. During that time we had an opportunity to dine with him informally in little Hungarian restaurants. Anna Freud was there, too; that was when I first met her. Geza Roheim was already in the Society. This was the occasion when we really first could talk to Freud confidentially and privately around a big table under a walnut tree in the garden of one of those wonderful restaurants in Budapest. Life was soon hard in those days. We had terrible inflation and then various social upheavals.

Once the war was over, psychoanalytic work could be reassembled. Ferenczi had been, for practical purposes, separated from Freud for years because of the war. Ferenczi had his military place, and Freud was off in Vienna. They must have had correspondence between them, and on some furloughs Ferenczi might have been able to see Freud. I do not know these details. During the war itself, to make a trip which now takes half an hour by plane could easily consume two days' time. Hungary had few trains, and to undertake private pleasure trips was not exactly consistent with the program of the war. Afterwards it was clear to both Ferenczi and myself that the experience of being somewhat removed from Freud's immediate personal influence did a world of good. I grew up a bit and Ferenczi, with his extra twenty years that he had on me, also matured somewhat. His fiftieth birthday was in 1923, and I made a *festschrift* for him. So during the war itself he was in his early forties and therefore still a young man.

The name Freud remained unknown to the vast majority of members of the medical profession, not to speak of the general public, until after World War I. The first popularization of psychoanalysis, advertising of his name if you so please, came from people who read psychoanalysis and happened to be writers or newspapermen; these were the literature people who became disciples, joined the movement spiritually, or actually sought formal membership. Freud loved these people and was enormously pleased that they spread the new knowledge. It all seemed perfectly normal and healthy.

The Budapest psychoanalytic convention took place about two or three months, as I have said, before the collapse of the war effort and the revolutions; Kaiser Wilhelm ran away, and so did the Hungarian king.

Especially after it became known that Freud had been invited to America for a lecture in 1909, there was already an effort afoot to get him to Budapest. By the end of the war Freud had published most of what he had written; what came afterwards was relatively insignificant compared with the total body of his work.

By late 1918 some people were clinging to the idea that psychoanalysis was a new branch of medicine but that it was stubbornly opposed, like anything medically new. Ignatz Semmelweis was a Hungarian. He was the one who discovered how it happened that out of a hundred mothers who gave birth in the university hospital, sixty or seventy, if not more, died. From eight until nine young medical students went into pathological anatomy to work on cadavers and, with their filthy hands, then entered the obstetric clinic to examine women in the process of giving birth. It is a miracle that not a hundred percent died. This man was persecuted because of what he found out; eventually he died in an insane asylum. So the Hungarian public was indoctrinated with the spirit that all you have to do in medicine is to make a great discovery and you will have the whole profession against you. That had been demonstrated to them half a century before by the Semmelweis story.

Also around then, Albert Einstein was achieving world fame; that happened after World War I. There was an eclipse, and the first observation confirmed Einstein's calculations. That fact was printed on the front page of *The New York Times*, and overnight the name Einstein became known around the world. He had been as obscure outside physics as anybody could be. And when it became understood that there were things going on in the heavens that he had foretold and computed, thanks to the newspaperman who made this scoop in short order, other papers took it from the *Times*.

Freud's name at that time was far from world-famous. Nobody in psychoanalysis made any observations comparable to those in astronomy. But all the medical students knew this Semmelweis story. The peculiar thing is that then, at a time when the operations of the Budapest Psychoanalytic Society were a hundred percent on a humanistic basis, and when it was more or less a complete cult, the public still believed that this must be some new branch of medicine. Freud was a professor in Vienna, and Ferenczi was a doctor; so psychoanalysis had the credentials for being a medical science.

The more informed people who wanted to establish Freud's fame made incredible efforts to get the Nobel prize for him. Every former Nobelist who has once been honored by the prize is entitled to make recommendations for the future. I remember how they were trying to dig up as many people as possible, who had once received a Nobel prize, to have them send in Freud's name. They were guided by the hope that the more such recommendations arrived, the greater would be Freud's chances. Then they made a catastrophic mistake, in trying to get the medical Nobel prize for him, in that they had mobilized opposition to Freud.

Then they began to work that he should get the literary Nobel prize, like Russell later. Freud was after all a writer. Martin Luther King eventually got the Nobel prize for peace. But the antagonism to Freud was so stubborn that he never even got into the neighborhood; he was not seriously considered. But the fact that he could have been brought into the Nobel prize possibility still showed that there persisted a strong popular belief that psychoanalysis was a medical science. The development of psychoanalysis away from science into becoming a movement did become acknowledged to some extent in Vienna and Germany; but it never was understood in Hungary, nor in France or England either. In France then so little attention was being paid to psychoanalysis, and in England at the beginning, psychoanalysis was so unimportant that nobody much bothered to try to establish its status. The clarification of this whole story actually took place later in the United States.

Here we had huge psychology departments, a national association for psychologists, and a number of renegades, including myself, who took Freud's early discoveries for what they unquestionably were: a contribution to investigative science. And then it was seen that psychoanalysis went into a direction which was romantic or mystic. If I had had more knowledge of the Jewish mystical tradition, I would not have troubled with it, for one would have had to be careful about being exploited for misunderstanding the situation. So ignorance was much nicer.

Bakan's book is full of errors, and he naively accepts psychoanalytic concepts. But this has nothing to do with what is essential in his book, namely, the relation of Freud to the Jewish tradition. How much Bakan understood of psychoanalysis, and the extent to which he tries to show that much of the contents of Freud's work are determined by the oral tradition of Jewish teaching, is for me, personally, a subordinate point. To my thinking, there is just one key thing: reality testing, the observations of science. If a scientific idea is fruitful, it would not matter whether Freud took it from the Koran, or the Jewish mystical tradition, or from Hindu philosophy.

In my time, however, neither in Hungary nor Germany nor England was there an adequate attempt to separate the scientific part of Freud's work from this later movement aspect. In the beginning some single attempts were made in France. In 1913 Regis and Hesnard wrote on psychoanalysis, and they formulated the demand that it should be more precise. All their efforts went under the name of their pride in Gallic logic. These people were both professors at the university in Paris; they were academicians. For them the whole idea of validation and evidence was in their flesh and blood, and they tried to rewrite what Freud said in order to give a sound presentation of psychoanalysis. They were working at a time when I had never written a word yet and was still a medical student.

Even though these two French writers were trying to bring psychoanalysis over to science, there was no reaction to their work within Freudian circles; it was said that they just overestimated logic in the Gallic spirit. I remember that argument: "They think that if it is logical, it is also scientific." Analysts talked about science in such grotesque, nonsensical statements. It is of course true that science has to be logical; but their 1913 book, as far as the development of psychoanalysis in Europe was concerned, had no influence that I know of.

The grandiosity of these central European analytic groups was something that has to be studied. I do not think the Christian apostles went that far. Within psychoanalysis there was an almost apostolic activity which affected both the stands people took as well as the status they attained. It seemed as if compared to psychoanalysis, nothing that men had produced before had any significance. Mankind now for the first time had become aware of itself, and Freud was thought to have disclosed the secret powers that dominate us outside our consciousness. In contrast to the greatness of his discovery of the unconscious, everything else was dwarfed into insignificance; at least that was the spirit with which the early psychoanalysts were imbued.

6

EDITOR IN BERLIN

In the fall of 1922 I decided that I must be analyzed. My training up until then had consisted in reading everything that had been written by Freud and all these journals as they gradually came into being. My education in psychoanalysis consisted of dinner and coffeehouse parties with Ferenczi; I met him as a rule at least twice a week socially. In the early period of our acquaintance, I told him about everything I knew; and he reciprocated with his own observations. I discussed with him dreams and symptoms. It was a kind of supervisory situation, and our sessions were conducted in the most informal and casual manner. Then I decided that since everybody gets analyzed, I must too. It was impossible for me to be analyzed by Ferenczi; by that time we were bosom friends except for the years we were separated during the war. I told him I was planning to go to Karl Abraham.

I chose Abraham, who was the leading figure of the Berlin Psychoanalytic Institute, which was just in its beginning period, because he was the only clinically oriented analyst that I knew. That meant he did not neglect concrete opportunities for observations; Ferenczi was too apt to jump right away into evolutionary speculations about what happened millions of years ago. I loved Abraham's case histories; they were the first ones I had read. Freud had, at the time, only a few case histories; and that was the total clinical knowledge anybody could have.

So I went to Berlin and was analyzed by Abraham for two years.

Two months after my arrival I was invited to join the faculty of the newly organized Psychoanalytic Institute, and that was the time when I started my teaching activities in January 1923. In Budapest I had started a psychoanalytic practice after World War I was over; I began also to work there as a doctor. I treated my patients as best I could; so did everyone else, still as yet there was no organized training of any kind.

But then when I came to Berlin that was a period when we began to build up the idea of a psychoanalytic curriculum. And that was a time when I started out teaching. A few years later an international committee worked out the first plan that there should be a personal analysis, supervised work, and theoretical as well as clinical instruction. The whole basic outline of training, including what should be taught as well as the required analysis under supervision, was worked out then for the first time.

In the midst of all this activity of mine, Freud was already having a fight with Rank, who had come over temporarily to the United States. In 1923 he had written a book called *The Trauma of Birth*, which was vehemently attacked by the other doctors. So one day in 1924 I got a wire from Vienna saying I should come to see Freud and take over the editorship of the *Zeitschrift*. I was stunned at the idea of filling the position that Rank had held. The invitation came out of the clear blue sky, without any preparation.

The job Freud was offering me was unusual. There were three names on the magazine. Besides myself, the other two were Max Eitingon and Ferenczi, but both Eitingon and Ferenczi were superfluous to the actual workings of the journal. In actuality I was the executive editor. My name was printed as the person to whom manuscripts should be sent.

I had to read all the submissions to decide what was bad as opposed to what was worth publishing. It was my place to re-do the German papers of the doctors who did not know how to write a scientific paper. I had to read all the proofs and carry out the correspondence; I had no secretarial help and not a penny either of salary or expense account. With the result that a few years later, I got in 1926 a letter from Freud when I congratulated him on his seventieth birthday: "to you who contribute by far the greatest unselfish work to the cause of psychoanalysis." This praise was merited. My daily work in those days started around seven in the morning and finished at two o'clock the next night.

In the meantime I increasingly taught classes. We had three Society meetings a week, and I had my teaching schedule; there was my editing of the *Zeitschrift*, and I had my private patients. In the meantime Hungary collapsed. I then had no money coming from home; that had to stop, and I lived from hand to mouth. In the meantime my own analysis went on from Christmas 1922 to Christmas 1924; a year later Abraham died. It was a training analysis, at an irregular time when there were no rules established yet for how to become an analyst.

When I had gone to Vienna and Freud asked me whether I would take over the editorial job, I had accepted the position. In the Vienna Society the establishment of an institute in Berlin, which was due to Eitingon's having given the money for it, created terrific jealousy and rivalry. Vienna thought it had the birthright to have the first institute. Through the establishment of that path-breaking institute in Berlin and all the help Freud gave to it and the Berlin Society, the Viennese were unspeakably jealous.

Then came the news that Freud was willing to have the editorial office of the *Zeitschrift* move from Vienna to Berlin because he wanted me to be the editor. There were at least ten people in Vienna who each expected to be made editor instead. That was a major tragedy in the story. On the one hand, they kowtowed to Freud because that was his decision in picking me; on the other hand, they wanted to murder me. They tried to tell Freud what an absurdity it was, that the journal, printed at an office in Vienna, had its editor in Berlin. The manuscripts had to come to me in Berlin, and I had to then send them back to Vienna; all the page proofs had to be forwarded to Berlin. The arrangement involved immense complications, but Freud silenced all those who objected.

I said to him, "How did you pick on me?" At that he smiled and said, "I am not going to tell you." He had gotten detailed reports about me from both Eitingon and Abraham. Since he could not give me any salary or money, he had wanted to tease me. When I had first gone to Berlin in 1922, it was a convention that to become a member one read a paper; I gave one on the pathways of natural science in the light of psychoanalysis. So my biological orientation existed from the first day on, long before I was analyzed.

The original title of the journal I was to edit had been *The International Journal for Medical Psychoanalysis*. In those days, despite the many names which appeared on the cover, the man who actually did the work was Rank. And he had persuaded Freud to drop the word *medical* from the title, despite the fact that an extra journal, called *Imago*, had already been created for the application of psychoanalysis to the humanities. Rank was the editor of *Imago*, too. Freud, knowing my own orientation, said: "I will give you a present. If you wish, you can restore the term *medical psycho-analysis* on the title page. But you have to arrange that with Storfer."

A. J. Storfer was Swiss, a schizophrenic patient of A. A. Brill's at the Burghölzli at a time when Brill was working in Zurich. Storfer was a charming guy, a journalist, a dilettante in all the cultural sciences. He wrote about mythology and culture, in fact on everything under the sun, but he was schizophrenic. At the same time, he was director of the International Psychoanalytic Press, which by that time had been brought into being thanks to the financial contributions of Marie Bonaparte, the Princess George. Storfer was the director. So I came to him, who was also jealous that I had become the editor.

I then made a terrible blunder. Instead of my saying that the professor had ordered the change, I stated, "The professor left it to me to restore the word *medical*, and I want it." But Storfer exclaimed "No!" He was a man whose life revolved around printing and the particular type used for the journal. He was what we called a *typomaniac*. He had had an artist design what type of letters should be used. Only one type of letter appeared in all the volumes, and he had had the title page designed. By that time he had that work done. He protested, "I should destroy the color and this magnificent page! Where would you put this word *medical?*" I said, "On the same paper." He replied, "Show me where! That is impossible!"

It was fantastic. I had the choice to start out my office as editor with a bloody fight with Storfer or say, "All right. The word *medical* will not be in the title." So I just dropped the whole business, and it never got restored. After I had made that initial blunder, there was nothing I could do. It was impossible for me to lie to him and say that Freud had ordered this. That was not up to me; he would have been capable of going to Freud and pestering him with the same typographical business, that the title page should not be changed because it was such a beauty.

It may have been well laid out, but to Storfer it was a life and death question: "How can you put in *medical!*" It was also characteristic of Freud that by trying to do me a favor he knew I wanted, he did not succeed in accomplishing the objective. The jealousy and envy of the Viennese crowd increased as the significance of Berlin as a center of psychoanalysis grew. The lion's share of the work fell on my head. Storfer, not a doctor but an amateur humanist, was also a member of the official editorial board. He said to everybody, "Everything that goes on takes place in Berlin and is done by Rado." All the Viennese hostility was concentrated on me; it was a repressed anger.

Abraham died in 1925 and then Ernst Simmel became president, and I stayed secretary of the Berlin Society. Throughout these years I made regular visits to see Freud. I think it important to record that Freud paid no attention to the journal itself. He got one copy of every proof that came out of the printing office. All the other proofs came to me in the usual routine fashion. Sometimes months and years passed by without Freud making any remark about the journal. He said he was pleased, everything was fine, and that and that was good; this remained our relationship until the last day. So I was left completely alone as editor. If I wanted any decision to be made by him rather than myself, I had to write a letter and ask what I should do. Most of the time the answer was, "Do what you want."

He always tried to please me and to give me some reward for this murderous work. I finally got a secondhand portable typewriter; that was the editorial office with which I operated. Freud was overwhelmed with what I accomplished—how magnificent was the memorial edition we had after Abraham died, how splendid the volumes we published for Freud's seventieth birthday.

And then came a lot of fighting about the issue of lay analysis. He published his booklet *The Question of Lay Analysis* in 1926. Freud became a vehement proponent of nonmedical psychoanalysis. I was supposed to organize, and did so, a collection of papers on this educational problem; at that time I was also secretary of the International Training Commission. Freud had asked me, as editor of the *Zeitschrift*, to publish a debate about the problem of lay analysis—that is, about his pamphlet—and I was supposed to try to get statements from the most prominent analysts. This I did in two issues of the *Zeitschrift* in 1927. He then published a reply, restating his case.

Almost every important analyst had a contribution to the discussion, pro or con; the only one who wrote not a line was myself, and I was the editor. There was opposition in this debate, semicamouflaged and open, and I was left in a terrible fix. I knew what Freud wanted, but as his official editor I could not write against lay analysis and also was unable to bring myself to make a phony endorsement. I could not have opposed him; everybody would have laughed. But I was against lay analysis. I do not know whether he noticed that I wrote nothing, but I assume so; others certainly did.

In the meantime a wonderful Society in Berlin had been organized. Almost all the members became prominent in the larger psychoanalytic movement. Franz Alexander, for instance, had already won a prize; he had just finished his psychoanalytic studies. Alexander was in training at the institute and became one of the first graduates, and when we had the international convention in Berlin during September 1922 (that is when I went to Berlin), he got an award from Freud. Alexander was already slated for a big career. After the death of Abraham the entire command of the institute was put in the hands of Eitingon, who paid every nickel that was spent there. He was philosophically minded and not an active man, so in actual practice that meant that everything under the sun in Eitingon's name was done by myself. Everyone knew that.

The extent of my own accepted loyalty to the group can be gauged by Freud's initial choice of me as editor. When Rank had still been in that office, I wrote him a letter that since Wilhelm Stekel and Alfred Adler's departures from the movement, they were considered dead. I said this was scientifically impossible. And I remember the phrase that I used: "We are entitled to disapprove of certain contributions, but we are not entitled to repress them," because if we do that to them, we damage psychoanalysis as a science. Rank replied that he completely shared my view, and then nothing happened. I criticized the fact that no paper ever written by Adler after his departure was even mentioned in the psychoanalytic journals.

When I became editor myself, in the first issue I introduced an innovation. I divided reviews into three groups: psychoanalytic literature, other psychiatric literature, and related literature. And I began to bring in reviews about psychiatric contributions which had nothing to do with psychoanalysis. But I could not get anybody to write a review about anything that Adler or some of the other "dissidents" had written. The nicest thing is that I got a congratulatory letter from Freud that I had done this, and the matter was left there. Not because anybody opposed my suggestion; I could not get someone to write up an Adlerian contribution from the psychoanalytic point of view. Occasionally on Freud's instigation Ferenczi wrote disapproving criticism of one or the other publications by Jung.

So these people were dead, the same way as I later died in 1931 or 1932 after I decided to come to the United States. The whole system of ostracism had started earlier. You can read in Freud's *On the History of the Psychoanalytic Movement* that in the beginning he was tolerant of views differing from his own. But then he felt that it is so important to have a group with unanimous agreement that he became stiff, and that led to the departure first of Adler, then of Stekel, and finally Jung. Years later I heard Ernest Jones every decade or half-decade on one occasion or another saying, "We cannot go on with this business. We cannot continue

excommunicating people and considering them dead. This is a scandal."
And every time he made this announcement, anybody could have expected that he would do something about it; the whole thing ended with his expression of pious sentiments, and he never followed up on it. Occasionally in international journals tolerant reviews appeared, but the spirit of a cult, a completely isolated ethos of a sect, remained unchanged.

The admission of nonmedical people to therapeutic work also started out early and only later became known under the heading of *lay analysis*. Rank was the one who made a beginning with that, and then Anna Freud, under Freud's ·pressure, came into analysis without ever having had anything to do with the medical sciences. My personal situation on this issue was terribly difficult. I had insisted that psychodynamic psychoanalysis and psychoanalytic therapy are part of medicine. Who does what in practical life is another question. But one thing is sure: the same way as someone who practices medicine must know the basic sciences, this new field of Freud's should also be part of the scientific world, and there are just no two ways about it. In my view a sociological or cultural orientation cannot replace the knowledge of brain physiology.

But I had written nothing on the issue of lay analysis, although about thirty people participated in the symposium in the *Zeitschrift*. This is how the few oppositional spirits within psychoanalysis behaved. To some extent Jones shared my view, but he was forced to remain silent much in the same way I was.

Coming back to the early spirit, so far as the medical nature of psychoanalysis is concerned, the idea was to be a psychoanalyst and nothing else. Around 1924 I had become the editor. Freud had been trying to please me by offering to put back the word *medical* in the title of the *Zeitschrift*, but that was prevented by Storfer. At that time Freud had already issued the complaint that medicine wanted to swallow up psychoanalysis; it was like saying medicine wants to absorb anatomy.

Many years later I understood Freud's absurd fear. Up to this day now in 1963, nowhere did I ever see a medical person saying a word about the application of this basic science of psychodynamics – or, as it was called at that time, dynamic psychology – to any aspect of culture. So Freud's complaint possessed no objective meaning. Medicine had no interest in what results analysts were able to achieve by using psychodynamic psychoanalysis and applying it to their heart's desires. So this idea that medicine wanted to swallow up psychoanalysis was empty.

It was decades later that it became clear to me that Freud's statement was a reversal of the truth. Psychoanalysis wanted to swallow up all medicine and the other sciences. According to Freud's feelings, the moment medicine was used as a point of orientation outside of psychoanalysis it became a hostile force. He wanted to conquer the world. All the departments of medicine were secretly viewed by him as subdivisions of psychoanalysis, and likewise all the cultural sciences.

Even this grotesque absurdity had a scientific basis, in that the behavior of the human organism is dominated by the cerebral cortex, in particular by what we call the mind. So if that be true, then it follows that the entire system of medical science and all cultural studies must be subordinated to that science which specializes in the study of the psyche.

7

ANALYSIS WITH ABRAHAM AND THE BERLIN SOCIETY

An international psychoanalytic convention had been scheduled for Berlin in September 1922, and the preceding May I had written to Abraham from Budapest, saying that after the fall meetings I would like to stay on in Berlin to be analyzed by him. He replied that he would be delighted to have me do that, although he was uncertain whether he would have time available early in October or not. I might have to wait for a few weeks until the changes, giving him an opening in his schedule that he was looking for, would have taken place. He hoped that this uncertainty would make no difference to me, and it did not.

I arrived in Berlin for the Congress and remained there; I started my analysis a few weeks later. It is extremely difficult for me to reconstruct after so many years the actual analytic procedure I underwent with Abraham. But I can say for certain that features about the approach to the life of a patient which are taken for granted today in any psychiatric school, or at any social work institution or as any variant of the practice of psychotherapy in the United States, were not known or in existence then.

Nobody had an idea then about how to approach a patient or to find what was more, rather than less, important; nor was it understood what the therapist should deal with as opposed to leave alone. So without my being in any way unjust to Abraham personally, because we all more or less did the same thing as he tried to to do with me, attention was focused on phenomena about which Freud had written and for which we had an explanation. It was not a study of the life of a person, digging out what were the turning points, or the central problems, and then seeing what we could do about it. Instead it was a search for opportunities to apply certain Freudian insights to a human life, which was a total reversal of the therapeutic procedure known in the United States; in one sentence, that describes the Berlin situation then.

There was a quest for signs of the castration complex, oedipal conflicts, narcissism, oral and anal eroticism. But none of this was so much an application of theoretical so-called insights to the problems of a patient. Both the listening to the patient as well as the patient's productions of thoughts were oriented by theories, since everyone found it fruitful to talk about such matters. So that problem finding was not germane to the life history and the actual therapeutic needs of the patients. The problems were found according to what occurrences or symptoms could by that time be interpreted according to Freud's writings, which was the opposite of the whole situation as it should be.

My analysis was personally helpful to me in a limited way. For when I began to analyze myself, which I am still constantly doing to the best of my ability, I started to see, as the years passed, what vitally important events and turning points took place in my life which never came out with my treatment under Abraham, even though I was in analysis for two years. In those days that was a long analysis, and sessions then were six days a week.

We did not come anywhere near the real neighborhood of my conflicts, because I had no idea of them nor did Abraham, and Freud had not happened to write about such issues. So it can be stated that my analysis fairly reflected the state of knowledge and therapeutic skill of that period. And that applied by and large to all the analysts working at that time, and the deviation from that model took place only with analysts who went up to the sky because they used the patient to discuss the analyst's own new papers. Analysts could be carried away by their own research interests, as Freud himself often was. But there was no great exception to that way of proceeding.

The first attempt to give a more or less coherent, integrated picture at least of that which Freud had found, rather than piecemeal bits, was by Alexander. That was his great merit at the time. He published a book *Psychoanalysis of the Total Personality*, which was a monstrous title. (Whenever I was angry at Storfer I wrote him a letter: Dear Total Director of the Total Press.) Aside from the bombastic title to the book, Alexander had made a serious attempt to outline something like the pathological development in a person.

Alexander's books were composed only of elements which Freud had found, because nothing else was available. But it was a first attempt at a certain organized, integrated presentation which could guide the student in following a certain line in his mind. Why is this person here in analysis? What comes first, and what later? Which elements should be treated? The technique of interpreting free associations meant that the analysis practically started all over again in every session; and what had come about in a week or a month or a year was a haphazard performance.

It might be thought that the libido theory gave a framework. But it could never tell you how it happened that a person suddenly at this point did such and such. The actual development of symptoms was a mystery. The libido theory underplayed the whole idea of pathological inhibition. The first understanding came when Freud began to emphasize inhibitions, symptoms, and anxiety; but that was in 1926. The first real insight came when we grasped that pathology starts when useful healthy activities which are being carried out by all normal people suddenly become impossible because the person is inhibited.

The compensatory miscarried repair work, the symptoms and fantasies of the patient, completely diverted attention from the fact that without inhibition there would be no need for symptomatology. If you begin to remove by analysis the consequences of the inhibition, without touching the root cause, it becomes an endless process. As long as the inhibition exists, its consequences will only be revived. When I finally described that in a paper written in New York, it made people panicky, and they decided I was not a real Freudian.

For quite some time in psychoanalytic therapy it was not the discovery of the significant problems in the life of the patient, Freud's original objective, which was guiding his pupils. The disciples were following up on applying existing knowledge to their patients. Issues were examined or overlooked in the light of what was already known or then understood. Application of previous ideas was undertaken whether or not it fitted or was important for the patient.

My own analysis was helpful to me in coping with certain emotional reactions in my life. It might have been better if Abraham had interpreted my quick temper rather than my Oedipus complex. But he was constructive for me, although it is difficult to separate out how he succeeded. I think now of his cordiality and friendship, which he extended to me from the first moment we started. I do not doubt for a minute that it must have been the enthusiastic descriptions of me he sent to Freud that led to my appointment as editor.

Similar letters must have gone from Eitingon to Freud. By the time Eitingon was half-ready to see a problem, I already supplied him with the solution. I was young and fast in those days. It has to be extremely difficult to isolate the situational benefits I derived from being in Berlin from what was, actually speaking, the result of the therapeutic procedure itself. Summing up both sides, I did definitely benefit. I can testify to the fact that Abraham was a man of impeccable integrity, with an honest scientific interest, even if he was of limited special talent in grasping unusual motivations and the like. Abraham did cling to methodological principles, but they were naively held and based on what he had learned in medical school. I doubt that he ever read a philosophical paper on scientific methodology. But he opposed and was afraid of Ferenczi's speculations. This sort of wild thinking could have a devastating influence, and Abraham feared that, like Jung, analysts will forget that psychoanalysis is a clinical discipline.

As compared with the early days in Budapest I found a completely different atmosphere prevailing in Berlin. From the first meeting Abraham came in and began to talk about the cases he had analyzed; he described what he found, how he explained it, what might or might not be true. And naturally the others followed suit. So that was a domain of clinical psychoanalysis which I welcomed with enthusiasm. Since it was highly clinical practically nobody bothered with the theory, and most of them either did not read or failed to understand the conceptualization. They began to ask me that I give lectures on theory, which I knew inside-out. For years my chief activity in teaching was to supply the theoretical foundations which almost everybody else neglected.

As I have already mentioned, by January 1923 I was a member of the budding faculty of the Berlin Psychoanalytic Institute. And from that moment on, the essential work in organizing a curriculum was done by myself. I had patients at the same time; I was making a living through my psychoanalytic practice. I had my own analysis, too; and I also worked at the Psychoanalytic Institute itself, which included an outpatient clinic.

It makes no sense that we should promise people treatment and then, like Ferenczi, talk about what happened two hundred million years ago in the evolution of the species. Abraham was genuinely wary that in a young science, the character of which was not yet settled, this sort of thing would be injurious. Everything was in flux, and each powerful individual was able to mold at least the interests of his own pupils in a local group. Abraham was afraid that what should be an empirical science would become sort of a speculative system, like the many semi-Talmudic schools organized by religious leaders in the course of history.

Although Abraham is sometimes credited with being the father of the libido theory, that bit of credit for him is unrelated to the facts. Freud himself created the theory of the libido. The first edition of Freud's *Three Essays on the Theory of Sexuality* came out in 1905, and there were subsequent editions of that book. By the time Abraham started to write about the libido, the theory was fifteen years old and included everything that it today encompasses, with one exception: Abraham divided both the oral and anal phases into substages.

All Abraham did was subdivide these two steps. The systematization had all been done by Freud. And then in 1925 or so, Freud prepared the last edition of his three contributions on sex and completely included Abraham's points in the course of one paragraph, without leaving out one word. So in this book by Freud, Abraham's part consisted in one additional paragraph.

If somebody knew nothing about the literature and arrived at the Berlin Society meetings where Abraham's innovations were much discussed, he could have thought that this was all Abraham. I have to laugh about that because after Abraham made his contribution, that there is a sadistic phase and a postambivalent phase of the oral libido and something similar in the anal libido, Freud later talked about narcissism, oral eroticism, the pregenital and the genital. And then came the elaborations of all that in so many papers and books.

Abraham, who died at Christmas in 1925, had started writing these papers of his around the early 1920s. I remember when he wrote one of his last essays. He also was in the habit of showing me his manuscripts. Freud had turned that way to Ferenczi, and Abraham, ever since I had been with him, gave me manuscripts of his before sending them to Vienna. So I somehow read all the papers of Freud before they were printed, because soon after I left Budapest I had become the editor; Freud then sent me his manuscripts from Vienna to Berlin, and I sent them back there to the printer.

Abraham showed his manuscripts not only to me but first of all to Freud. And he gave me a letter to see, in which Freud said, "This is all nice, but I do not think you have made full benefit of the libido theory." Of all things! And then Abraham asked me, "What does he mean?" And I supplied him the information that I presumed Freud thought of at various points, and Abraham went ahead and rewrote his paper.

It is true that, as you seem to know already, Helene Deutsch and I were in analysis with Abraham at one and the same time. That is where we became friends, and we remained close until our scientific work parted. But that has nothing to do with libido theory. After she had been analyzed by Freud in Vienna there was nobody else in the city she trusted for herself. Freud could not take her again, in part for financial reasons, because by that time he was making a living on foreigners who could afford to pay him in their own currency. Helene had the choice between Abraham and Ferenczi and chose the former because he was a clinically oriented man, which everybody knew and could see. And she went to Freud and said, "What do you think of my going?" And he said, "Fine, that is a good choice."

The main point is that the Berlin Society established the model of a psychoanalytic group in which at least the clinical empirical spirit was deeply rooted and which was not carried away with the speculations of Ferenczi reaching too far out into other areas.

Erich Fromm originated at the Berlin Society; he read his first psychoanalytic paper at one of my seminars. If I remember correctly, that was when he attacked the easygoing manner in which the religion of the individual, what Freud saw as obsessionality, got equated with the development of historical religions. That was one of the interesting topics at that time, in the wake of *Totem and Taboo*. Freud, in one of his papers, made some such remark that you could describe obsessional neurosis as a private religion of an individual and, in reverse, the historic development of religions as an obsessional neurosis.

Fromm's thesis was that this was a dangerous analogy because the environment of the life of the individual is one thing, and the organization of a society something incomparably different. Unless all the influences are recognized that lead to the invention and spread of religion, we are arriving at a valueless game. I recall having cautioned Fromm that the only explanatory phrase taken from psychoanalysis in his paper was that of libidinal gratifications. Everything a human being did was being described in a generic way.

The characteristic of that time was a neglect of a human being's emotional life. Everybody was looking for oral, pregenital, and genital components in motivation. But that some people are happy, others

unhappy, some afraid, or full of anger, and some loving and affectionate –
read the case histories to find how such differences between people were
then absent from the literature. So in my opinion the word *libidinal* came
to mean nothing.

That is where Fromm started. And when he left Europe and came to
the United States with my help, he and I met. I had given him an official
invitation in my capacity as educational director of the New York
Psychoanalytic Institute. It was our last get-together in pre-Hitler times. It
was in 1932 I believe. Somewhere in German territory Hitler was already
at the door. After that, Fromm wrote me a letter: "I have to tell you what
I learned in psychoanalysis." He arrived in New York, and that was the last
I saw of him. The invitation from me was helpful in getting his visa.

The books he has been writing, which have made him famous in the
social sciences, are all part of his development since he arrived in the
United States. Not a trace of that was in existence beforehand. He was
trying to be a lay analyst; that was how he made a living. Here it was
possible for the first time for him to get jobs for which he got paid, and he
began to write books; one was more successful than the next. The first
book was, I believe, *Escape From Freedom*.

Nowhere did I see in his writing an insight that was not available
before. This was all the application of knowledge, mediocre journalistic
writing which was influential because sociologists had nothing and he had
something they could understand. He wrote a book recently on Karl Marx
and Freud as philosophers, and I heard two interviews where he talked
about his work. His statements about Marx were based on texts which had
not been published until recently. But what Fromm said about Freud was
hair-raising! Fromm's speculations about what Freud wanted, without
Fromm anywhere making an attempt to supply evidence, were like sitting
Sunday afternoon on the porch smoking a good pipe or a cigar.

Alexander was, of course, also a member of the Berlin Society, and
so was Ernst Simmel, who later came to this country, too. Carl Müller-
Braunschweig was by profession a philosopher, a Ph.D.; but he had little
known influence. Otto Fenichel was also in Berlin, he was a pupil of mine;
and also Edith Jacobson, who was first a student and then a member.
Then gradually a number of people moved from Vienna to Berlin, like
Wilhelm Reich and Theodor Reik.

In 1930 Reich arrived from Vienna. I have forgotten who was his
original analyst; perhaps it was Paul Federn. At any rate, Reich came to
continue analysis with me. By that time he was heavily involved in

communist propaganda; he was both leftist and outspoken. To my knowledge he was not a party member, but he was an admirer of Lenin and Stalin. I had him in analysis for perhaps three or four months.

Then I asked his wife, Annie, to come from Vienna to Berlin; I had to make an important statement to her. I said to Annie Reich in the spring of 1931, a few months before I left Berlin to move for good to the States, "I have very bad news. This man is a schizophrenic. And not a schizophrenic in the coffeehouse sense. He is a schizophrenic in the most serious way." She was knocked out; nobody had ever suspected any such thing, and he was at the height of his medical reputation. People were already uneasy about his involvement in political matters, but his scientific contributions and his clinical gifts were widely acknowledged. He had already written *Character Analysis*.

Annie Reich was unprepared for a statement like mine. She said, "Thank you very much for telling me this." She went home to Vienna and instituted divorce proceedings and, in no time, was divorced from him. That was the only decision she could make. As much as it was possible, I gave her a few examples to support my diagnosis. I said to her, "I would not make a statement like this without weighty reasons and here they are." After that, it took about ten years until the world discovered that Reich was psychotic. And since she kept her mouth shut and I did, too, nobody knew that was the issue. It was in the 1930s that he started his "orgone" business; I thought then that it was a paranoid fantasy. I was the one who had had the bad luck to discover his illness, and the good fortune to help save his family.

Theodor Reik was also in Berlin and continued to write along his own lines; I have already touched on what I think of him. Originally he was a psychologist and a recognized writer, so he had an easy time going on about psychoanalysis. In those days he never wrote a line about clinical analysis. He analyzed in order to make a living. He made a contribution in his anthropological books but not in his later works. I got bored by reading them. He can be witty, but his works contain too much padding; everything gets stretched out, so that things that would be nice to read in an article of twelve or fifteen pages are 350 pages long.

I never doubted the seriousness of Reik's intentions. But I did not take him to be a contributor to medical psychoanalysis. In his own field I consider him a worthwhile man. Whether or not he is a good therapist I have not the remotest inkling because I have never seen anybody who was analyzed by him. He had a definite scientific integrity. When the New

York Psychoanalytic Society did not want to accept him as a member, he told them to go to hell and established his own organization. He published one book after another; he is guaranteed to be better known in the United States by his books than the entire membership of the New York Psychoanalytic Society.

8

ABRAHAM'S DEATH

The problem for me with the atmosphere of the Hungarian Psychoanalytic Society had been, as I have said, that clinical interest, not to speak of therapy, in the patients' case histories, in what went on in the lives of human beings as revealed by psychoanalytic investigation, was practically crowded out of the meetings. Nobody would have dreamt that the people who were conducting these strange discussions were M.D.'s who were treating their contemporaries because of the presence of specific neurotic disorders. On one occasion in Budapest, I remember, a doctor came and began to talk about clinical observations. It was a stunning novelty. A characteristic of the Hungarian group was not only an absence of interest in therapy, but of any concern with clinical psychodynamics or case histories.

That was the original reason for my going into analysis with Abraham in Berlin. This choice was self-evident to me. An analysis with Ferenczi was inconceivable. We had been together day and night. I chose Abraham because he was the first man of whom I knew, and who appeared in the literature, as someone who wrote about clinical psychoanalytic training. In every one of his papers, rarely did he indulge in what you could call a speculation. Like every recently trained psychiatrist, he was interested in patients, in the history of various illnesses, in how they developed, in what we could find out about the causation and the treatment. He was not much concerned with technique or treatment in general.

Hardly had I started on the analysis with Abraham, when Max Eitingon extended to me an invitation to settle there and become a faculty member of the Psychoanalytic Institute, which was at the time in the process of organization. Naturally I gladly accepted the invitation and chose to stay there.

Abraham, who began his papers with saying, "in a case I found such and such," was the one who invented how to write psychoanalytic case histories. By that time Freud had already published all his big case histories, including the last one on the Russian Wolf-Man. I do not recall that afterward he published any case history in great detail. He presented certain aspects of cases or used them for the illustration of some theoretical propositions, but the last explicit case history was already a few years old. It was impossible for any ordinary person to follow in Freud's footsteps here, for his own cases were overdramatized and presented in a manner for which no space would have been available for others to publish similarly.

Abraham invented a use of the Freudian language, combined with the ordinary clinical terms of psychiatry, to be able to tell the essential story of a patient, sometimes in a few paragraphs and often in a few pages. While I was myself a teacher, I regularly attended his lectures for a few years, for the simple reason that I had never attended lectures of this kind. In Budapest they were nonexistent; and when I went to Vienna to listen, which was rarely, it was usually some special occasion and no case histories were reported.

Abraham was not very deep, but he understood motivation you can get hold of more or less on the surface, including many things which are repressed but still superficial. He became the great master in presenting these case histories and giving the newcomer the idea that psychoanalysis is a medical science, a clinical discipline, and a branch of psychiatry. It was from him that I learned how to handle this type of material.

I did not know this then. But I understood that I could not start out writing case histories like Freud, all jam-packed with theories. And the same thing was true about the meetings of the Berlin Society. That group suffered from over-zealousness. They had three meetings a month—one was reserved for *small communications*, in which people just came and said, "This and this I observed, and the significance of that is such and such." And that was the sole training and self-education of every member of the Society in clinical practice and psychoanalysis. After about half a year, I looked back from this vantage point to the Hungarian Society, and I said to myself, "Almighty God! We were not in the clouds, we were beyond the clouds somewhere else."

Unfortunately around Christmas 1925 Abraham died. He was sick for eight or nine months. That was a tragic story which itself would require a volume to describe. His illness started allegedly – nobody knows – by his having eaten chicken and swallowing a bone. That led to some bronchial or lung complication with the development of lung disease, which was not ever clear what that was. He just could not get well.

Then came the complications. The doctor shifted from this lung business and said he had a gallbladder ailment, possibly stones. And the diagnoses went back and forth, both doctors and the family in a state of helplessness. In my mind at the time the family did not turn to the proper physicians, not out of evil intent but because of ignorance. This desperate situation went on for months and months, all of 1925. In those days Felix Deutsch still lived in Vienna. He was an internist, not yet a psychoanalyst. I persuaded Mrs. Abraham to ask Felix Deutsch to come and take a look at what was going on. By my making this move I got close to Abraham. I respected him immensely; he lacked Ferenczi's brilliance, but you got the feeling "this is a dependable man." To make a long story short, Felix Deutsch could not do anything either.

And then came a fatal mistake. They decided to operate on Abraham's gallbladder, which was a serious abdominal operation, while the lung was still sick and he had to spit out pus. What the operation found I do not remember, if I ever knew. But we all understood was that this was a medically impossible business. The scar from the operation had to heal; on the other hand, he had constantly to cough in order not to choke. So every time he had a coughing spell, the cut opened up. Then they sewed it together again, and there was trouble with the lung, and it went back and forth this way.

This was such a fantastic story. Eventually he died while I was on a Christmas visit to Freud. By that time I was editor and therefore went to see Freud on business. I was with Freud when the telephone call or the telegram came that Abraham was dead, and became an eyewitness to Freud's first reaction. He immediately sat down and wrote a statement which was hurriedly put into an almost fully printed copy of the *Zeitschrift*, and he discussed the matter with me at great length.

I was close to Abraham, desperate about this terrible medical history, the like of which I never heard either before or since. I remember that Freud wrote a warm eulogy of one or one-and-a-half pages. I recall one sentence: "With the death of Abraham, psychoanalysis possibly lost an irreplaceable part of its future." And that was the way he felt.

Despite that reaction, five minutes later he turned to me—I was by that time an important member of the Berlin Society—and asked, "What is going to happen to the Berlin Society now that we have lost Abraham?" So Freud's mourning seemed over after five minutes; I was amazed by that. Freud's relationship to Abraham was naturally older than my own. Abraham had brought to Freud all the adoration you could expect from a devoted disciple.

Abraham was a few years younger than 50, perhaps 46 or 47. Freud's immediate reaction was almost verbatim set down into the euology, which was squeezed into the new issue of the *Zeitschrift*, the first one of 1926, which was almost completed and ready to be printed. Freud was deeply moved and still, five minutes later, he asked me about the future of the Berlin group.

I went back to Berlin and participated in the funeral, and Ernest Jones naturally appeared. I remember that I settled down with him and told the true story of Abraham's death, many details of which have left my mind now. Jones was stunned and said, "Write that down. You do not need to publish it, but record it." And I had in mind to do so, but I did not. In particular, I had described to Jones all the details, the ups and downs, and the lack of elementary medical common sense in the treatment. Who in heaven's name was the family physician, or the other doctors who they brought in! They called for a surgeon; he said there is a gallbladder affliction, and we should take that out. To add to everything there were all the problems and worries of Abraham. I remember that he was just on the verge of a conflict with Freud. And my theory at that time was that he killed himself to avoid the struggle. Jones was struck because the whole evidence was such that it was difficult to arrive at any other conclusion.

Abraham's difficulty with Freud was not of his own making. That struggle was the result of the machinations of the Viennese *camarilla*, intrigues by people who wanted to ingratiate themselves with Freud and who were all the time in search of where they could find an item that would shed bad light on one or the other of the older men who they knew were closer to Freud. That whole business came from the *camarilla*, some members of which later arrived in New York, thanks to the efforts of Lawrence Kubie, who was head of some refugee committee at that time.

To give the full background, Freud had become angrier and angrier with Otto Rank, who by that time was definitely out. I had come to take over the function of Rank as editor. And while Abraham had disliked Rank's theory, he was desperate about the procedures against him which were followed. At that time I had no inkling that in 1963 I would read the letter which Eugen Bleuler wrote, years earlier, resigning from the Vienna Society because of the disgraceful manner in which Freud and the local people handled a man in Switzerland. That letter is coming out in print; Bleuler read Freud a lecture that in science these things do not exist and that Bleuler did not intend to get involved in that sort of thing. Franz Alexander got hold of this letter; everybody realizes that here is the nucleus of the whole tragedy of the psychoanalytic movement. And it is equally clear that Freud's attitude was formed under this pressure of the evil group around him. Like me, many were gasping when Bleuler's letter, written way back in the teens, was first read.

Now in 1924 and 1925 Abraham was in despair about the personal persecution to which Rank was exposed. Abraham wrote about that to Freud, who did not like it. I do not know whether Abraham had any idea that Freud, ten years earlier, had had a similar letter from Bleuler about someone whom we did not know. Freud used to talk about things that occupied him, and he probably dropped a few words about it, that Abraham is "ambivalent," that he really does not share the theories of Rank but that he does not like such and such things done against Rank either. That started the trouble. All Freud had to say was, "There are some moral obligations in science," and that was enough to set the gang to kill Abraham. Al Capone in Chicago had the criminal morality, but this is all incredible in a science.

Then came some less than trivial incident, which I am not sure I am capable of reporting accurately, but I know the issue. In that year, for the first time, a motion picture of psychoanalytic content was produced by an excellent director who much later had a career in Hollywood. The story was of an obsessional person who could not touch a knife. When this film was finally presented, in a special frame there was the news that Hanns Sachs was a scientific advisor, and I believe that Karl Abraham also got mentioned. Sachs was listed as training analyst of the Berlin Psychoanalytic Institute. At any rate there was immediately an envious, violent attack from Vienna. That Vienna group was really impossible. They objected that the title *Training Analyst* was for consumption inside the Society and not to be used with the general public. They always found some such thing to raise.

Abraham in some way was involved in this matter. On this occasion there were a number of conversations. Abraham began more and more to discover the soul of the Vienna Society, which was of the utmost corruption. They were like babies fighting each other to see who should be the favorite son of Freud. Federn was then presiding chairman of the Vienna Society.

Abraham had begun to worry about Freud, who was just about at that time ready to celebrate his seventieth birthday, which was in May 1926. Abraham put in some words in behalf of Sachs. I do not think Abraham participated more than that. Sachs had actually gone to the film studio and helped them; and the picture was a good one. The question was not whether it was wise or unwise, tactful or untactful, to use the title of *Training Analyst* in a credit frame to a movie. Remember, the motion picture industry was about 10 years old then. But this whole procedure on the part of the Viennese was incredible!

I developed this whole line of thought to Jones, and I maintained that this man killed himself. Abraham did not want to see these things taking place. He mentioned to me, a year before he was ill, that he wrote Freud a letter saying that Rank was being exploited. I do not say let Rank be allowed to do anything for himself. But Abraham already, a year before it happened, wrote to Freud that they should change the editorial arrangements while Rank was still in the group. You cannot in fairness expect a man to sacrifice himself completely.

So at certain intervals Abraham had issued some warnings to Freud about these things. But somehow it came to a critical point over this motion picture. I remember I took at least two hours to describe this whole incident to Jones. He did not know to what extent machinations against him, too, were at work. He had no idea that 90 percent of the things he describes about the secret committee were invented for its purposes, and that he was lied to the whole time. They kept from him what was going on in the Vienna Society and the continent in general; they did not consider him as belonging.

Not only was the death of Abraham untimely and tragic, costing us a fine person, but there was plenty of evidence showing that a terrific conflict went on inside Abraham which undermined his trust and confidence in Freud's judgment. By that time it was widely accepted that Freud was a genius but that his knowledge of men was poor. It was true, because he never took the time to penetrate into anybody except into his own theories. And Abraham worried to death that this great idol should appear in such a human stature.

So I maintain that Abraham died in order to avoid a conflict with Freud. I remember one of the remarks, whether Jones said it or I is unclear, but we quoted the saying that Kronos eats up his own children. So you can imagine how happy I was when I later came to the United States. I thought this was far enough away and did not know that the whole *camarilla* would arrive in New York and, thanks to the brilliance of Lawrence Kubie, they would be settled right here and given a free hand to prepare the ground for undermining Kubie himself. He remained a member but withdrew all his interest from the New York Society; it was this bunch that squeezed him out.

In Vienna the "they" I refer to included Federn, Edward and Grete Bibring, Robert Waelder, and to some extent later, though not at that time, Hartmann. Hartmann was in analysis with me in 1925 or 1926, and then in the '30s, at the request of Freud, he went into another analysis with Freud. Hartmann told me, "Freud asked me to come." There was no answer to that, and it ruined Hartmann's whole life. Then Freud died, and I talked to Alexander, and we were wondering what Hartmann's reaction to Freud's death would be. And I said, "It is too late. He committed himself too much. He cannot admit to himself what an idiotic thing that was, to sell himself to a dying man."

I was in Europe at a convention in Switzerland when in 1934 Hartmann told me he went into analysis again. Freud was 78 years old, and I later said to Alexander, "This man faces now the job of admitting to himself what a mistake it was. But to turn his back on Freud the moment Freud died was to destroy Hartmann's own reputation with the gang. Everybody knows better."

Freud had two tragic weaknesses. One was his fear of anti-Semitism that went through his whole life, which I have already touched on. The other was his weakness for rich people. Brill told me endless stories from earlier years of Freud's inabilities on the point of wealthy patients. Freud had wanted Jung to be president originally because he was a Gentile, and Freud wrote that "he seemed to have relinquished racial prejudices," namely, anti-Semitism. Freud thought Jung had given up such ideas for Freud's sake. And he wanted Hartmann because he was mainly Gentile.

Hartmann was bright; he was a half-psychoanalyst when he came to me. He had written a book in which psychoanalysis does not really appear. He wrote on a topic for which he got a fellowship from the Rockefeller Foundation about the psychological schools in existence at that time and the relationship of psychoanalysis to the current problems of the psychological literature. This was an enlightened, scientific book; there was not an iota of psychoanalytic prejudice in it.

And then, after a year-and-a-half or two years of analysis with

Freud, he had been transformed into a caricature of his former self. When Freud died, I had this conversation with Alexander about Hartmann. That's when I said, "You will see. He is hooked. He is such a narcissist he would be unable to admit to himself what a blunder he committed. And in order to protect himself against the self-reproach of having been such an ass, he will stick to this." And that is what happened.

I still have respect for Hartmann's mind, but I am not so sure about his mental health. He has written one obscure article after the other. I am never able to find out what he is talking about; all is schizoid confusion. And Alexander did not oppose my viewpoint.

Freud had feared that psychoanalysis would be viewed as an all-Jewish science; secondly, he hoped that if anybody came to him then it would be a Gentile, as it actually happened, who opened up the situation at the university. Jung had been under Bleuler at the Zurich Psychiatric Clinic. Freud wanted that psychoanalysis not be identified with Judaism, and that it should have a Gentile president who sooner or later would open up the university doors. So this choice of Hartmann by Freud was made with this idea in mind. He was a little unhappy that Hartmann married a Jewish girl.

To the best of my knowledge, one of Hartmann's grandparents was Jewish; he was mistaken if he thought he would not have suffered at the hands of the Nazis. One Jewish grandparent was enough.

Let's go back to the Berlin Psychoanalytic Society and what followed Abraham's death. Eitingon owned the institute because he gave the money and nominally was the director of the institute. Somebody wrote to Vienna that it was time they pay me something for all this editorial work. I bought the stamps and the stationery; at least my expenses might be covered. Storfer's reply was that since everything that comes out of the institute appears under the name of Eitingon, although actually done by Rado, and since Eitingon pays for the whole Berlin Institute, Eitingon should reimburse Rado. Storfer had a point.

After Abraham's death, Eitingon remained in the background. Simmel was elected president, I was elected secretary, and Karen Horney was elected treasurer. I remember that it was a memorable evening. Everybody was shocked by the death of Abraham. There were twenty-one members at that gathering, and all three of us got twenty-one votes. In a secret ballot each officer got every vote. So there was unanimity and a great development of the institute followed. Alexander rose rapidly. And I must say that the clinical spirit, which Abraham had established, remained. That was the society which remained closest to medicine, psychiatry, and psychotherapy.

During this decade, especially after Abraham's death, with no causal connection but just coinciding with it, a nonpsychoanalytic psychotherapy society was for the first time organized in Berlin and created the group of which later, after Hitler, Jung became the president. They and the psychoanalytic society were in murderous competition, which was a one-sided race because the other society had no standards of admission of any kind. If you were interested in psychotherapy, you could become a member of their society. They were incredibly envious of the members of our society.

Then came, in an article by Freud, a sentence which suddenly said, "We psychoanalysts should go together with the psychotherapists." He was writing this out of the clear blue sky, without knowing or not having enough care to have the interest to spend two minutes thinking about our situation. Naturally, if there is a nonanalytic psychotherapeutic society in Berlin and an analytic society, there must be warfare between them. Freud did not take the trouble to ask anybody and he did not figure it out for himself. He did not know his own pupils.

9

THE BERLIN
INSTITUTE

It was during my years in Berlin that both Reik and Alexander got special recognition there from Freud. Alexander was one of the early graduates of the Berlin Institute and received an award which Freud was able to distribute to him at the Berlin Congress in 1922. Alexander got the prize because he wrote a paper that Freud had liked, and also Freud wanted to push the Berlin Institute. Reik, too, got an award then, on the grounds that he had already a lot of accomplishments and wrote beautiful articles on the application of psychoanalysis to Jewish ritual, and so on.

Alexander rapidly became a favorite. He was a model product of the Berlin Institute. And then he went to Eitingon and said that he should be entitled to teach. Eitingon was frightened by Alexander's rapid progress and resisted Alexander's request for at least two years. I can assure you I constantly had to hammer on Eitingon. I said, "This is absurd. Alexander is the best man that the Berlin Institute has produced. No school can hope to exist if it does not develop its own teachers from its graduates." That applied even more so to psychoanalysis, which cannot recruit people anywhere else. And I pounded at Eitingon until finally he accepted the idea.

The same procedure was repeated in regard to Otto Fenichel. Eitingon put up a similar sort of resistance, and it was due to my stubbornness and his inability in the long run to deny such requests on my part that Fenichel was made a member of the faculty of the Berlin Institute.

I was in those days quietly and somewhat effectively working against the whole cult atmosphere. I remember when I arrived in Berlin the Society had a variety of membership categories. I said, "I do not understand it. Either someone knows psychoanalysis or he does not. If he knows his stuff he is a member, and if he does not he cannot belong. This is a nursery school here: ordinary members, extraordinary members, out-of-town members. A scientific society has people who are members and others who are not."

This tendency to establish categories and ranks was involved with Sachs's using his title as a training analyst in the making of that film. I think that only one of his speeches which was printed said that Sachs and I were two training analysts of equal rank, neither coming first. And then Sachs was asked to help in the production of the first psychoanalytic film; in all the theaters where this film was shown you could read an extra credit given to Dr. Hanns Sachs, training analyst. Then the scandal broke loose; the analytic people argued that the title was for domestic use and not for public appearance. Eventually this whole fight quieted down, but Sachs won because at that time to be a training analyst was a sort of baronial status as compared to the regular members.

So all the evil aspects of a patriarchal family organization, the mutual jealousies of people, so that nobody wanted to quote anybody else, and everyone wanted to out-do the others in citing Freud, were present then. This whole spirit, by the way, was superbly described in the first book, by Fritz Wittels,[1] on Freud.

There were parallels in other fields at the time; a general authoritarian spirit permeated all the sciences. Where opinion was heavy, facts were few. For instance, Adolf Meyer, in private conversation, often referred to Emil Kraepelin as a German imperial psychiatrist. Nobody could get an appointment in psychiatry in Germany without having the endorsement of Kraepelin. If you wrote a line in which you in any way criticized or disapproved of Kraepelin, that was deadly. So in this respect there was a similarity to what was true in psychoanalysis, although the authoritarianism was worse in Germany than Austria. The German army was so much stronger than the Austrian. This whole authority rested on the German bayonet because the empire itself was dependent on German

---

1. Fritz Wittels, *Sigmund Freud* (New York, Dodd, Mead & Co., 1924).

power. But this kind of thing in psychoanalysis was due to its isolation and was a defensive feature against a more or less hostile world.

As time went on I watched over the years the gradual narrowing down of Freud's interests, which in the beginning—the first time I met him—were still encyclopedic. I originally met him in 1913 when he was 57. By the time he was 70 in 1926, his withdrawal became more and more rapid. Whatever you talked to him about, the most he could do was politely listen for a few minutes, and then he came back to the libido theory and his own work. By that time he was completely absorbed by his own greatness, which gave the men hanging around him and trying to be in the first ring an impossible task. There became a second, a third, and an outer ring, as they all tried desperately to belong to the first one; the result was a Byzantine performance, the like of which I have never seen anywhere. Incredible flattery took place at that court.

Also to a small extent there was patronage too, though I believe Freud preserved his personal integrity in the course of this organizational deterioration. When he was unable to hold office hours for seeing new patients, which were not as numerous as you would think, they were all sent to Federn, who was the president of the Vienna Society. It was then Federn's job to assign these cases. Rarely had Freud an opportunity to send a so-called training analysand to A or B or C, but the bulk of the passing on of these few patients was assigned to Federn; what Federn could not take himself was further distributed by him.

What counted more was to move Freud to mention somebody's name in one of his papers; to be quoted was what mattered. It was a form of patronage in that to appear by name in one of Freud's papers was to become immortal. This system was almost unbearable. Freud knew what was going on, and eventually he got tired and gave in. He became a captive of his cult. I think I last saw him in the flesh in 1932, my final visit to Vienna. It was summertime; he had rented a house in the suburbs. It was a beautiful day, and he proposed that we should walk in a huge garden that surrounded the house. He had already a dog, who was jumping around; about 90 percent of his affection went to the dog and the rest to me.

At the time I was still responsible for the contents of the *Zeitschrift*. I said, "Professor, do us a favor and send us a manuscript. We do not have very good papers." He said, "Nothing comes to mind." "And," he continued, "even if I would write a paper, my pupils would not approve of it." He knew what was going on. He saw the confusion he created in 1926 with his book *Inhibitions, Symptoms and Anxiety*. (That title got artificially changed and mistranslated in the American edition to become *The Problem of Anxiety*, but in Britain the correct title was restored.)

He thought his pupils would not approve of what he might write, because by that time the dogma making was already so strong; when Freud came along and reversed himself on a fundamental issue, the questions arose: "Whom shall I trust? Where is the rock of Gibraltar?" When he published *Inhibitions, Symptoms and Anxiety*, he was saying that fear is a response to danger. Within his school the response was confusion. Everybody but the psychoanalyst knew that fear is a reaction to danger; the old theory of Freud's had been that fear must be understood as a fermentation product of repressed libido. Volumes of psychoanalytic articles had dealt with the treatment of fearful patients; the main problem had been to find out which part of the libido was repressed to give rise to fear. And then suddenly Freud was coming along to innovate by saying that fear is the ego's reaction to danger. That had to be subversive. And by 1932 this reaction to what Freud had done had by no means subsided.

That such a thing as rage exists, that rage is also a reaction to danger, and not a manifestation of the death instinct, and whether or not it is an expression of the death instinct, it is really a reaction to danger, were all points Freud never wrote about.

The spirit, by that time, was authoritarian. There was no question about any attempt at bringing psychoanalysis closer to the procedures of the other disciplines, though in Berlin that competitive group of rival psychotherapists had arisen. They had a journal and also sometimes called themselves psychoanalysts. That led to fights. They called the Freud group the analysts of the Psychoanalytic Society, and they were the free psychotherapists. That society exists here in New York, since some of these men came over. They have a Society for the Advancement of Psychotherapy, which is a historical continuation of the group that started in Berlin. There was a branch in Zurich of which Jung was a member.

So competition already at that time had started out. The outsiders, in part, envied the special training and the rank of being a member of the psychoanalytic organization. What you see today in the United States, that psychoanalysis is now a trade union, started out in Vienna. The gradual replacement of feelings of devotion, enthusiasm, serious loyalty to Freud and his tenets, and the substitution of trade union interests was a contribution which was made in America.

People with a genuine, honest emotional attachment to Freud's work became fewer, and a new breed appeared: the pretenders. People had a private view which they swallowed and the public outlook which they wrote about and spoke to at meetings. This is where we are now in 1963. This started out in the United States because even those American doctors who came for training to Vienna and later to Berlin were for too short a time in contact to get really fully caught up into this religious type of adherence. They did not become true members of the sect. They were tourists, visitors who participated for a short while in the appropriate rituals.

Eitingon, on the contrary, was an authentic apostle of Freud's. He was philosophically excellently trained, cultured, enormously inhibited, but extremely good as a man who could build an organization; and he idolized Freud. At the time when he had financial resources he put them at the disposal of the psychoanalytic movement. He was thoroughly good to me. But he never claimed to make a real contribution. He never in his life wrote a clinical article or ever delivered anything but a general speech. He was an organizer, which meant that his name was put on paper while other people did the work. But do not get me wrong. He was a man of high integrity and encyclopedic interests; but he was without a trace of originality or scientific imagination.

The greatest contribution among the Berlin school was made by Otto Fenichel, who codified orthodox psychoanalysis. His book *The Psychoanalytic Theory of Neurosis* was the outcome of his lectures; I gave him that assignment myself. I delivered the general theory, and he wrote the special one of individual diseases. And then his book came out, he revised it, and had a spectacular success. I saw its growth from the beginning. When it appeared in 1945, I still had a close contact with Heinz Hartmann here, and he asked me what I thought of the book. I said it was a remarkable record of all the errors in psychoanalysis. And Hartmann thought so, too.

But Fenichel appeared to have produced, for those who wanted to know in a hurry, the psychoanalytic theories about hysteria, stammering, et cetera, the fundamental source book. So his influence in spreading psychoanalytic doctrine was great on the illiterate outside world. There is no question about the impact his work had, but in the last few years it is diminishing.

Hanns Sachs was in Berlin too, and later he went to Boston. He had a journalistic ability and wrote a number of nice chit-chat books. For years he was teaching the technique of psychoanalytic therapy; but that was a unique historical event because it was clear to me already at that time that he had no conception of what therapy was, no understanding of medicine, and no familiarity with the most elementary practices in a clinic or a hospital. Yet generations of analysts got their introduction into psycho-analytic theory from this man.

Sachs analyzed Alexander for three months. Naturally, Alexander paid no attention to Sachs's theories. This was the coffeehouse hokum of someone who had knowledge only from reading. Even to raise a claim that Sachs was a scientist is an absurdity. He never in his life had any scientific training. He did not know what physics is or chemistry. Nor did he understand biology. He had training in law; and with that background he dared to write about the technical procedure of psychoanalytic therapy.

The true impact of Sachs started out when he settled in Boston after I declined the invitation to move there because I was established here in New York for good. Then they invited Sachs from Berlin. At that time Alexander was already in the States, and Sachs was the third one to be brought over for training purposes because they could not find anyone else. He had the advantage that they knew who he was, and he was fluent in English. And until his death he was an influential member of the Boston Society.

Helene Deutsch, who also wound up in Boston, was for about two years in Berlin; her stay there coincided with my analysis about to the hour. During that time she was a regular functioning member of the Berlin psychoanalytic group. She wrote papers; her favorite subjects were on the psychology of women.

Helene Deutsch had temporarily come to Berlin from Vienna; Hans Lampl was a Viennese also in Berlin during my time there. He was in pathology and then decided that he wanted to jump on the bandwagon. He saw that Freud was an important man, and overnight he became a psychoanalyst. He was analyzed by Sachs. Lampl had an existence in the Berlin Society due to his connections with the Freud family, otherwise he was a zero. His wife, Jeanne Lampl-de Groot, was in a training analysis with Freud. She is an obsessive, opinionated, scientifically worthless person; still today she is a friend and competitor of Anna Freud's and a member of some of the inner circles.

At the time the one I had the most regard for was Alexander. I fought for him. I struggled, among those people I analyzed, for Hartmann; but of those I worked with it was self-evident that I ranked Alexander first. He turned later to psychosomatic medicine. He wrote a huge number of books and popularized psychoanalysis; he created and supported a great number of psychosomatic theories, the value of most of which is gradually going down because better methods bring truer insights.

Alexander actually made little contribution to psychoanalytic theory, or to psychodynamics. And that which he considered his special point of view had been written before him by Ferenczi. Alexander's whole theory of surplus energy was all anticipated by Ferenczi. But Alexander is one of the brightest people in analysis; he was a devoted and enthusiastic worker. He managed to enlist the interest and support of the Rockefeller Foundation to create and bring to heights the Chicago Psychoanalytic Institute, which collapsed the instant he decided to move away to Los Angeles.

What went on here in slowly building up the Columbia Psychoanalytic Institute took place there rapidly, almost overnight. But his successor at Chicago is dishonest; he knows that this orthodoxy is nonsense but he goes on pretending. Still that Chicago Institute remains one of Alexander's achievements. Now he does a lot of work in Los Angeles. He is silent recently about therapy. I was, and am, increasingly pessimistic that the problems of psychoanalytic therapy can be solved by taking sound recordings and making movies of the interaction between patient and analyst. Although I would not say it is a worthless undertaking, I do regard it as peripheral.

This is my description that I am able to give about the Berlin Psychoanalytic Institute in those days. On the tenth anniversary of the institute in 1930 we published a book—*The First Ten Years of the Berlin Psychoanalytic Institute*.

10

THE STRUGGLES OVER RANK AND FERENCZI AND MOVING TO NEW YORK CITY

Rank was himself not ever part of the Berlin Society. But I followed the Rank affair. He wrote a book in 1923, *The Trauma of Birth*, in which, contrary to the original intentions of Freud for Rank and Rank's pledge to Freud, Rank turned to clinical matters and conceived a theory which made no smaller claim than that the whole behavioral future of an individual depends on how he manages to get through the process of getting born.

Rank's book was scientifically absurd. In those days I read a lot of medicine. I saw in a medical journal a paper by a pathologist who dissected the brains of many people who died of concussions. This man had also studied the brains of many babies who died during childbirth. All hemorrhages in the brain, the visible damages of tissue due to severe cases of concussion in adult life and those concussions produced by childbirth, so closely resemble each other that they could be almost identical.

So I went into the Berlin Psychoanalytic Society and said, "The initial sign of such a serious concussion is loss of consciousness. For that is the first thing that happens. It looks, on the basis of these pathological findings, that the more severe the birth, the surer it is that the babies go through the whole of childbirth in a state of natural anesthesia. When and how the baby thereby acquires a trauma Rank will have to explain. The impression is that the more severe the childbirth, the surer the baby knows nothing about it."

Jones himself did not have the material that I reported, which was published in a fine German medical journal by a highly respected professor of pathology. The accuracy of these findings was beyond doubt. So Rank's theory was worthless, and Jones conducted a campaign against Rank. Freud himself had originally liked Rank's book.

That conviction of Freud's was deep-seated in him, for two years later, when he wrote *Inhibitions, Symptoms and Anxiety*, at least two chapters dealt with Rank's theory, which Freud could not completely reject. But Freud marshalled all the arguments against it. Only I and a few others know that these two chapters, which were out of all proportion in a short pamphlet, were actually written by Freud to persuade himself that Rank was wrong. He remained closely divided against himself. There had been a close personal tie with Rank. Freud saw in Rank's book some bright sentences and was inclined to take it seriously in the sense "this is a scientific contribution and we will have to see what happens." But under the pressure of the entire psychoanalytic group, Freud broke this whole relationship to Rank and practically kicked him out.

This extreme reaction presupposed that he should first persuade himself that this is indeed a lousy book. That Freud succeeded in doing in those two chapters of his in *Inhibitions, Symptoms and Anxiety*. Later Rank came to the United States and began to teach, instead of psychoanalysis, the significance of the trauma of birth. According to Brill and others, Rank created such terrific confusion that after his teaching activities at the New York Psychoanalytic Society, they felt they had been cheated by him.

Then Ferenczi was invited here. That was, I think, in 1926 or 1927. Prior to that, Ferenczi and Rank had joined together to co-author another book, which thereby became suspicious and cast the first shadow on Ferenczi's undisputed reputation. Because Ferenczi had written a book jointly with Rank, the man who became an outcast because of *The Trauma of Birth*, the first doubts began to fall on Ferenczi himself.

Ferenczi had become a little more adult and mature while he was cut off from Freud during World War I. That trend was increased by a spectacularly successful year in New York. He could accumulate there, and save, a good deal of money. He met I do not know how many people, and he saw what the world looks like outside of Budapest and Vienna. It was the first time he had lived abroad for a year. And he was increasingly dissatisfied with the therapeutic results of psychoanalysis. We are living in the same period here now; the young men are in despair about the lack of therapeutic results.

This dissatisfaction and unhappiness is not limited to any one group of analysts. You hear the same thing from the classicists. At any rate, Ferenczi, in the book he had written with Rank, already discussed technical questions. Ferenczi was the first to call attention to the fact that in Breuer's original procedure everything was emotional; in Freud's approach, therapy got turned into an intellectual exercise, a rabbinical study of the life history of the patient. Ferenczi invented, together with Rank, even though who contributed what I would not know, the catchword idea of the need for *experience* therapy. It is an emotional experience that does the trick for patients.

Ferenczi was working alone now, surrounded in Budapest by a group for whose members he had little intellectual respect, and with no emotional attachment like he had had to me earlier; I was a boy of 20 when he picked me up. Let me try to formulate his new idea clearly. (I was then in Berlin, and a few years later came to the United States.) All neurotics, Ferenczi felt, suffered from the frustrations of the child by the parent, who denied the warmth, the affection, and the love that the child wanted. The parents paid no attention to the children, left them to domestic servants, and were busy anyhow. By the time Ferenczi's ideas had led to a crisis with Freud, that was my last year in Berlin and the first or second year I was in New York.

Ferenczi's proposal was that the basis for this despair was realistic. At the time it could not exist within psychoanalysis that there is such a thing as anger, resentment, or rage; all of this was buried under the concept of the death instinct. I was the one who proposed that there is an emotion like rage. In the absence of the concept of rage, naturally there was no problem about what to do with it. So the only therapeutic idea Ferenczi could invent was that the doctors should give in actual life, during therapy, that which would satisfy the cravings which patients had carried along since early childhood.

One of the people whom he analyzed at this time, and treated with this new technique, was Clara Thompson. Years later he told me that they had wandered about the streets of Budapest in a half-delirious state, completely confused. But the implication was that if the patient wanted to be put in the therapist's lap, he should without hesitation do it and give them a kiss or I do not know what. The therapist should forget that this is a grown-up person, treat him as if actually he were the child whose frustrations he is still suffering from. And now, decades later, the therapist should try to put an end to this frustration by belatedly supplying the child with the desired satisfactions.

Ferenczi began to write about this to Freud. Freud naturally told the news to the clique who came to meetings at his apartment. Freud was beside himself, perhaps exaggerating what Ferenczi was doing. That Ferenczi was engaging in a scientific monstrosity I do not need to tell you, but that was not so clear in those days. But another thing was evident: the social danger. Suppose that the patient were a young woman; Ferenczi could have kissing parties with his young patients. Freud was afraid that even the knowledge that psychoanalysts experiment with such crazy ideas was to expose his cause to a then still hostile environment. Freud's objection to Ferenczi was not on scientific grounds.

I talked to Freud at that time. I had come back to Vienna from New York. The topic of Ferenczi's technical innovations came up, and Freud said we cannot make a whorehouse out of the psychoanalytic situation. But I thought Ferenczi was incapable of turning his practice into what Freud called a brothel, considering that a number of Ferenczi's patients were men and some were older women—unless one presupposes that he was a sexual acrobat.

Even though Ferenczi's recommendations resemble later theories about how to treat schizophrenics, the Freud–Ferenczi relationship never recovered from this fight. A year later Ferenczi was already sick with pernicious anemia, and in the spring of 1933 he died. I gave as a memorial a speech at the American Psychiatric Association meeting in May 1933 in Boston, and I rewrote it for publication. It was a scientific obituary and expressed reservations about Ferenczi's theory of genitality. It is a fascinating conception and a challenge to future science.

Freud also wrote an obituary notice, much cooler than mine. Then the message came to me that Anna Freud did not like what I had written. It was too warm for her. One of the greatest mischiefs in all these problems was Anna Freud. The nightmare was that she had no inkling what science is. She was educated to be a nursery school teacher, not even a grammar school instructor; that was the extent of her scientific equipment. And all she could see is whether or not her father was angry, and she became a magnifying glass for all such reactions. She was particularly dissatisfied with my having said a kind word for Ferenczi, who happened to be a lifelong friend of mine and who also was her father's closest friend for so many years.

Before such difficulties had developed for me, in the late fall of 1929 I got an invitation to go to Washington, D.C., all expenses paid, for the first International Congress on Mental Hygiene. About three people from the Berlin Society were asked to attend. So Alexander and I, plus Helene Deutsch from Vienna along with a few others, came across. There had been a donation of a million dollars for the meetings before the stock market crashed. They were sitting there with all that money and did not know how to spend it. I got on the list of those invited; and I was given telegram blanks, to be able to send them out without paying anything.

I do not know who gave them the money, but Frankwood Williams was in charge of the whole thing. I was supposed to deliver a speech of fifteen minutes or something. The letter of invitation included first-class accommodations on the boat, hotels in New York and Washington, trips from New York to Washington and from Washington to New York. When I read it in a hurry in the morning, I thought it was a practical joke. You see, I had all the mail of the *Zeitschrift* to go through in the morning. I thought that one of the guys whom we had trained in Berlin was pulling my leg, and that the whole proposal was a fraud. I had taken the invitation and thrown it into the wastebasket.

Next day I got a telephone call from Alexander. He said, "Did you get an invitation to Washington?" I said I did. He wanted to know what I thought about it. He assured me it was all serious. Then Eitingon came and told me the same thing. Fortunately the contents of that wastebasket were still in the kitchen. I recovered the invitation and said, "Fine, I will go." And that is how I came to the United States for the first time. I participated in the convention, about which there are two volumes in print. I spoke in German and a translator put it into English.

When I came home, Freud was nervous about this meeting. He was afraid that something could happen to the status quo. I cannot give you an idea of what a decisive share of work rested on my shoulders. And Freud knew that. At Christmas 1930 I got a letter from Brill: in behalf of the New York Psychoanalytic Society he was inviting me to come for a year and establish an institute on the Berlin model, which I did starting in September 1931. Brill's letter had arrived just the day when we were leaving for Christmas vacation. In Europe we had two other holidays, an Easter and a summer vacation. Brill's letter came when we were all packed to depart. I was already thinking that I should accept the offer. Hitler then had 105 deputies in the German parliament; the whole political situation looked menacing to me. But I did not immediately answer Brill. We went up to the mountains where there was snow. And by the time I arrived back in Berlin on January 2, there was already a telegram from Brill: why hadn't I answered? So I got frightened and sent him a telegram saying I would come. My stay was supposed to last for a year.

I had in those days a terrific reputation as an ambassador of Freud's. I was not here for more than three months when two analysts arrived from

Boston to see me. One was Dr. Irmarita Putnam, the wife of Tracy Putnam who later became professor of neurology here at Columbia; the other person was a friend of hers, a doctor, whose name I have forgotten. They had come on behalf of the Boston Psychoanalytic Society. They wanted me to come there to set up a psychoanalytic institute and to remain for good. So I showed this letter to Brill, and to Bertram Lewin, who was the most influential figure in making decisions in the New York Society. They both got excited and thought it arrogance on Boston's part. To make the story short, immediately my one-year invitation to New York was made into an arrangement that would last forever, so that I should not even consider the Boston offer.

I went back to Europe after the first year here, 1931 to 1932. We had our apartment in Berlin; I brought out some of my furniture. This desk in my office now is part of my original furniture designed by Freud's son Ernst. This was my original analytic chair, covered with leather I did not like so it was recovered; and I am still using my original analytic couch in my office.

Freud was unhappy about this whole turn of events. When I arrived here I at first collected money for the Berlin Institute, since Eitingon's financial position was threatened. That was in the wake of the big crash of the New York Stock Exchange in 1929. His personal income did not come from his medical practice, which he did not have; but it flowed from a fur establishment his family ran in five cities. The Eitingons were one of the biggest fur traders. They had an establishment in Russia, one in Poland, one in England, two in Germany, and one here. The old man had died and Max Eitingon's brother-in-law ran the whole enterprise, and then came the years of the depression, during which all this began to collapse. For a while, even under the communist regime, they had the biggest contract with the Russians for furs. In any case, I collected money among my friends for the Berlin Institute, which survived me by two years. I left in 1931, and the Berlin Institute was finished with the advent of Hitler in January 1933.

Alexander had come to America a year earlier than I; he stayed on in the States after the Washington conference, while I had gone back. The loss of Alexander only increased my value and the need for me in Berlin. Freud increasingly became angry at me, who had been by far his favorite during the previous years. He did not want to believe that anything could happen to him. "Hitler comes in, so what, we will survive"—that was his attitude. When I began to see from here, reading *The New York Times* every day, what was happening in Germany, I began to write my friends. I said, "I came on a red carpet. If you still want to come in, you better hurry up." I sent them affidavits or whatever was necessary. I helped Felix and Helene Deutsch to come over. And Freud suddenly discovered that I was luring away his people from Vienna to the United States. He wanted to keep them there. I am talking about events in 1931, when he was already 75; an old man cannot start out to collect new pupils.

He had been sick since 1923. He wrote me increasingly irritated letters. He said I was seducing his pupils to come to America, and also that I was a bad boy. He had thought I would be some sort of emissary from Vienna here. The implication was that I should send money to him because at this stage of the game Hitler was already succeeding in Germany. Even in 1934 and 1935 he wanted to build an international institute for psychoanalysis in Vienna. People whom I talked to here all thought he was crazy. It was a preposterous idea that I should collect money for such an institute to be set up in Vienna just before Hitler arrived there.

I am convinced that by the time Hitler arose and Freud was already world famous, Freud's blindness to the true nature of the Hitlerian regime was a product of overcompensation. He never allowed his fear of anti-Semitism, which never left him, to come out fully. But he mobilized his own fame, brushing aside, overcompensating his anti-Semitic fears, and said, "Nothing can happen to me and my family." This blindness that he developed was based on his own inner denial of anti-Semitism, or rather his saying, "Anti-Semitism, yes, but me, no." This denial of his was in odd contrast to, and yet consistent with, his oversensitivity as a young man, possibly because he was overambitious, to the Viennese reaction to his visit to Charcot in Paris.

In those years of the mid-1930s I was still devoted to Freud's personal cause in analysis. By then Storfer was gone and Martin Freud had taken over the publishing company. He was a poor lawyer who never could make an independent living. Freud gave him the job to be director of the publishing company, and he could be paid because money came from the Princess Marie. And I, as a naive fool, wrote Martin an honest letter in which I advised him that the printing press had a huge stock of all the publications of psychoanalytic books which had appeared up to that time. Several large rooms were filled with those texts. And I told him, "Wrap that all up and ship it out to Zurich in Switzerland." I reasoned to him, "If by a miracle everything goes well and the Hitler era disappears and nothing bad happens, all that you will have lost will be the freight from Vienna to Zurich and back. Otherwise you run the risk that Hitler will come into Vienna, and nothing will remain in existence of what you now have."

He went with my letter to Freud. They decided that I was a traitor;

and they did nothing about the books. Freud became paranoid about this whole business. He trusted Hitler and doubted me, because I wanted to take away his friends and now sought to remove the publishing house, sending the stock of books to Zurich. Two years later Hitler moved into Vienna, and immediately the psychoanalytic publishing company was dissipated. Many of Freud's own books were sold on the market and by chance came to be bought by Dr. Schatsky and the New York State Psychiatric Institute. Everything they had had in Vienna was either stolen or burned.

This is when the Vienna group finally triumphed; they turned Freud against me. He could not have been blind to the historical facts. He so had his head in the sand that when the Nazis arrived at his house and plundered everything, Freud was with a patient then, and afterwards when his wife told him what had happened, Freud laughed and said, "Well, as a doctor I have never gotten that much for one visit." He expressed that sort of thing by the dozen. This joke cost not only the entire stock of books which were destroyed; nobody knows for sure how much the ransom was which Marie Bonaparte had to pay for him. It took lots of effort and money to get him and his family out.

After I had moved here I still remained the nominal editor of the *Zeitschrift*. The publishing house had only a business manager, Martin Freud; they brought out books which did not need any editors. The decision whether a book should be published or not was decided by him and earlier Storfer. I had had no word in that. I had also been made an editor of *Imago*. I decided what should be printed in these two journals and what not. And then Ernest Jones translated articles from the *Zeitschrift* and *Imago*. The first year of the English *International Journal of Psychoanalysis* contains a few articles in negligible number written by the British members; the majority were translated from the *Zeitschrift*.

And so my name was left. And then when I wrote that letter about the books being sent to Zurich, I mailed it to Freud's son, who was an idiot to show it to his father. Freud wrote me a very angry letter. He said, "It is now time that you should quit. You cannot do any work anyhow. You are in the United States." I did so. The *Zeitschrift* and *Imago* survived the move from Vienna by one year; they tried to publish them in London, but for whom?

I have had to talk a good deal about psychoanalytic politics, or more precisely, the jealousies among the early pupils of Freud. The waves of that jealousy extended from the first generation of pupils to the second, and there were cross-currents of jealousy that went from the second group to the first, and back.

11

TREASON

I do not know how many attacks have been printed against me in the various journals because most of these papers I never read. Occasionally people show me an article where I am way ahead of myself now. One piece attacks adaptation as a part of psychodynamics; the main argument is that Freud knew there was such a thing as adaptation, and that I have added nothing new. But the author has no true conception of the history of psychoanalysis.

The criticism of me has little to do with my trying to keep psychoanalysis within a scientific frame of reference and the medical community. I would describe the opposition to my work as that I am no longer a faithful follower of Freud's statements. I was accused of being a traitor to Freud's revolutions, an insider who had betrayed the cause; I can concede that it is accurate that I have different points of view than those to which he clung.

That is how the criticism started in the middle 1930s, when I came forward with a critique of Freud's case history of paranoia. Teaching at the New York Psychoanalytic Institute, I wrote such material on the blackboard; I said to the students, "Would you kindly put together the case history?" because Freud never did so. The case of Schreber contains his data as well as their explanation; but his account cannot be right, because he forgot what was the actual history of the person. That was the first openly critical presentation that I made; to this day I never published my

paper. In the meantime others have written about Schreber, but I still
have my original pages.

Brill then said to me, "I hear that in your lectures you attacked
Freud." I said to him, "If Freud published an addition in which he put
together three and four and got nine, and I called attention to this, would
you call it an attack on Freud?" That was the critical lecture in my heresy.
Either I was absolutely faithful to Freudian dogma—not to what Freud
himself did but to the official interpretation—or I was out. Dogma, as
taught in the American psychoanalytic institutes, includes all the misun-
derstandings of Freud. I did criticize and offer opposite views to many of
those upheld by Freud. I never did so without presenting my reasons; and
I was not negativistic but proposed instead what I thought was right. In
science such conduct is known as constructive criticism. You cannot show
me one single statement in which I have not done that, except when I
summed up previous positions. I could not always repeat everything in
Freud.

But my circumspection did not make any difference. The whole
attack was leveled against me anyway. I had some advantages; whenever I
stated Freud's views, which I did many times, no matter how sharply I
disagreed with what he said I never misquoted him. I was considered in all
my Berlin time the most orthodox Freudian. And I was always upset
listening to these psychoanalytic meetings and discussions in which he was
so often misquoted. People could attempt to quote, and my hair stood on
end. Sometimes they were arguing the opposite of what he had written.
Then I said, "Would you please take out volume so-and-so, page such-
and-such, and we will see the difference." That sort of comment brought
me the reputation not of a man well trained in Freud's writings but of
being an apostle. That was one basis, when the New York Society wanted
to establish an institute, for Brill writing me the original letter of invitation
to come and set one up on the Berlin model. They turned to me because
I was regarded as a loyal disciple.

The way I was able to quote Freud almost verbatim, without looking
at the book, was undeniable and obvious evidence for them. I was like a
rabbi who could cite the correct parts of the Bible. That was how my
reputation of being the greatest of all the orthodoxists arose—for in that
way I corrected the misquotations and in particular the misinterpreta-
tions. One of the people with whom that happened was Alexander. He
wrote something that Freud said, and I retorted, "What are you doing? On
page 72 of such a volume, he wrote exactly the opposite." "Oh," he said,
"this is wonderful, how you know the texts." I could not help that, it was

not my merit. I happened to have a good memory, which still, in many cases, is photographic.

The popular contention might be that somehow I met with disfavor with Freud, and therefore turned against him. But I have evidence to the contrary of why I began to move away from Freud. The letters I have from him in my desk, which nobody has read, show his support. For example, when I wrote a German book on the female castration complex, which in English is an article, Freud liked it very much. But then Anna intervened; I had inadvertently stepped on her toes. And she began to influence her father. My study was given to Jeanne Lampl-de Groot for a review; she was a loony, who once wrote that the most masculine act of a woman is to give birth to a child.

I admit I was angry about that review; it came out after I had come to the United States. By that time Heinz Hartmann was the editor, I think, of the *Zeitschrift*. To placate me he offered that there should be two reviews—one written by Mrs. Lampl, and one by someone of my choice. And I wrote him back: "I am sorry. This is not a question of choice, but a matter of the integrity of the editorial office." I never offered or allowed a counter-review to appear.

Nobody paid any attention to her review, as I knew they would not. She had poked fun at me because I was talking about trauma; that was in the years when there were so many fights about Rank's concept of the trauma of birth. I do not remember what I had written about trauma; she wrote one ironic paragraph after the other, the innuendo of which was that only two people advocate the importance of trauma: Rank and me. A few years later Freud's Moses book came out, and it was based on trauma from beginning to end; so her idiocy was proven by Freud himself.

I deny that Freud had slighted me in connection with this review of hers. He never wrote a line about my papers in public but sent letters to me about them. For instance, he mentioned my depression article, and that he was in full agreement with my conception. He always suspected that there were going to be conflicts within the person which are like the difficulties between the person and others, and that this represents an internalization. At that time I wrote within the terminology of the libido theory, and he said that he liked that.

He wrote that he could not endorse my derivation of the sense of guilt. But nobody could construe that as hurting my feelings; all the more so because it was written to me in a private letter. Once in 1927 or 1928, when Freud's son Ernst happened to be at my home in Berlin, I mentioned the lavish praise I had just gotten from his father. And then he said, "You know, when my father writes, that is what he thinks." In other words, Ernst Freud wanted to say that his father had not wanted to court me, but that this was his real opinion. In a paper at that time I had first described that in the mind of the child there is a good mother and a bad one, a giving and an angry mother, and that it takes a long time until these two images merge. This insight became one of the pillars of Melanie Klein's system, but my name somehow got lost. I wrote that years before she ever talked about any such thing.

The real opposition to me in New York was actually fed with the arrival of the refugees at the end of the '30s when, as part of the consequences of Hitler, most of the people who first went to London with Freud came over here; a good many of them remained in New York. The organized head of this opposition was Lawrence Kubie. He wanted to be everything; he was not against me but for himself. I do not recall what the formulation was—that I was no longer teaching Freud's views, or something like that.

Kubie based his argument on my lectures at the Society and my teachings then. When I saw what sort of man he was, I walked out of the New York Psychoanalytic Society and began to work to get another place started. It took a few years until we persuaded the dean at Columbia's College of Physicians and Surgeons to consent to a new Psychoanalytic Clinic.

I left instead of fighting within the Society; to remain would have been lunacy, spending my time and energy struggling to conduct a scientific battle against people who had no idea of what science was. That would have been suicidal; it was much better for me to try to get some other position established. I remained a member of the New York Psychoanalytic Society but did not go to meetings. There was nothing written by me that they could attack; it was all a verbal issue.

I was still at that time a member of the governing Educational Committee of the New York Institute. After I had secured the appointment at Columbia for the establishment of a new clinic, I got a letter in the late summer of 1944 from Sara Bonnett. The official beginning of the clinic occurred in June 1944, when the Columbia University Board of Trustees approved the whole proposition, which at the same time was a proposal of the medical faculty.

In June I had the officially signed document of my appointment. But we agreed that the whole matter would only be made public in September. Because of the war we could not start in the fall, and we decided that the whole year 1944 to 1945 would begin in January, and we would add

August to make it a full year. Two weeks after I had in my pocket the official announcement of the appointment by the Board of Trustees, I heard from Sara Bonnett. Our secret at Columbia was kept; the people (Abram Kardiner, David Levy, and George Daniels) I brought along from the New York Society knew the news and were the real founders, with myself, of the Columbia Clinic.

Although I had still remained a training and supervising analyst at the New York Society, Sara Bonnett's letter arrived. In two pages she explained to me that since it was essential that there be unanimity among the various teachers and they could not establish that with me, the Educational Committee had decided to terminate my being a training analyst at the New York Psychoanalytic Institute.

They had gotten the news of my "deviating" from the distorted reports of people who were in training analyses. The whole audience at the New York Society was full of students, and every one had a training analyst; so whatever I said one day was inevitably reported the next week.

I was not saying anything that disturbing but giving my views. For instance, I said, "Somewhere, something is wrong with this whole libido theory, because Freud nowhere gave a reason that would justify calling the suckling of the baby sexual." I was questioning some of Freud's statements. I would point out the various paragraphs where he discussed a question; I could do that because I said what nobody had. I have here twelve volumes of Freud's collected papers, printed in German, as well as what was supposed to be the closing volume, namely, the index to the set which was in proofs when I took them along from the *Zeitschrift* before I left. The last pages are "u," so "w" and "z" are still missing. If I wanted to know where Freud wrote about love, I had it. So I was using Freud's writings to indicate questions that I had.

For instance, I brought the book in and read; I said, "Now here, here, here, here — and that is all, according to the index, that Freud writes about it. There is nowhere a trace of anything that justifies calling suckling sexual." Then I made the statement that what Freud did was to discover the great significance of pleasure in human behavior, and he called all pleasure sexual.

But nobody dared to ask me a scientific question, because they knew I would find, in such inquiries, errors. They were so afraid of me that they could not enter into an argument because they would not know how to formulate the questions. Their opposition to what I was teaching was malicious propaganda and all behind my back. Nobody ever began to document anything. They never gave me an opportunity for a discussion, because they could not do so; they did not know what I was talking about. All they understood was that I was no longer quoting Freud verbatim. They thought I had different views, and that was the basis for the trouble. There was not one literate person among them, and they knew that I understood that.

There was no point in fighting. If there had been an opportunity, I would have gotten up and said what I thought of these people. But then the answer would have been that I accused them of illiteracy, which at that time would be construed as evidence of paranoia on my part. And since I had no intention of provoking such a situation, I just ignored them.

After that letter from Sara Bonnett in June or July 1944, terminating my teaching activities at the New York Institute, two or three weeks later the papers were full of the news that Columbia University had established a psychoanalytic institute for training and research, and that I was the director. I imagine that Sara Bonnett went to pieces when she read that; at the last minute she had written me that letter. I said to myself, "She probably would like to eat the paper on which she wrote."

Some other people, whom I knew were members of the Educational Committee, rushed to congratulate me, but I never went back. Once the new Association for Psychoanalytic Medicine got organized and was recognized by the American Psychoanalytic Association, I resigned from the New York Psychoanalytic Society. I remember that the president on that occasion was Philip Lehrman, who went out of his way for me then; but what could he do to prevent me from resigning? This was a personal action on his part; I left, however, and they were forced to accept the resignation.

Kardiner, Levy, and Daniels left to go with me, not because they were under attack for their teaching but for the sake of the opportunity to have psychoanalysis established at a university. It had been Daniels's dream; Levy was always opposed to any orthodoxy, and so was Kardiner, each on his own grounds. It was not that they were my pupils; some of them did not even know what my opinions were. I was way behind in my publications and needed a new start.

I remember that I had an article in 1939, "The Development of the Psychoanalytic Conception and Treatment of the Neurosis," and a vicious attack was organized at the Academy of Medicine. The proceedings were usually printed. When they got the usual request that they send in what they have talked about, my critics sent in discussions which were unrelated to the meeting and falsified. Luckily the secretary had stenographic notes, and we could prove that what these people were submitting had nothing to do with what actually happened at the meeting.

In addition to everything else, the submission was incoherent; it was written by Ruth Mack Brunswick, but Paul Federn was instrumental, too. I know that there was an investigation, and David Levy proved to the academy that this was all a fraud. The attempt was stymied by the vigilance of the neurologists in charge, not for my personal benefit but what was really at stake was integrity. So you can imagine that in the following years I was not anxious to publish.

My paper had been followed by favorable prepared discussions by Daniels and Levy, and then came Federn; honestly I do not remember what Federn said critically. This long alleged discussion was in print as lengthy as the two previous ones together and unrelated to what they had said in the academy. It was all presented to the president that this was a forgery.

For some reason they had sent me the proofs of the whole report on my paper: Levy's discussion, Daniels's remarks, as well as that which had never existed. A famous neurologist sent me the galley proofs from Chicago because I think they could not read the names. This president had no way of knowing what was up; he was an academic. These psychoanalysts had forged a discussion. Subsequently the neurologist in charge would not entertain the idea of a correction and insisted on omitting the whole business. What remained was the report of my paper, along with the comments by Daniels and Levy.

That had been the last time I presented a formal paper. Later, when I was not a member of the New York Society, I could publish again; they did not consider me a psychoanalyst anyhow, and the view was mutual, I did not think they were analysts either. There was that common ground, and the situation remains the same today.

12

FROM THE NEW YORK SOCIETY TO THE COLUMBIA CLINIC

I have paid no attention to the American psychoanalysts for decades now, but when I occasionally heard about their doings, I wonder whether they have ever written anything or contributed a sentence to a scientific discussion. Invariably the answer is no. The American situation was different from what we had known in Europe; the development of this new orientation was in part the reaction to our rising influence as a psychoanalytic school within psychiatric circles. But by the time that the New York Psychoanalytic Institute got founded, the hostility of the psychiatrists was much milder. Here there were fewer psychiatrists who ever read Freud. Those people in Germany who were hostile could be so because they had studied psychoanalysis; but here nobody read anything, so they were more tolerant.

As more and more residents in America realized the emptiness of descriptive psychiatry and insisted on being analyzed, psychoanalytic institutes were springing up; in this context the trade union aspect rapidly came into the program. So to talk today about orthodox psychoanalysis in terms of a religious faith or anything like that is an absurdity or, at best, a euphemism, because that is just a corrupt trade union. Vested interests have to be protected.

Until relatively late, the state of graduate psychiatric education was actually limited to descriptive psychiatry. In 1946, for instance, right after the war, John Whitehorn made a statement in a conference organized by the Orthopsychiatric Society that the residents' training consists of studying the patients' biographies and writing cases about them. He was somewhat shocked by the proposal submitted by myself, and also by Alexander, providing such a thing as training in which psychodynamics was supposed to play a cardinal part. Sixteen years later in the first Ithaca conference, Whitehorn was the leader in separating a science called psychodynamics. That showed all the psychiatrists the significance of psychoanalysis, led to a tremendous influence, and therefore multiplied the importance and power of the psychoanalytic organizations, which began to decline only with the advent of the tranquilizing drugs. That was the peak, and now in 1963 it is going down again.

The New York Psychoanalytic Society was itself composed of members who competed with each other in making idiotic decisions. The damage this Society did to itself from the beginning, considering the success they could have had, is beyond brief description. But who cares? The Society has been in a moribund state for decades now. You have there people like Hartmann, who was a brilliant boy. As I have already indicated, he was analyzed by me and became reanalyzed by Freud; Hartmann emerged as one of the faithful, and that ruined him for life. About five years ago I tried to read a few of his papers, and I could not do so. I still like Hartmann by far the most. He was and is a cultured, and fine person. But he got this indoctrination by Freud at a time that he was already at his worst; this was in the 1930s when Freud was in his eighties. And Hartmann never could get himself out of it.

Hartmann's ego psychology is not only scarcely a departure but a confusion, and the attempt to settle everything with high level abstractions is clearly valueless. Nonetheless, as concerned his private person as an individual, Hartmann was my pet, and he remained that, despite the fact that I saw with a broken heart how this so-called analysis with Freud destroyed a promising, wonderfully educated and gifted person. He is all that: educated, gifted, and paralyzed by this experience with Freud. But Hartmann was a visitor in the Berlin Society; he was only there as long as his analysis with me lasted. He came for the purpose of the analysis and left immediately afterwards.

Gregory Zilboorg, a particularly aggressive gentleman, played an important part in the development of the New York Institute. He had influential patients whom he collected. He was a resident at Bloomingdale Hospital, and by coincidence Bettina Warburg, who was also there as a young M.D. and a psychiatrist, befriended Zilboorg and introduced him to her family. Through her he got, as a psychoanalyst, into the Warburgs.

Zilboorg began with Bettina's father, who had become ill, and then treated some Warburg sons; Zilboorg analyzed one or two of her brothers. All of this triumph came from the chance acquaintance with Bettina Warburg. Zilboorg was an able man, a fairly good journalist, and a translator of Russian literature into English; but he was doing everything to build up a fantastic power position for himself.

The rivalry between Zilboorg, Lewin, and Kubie was enormous. When they first squeezed Brill out from the presidency, Lewin was elected chairman. They did everything possible to discredit Brill. He had possessed great merits in popularizing psychoanalysis in a country where no one knew what it was, but naturally his general scientific preparation was minimal; he understood little of the difficult psychoanalytic business which was more technical. So the attack on him was directed at a valid point, namely, his scientific ability. But the manner of this assault, and the tactics undertaken, were beneath contempt.

Brill was an older man who had created an opportunity for psychoanalysis to move into America. In those days A. A. Brill and psychoanalysis were identical. Their attack against Brill was inhuman, although the alleged reason for what they did was valid; the problem could and should have been solved without the fight. Not much silencing of Brill was needed because he never did anything except translate or have some books translated, and sometimes the opposite. I heard Freud say, "Oh, how my friend A. A. Brill translated *The Interpretation of Dreams* into the unEnglish." Freud knew what had happened but did not care. He thought that either this profession will survive, or not; if it succeeded there would be a better translation later. What was important to Freud was spreading the information. That was Freud's policy, and it was exactly what happened. Now we have all these volumes by James Strachey, who is capable of spending a few pages about the choice of *wanderer* over another possible word.

After Lewin served his presidency, which in those days was, I believe, two years, then Kubie maneuvered himself into office. He is bright and able. He was an excellent neurologist, a graduate of Johns Hopkins, a well-to-do Jewish boy in contrast to the ones who came from the Lower East Side of New York. His relatives were members of the Harmonic Club. These were his social credentials. But to me, since I still had European arrogance which was not yet eliminated, a Jewish club like the Harmonic was a great joke.

The Jews could settle down and copy the Gentiles; Jews who would never get into any decent club because of the anti-Semitism of the time, which was different from what it is today, made up such clubs. This whole business was fantastic to me, and naturally I never gave Kubie those honors which I imagine, in retrospect, he expected. Edward Glover analyzed him; since money was available, Kubie went to London. Back here he wanted to make himself king and use all these refugees as his devoted supporters. The irony was that I had been instrumental in bringing many of them over, which unnerved Freud; he did not realize I was trying to save the lives of these people but thought I was depriving him of them.

Kubie tried, gradually with success, and mainly with the new members coming in from abroad, to put up these people from Vienna as the great authorities. In exchange he expected them, to whom he opened up a living, to set him up as their god. But after they were established, the first man they pushed out was Kubie, because they wanted to be the leaders themselves. His presidency was not renewed; he had fallen into the trap he had made. And then he took his hat and went, paying no attention; the minute he saw he could not have what he wanted, he just left. On paper, though, he is still a member.

Zilboorg created more of a scandal with a patient he had who was a businessman. I think that Zilboorg gave him two kinds of sessions; one was an analytic one, and during the other Zilboorg was making himself the manager of his patient's business. The patient complained about this practice of Zilboorg's to a rich man who became furious. There was a formal inquiry instituted against Zilboorg at the Society, and in the end he was exonerated.

That was about the time, after I had been here ten years, when they did not renew my appointment as director of the institute. By then I was dreaming of building a clinic at Columbia. I had known Nolan Lewis just as a doctor and scientist. We had met at meetings, and I found him objective about the behavior of colleagues. His new professor of psychiatry at Columbia was a psychoanalyst member of the New York Society, but instead of the Society being happy to have this opening wedge into academic life, they paid no attention to him and behaved insolently. The analysts did not know what psychiatry is.

I continued on as a member of the New York Society, simply because that automatically made me part of the American Psychoanalytic Association, which in turn qualified me to remain in the International Psychoanalytic Association, which I had first joined in 1913. This is my fifty-first year as a member of the International; the last meeting I attended was in 1934, exactly thirty years ago.

At any rate, I worked out the new program at Columbia; there would be a clinic, actually a training institute but to be called *clinic* in order to emphasize the medical aspect. I was on good terms with George Daniels way back from Germany, when I was supervising him while he was being analyzed by Alexander. And he helped me with Lewis, who was discouraged because the dean, Rappeleye, was down on psychoanalysis. Then the war effort brought psychoanalysis to the forefront, especially psychosomatic medicine. Rappeleye realized that something was going on here.

By a stroke of good luck I had a patient who was a widow and for whom I did a lot of good, and she had friends, one of whom was a member of the board of trustees at Columbia University. This man wrote a letter to the provost of the university that such and such a bequest had been made, and that there were already two people in Columbia who were analysts. The provost called up the dean, Rappeleye, and said, "We have to do this." Next day Rappeleye telephoned Nolan Lewis, and then Lewis called me. He said, "I persuaded the dean," and I said, "That is wonderful." The whole thing was kept secret, as I have said, until the summer of 1944.

Then I brought in David Levy because we were friends; he was dedicated to scientific work. And Abram Kardiner was unhappy because he had had a terrific fight with Lewin. Kardiner gave a paper to the New York Psychoanalytic Society which was the germ of his contribution which he later jointly wrote with Ralph Linton. I was at the seminars where Linton brought the raw material of anthropological observations and Kardiner supplied the psychoanalytic interpretation. Finally Kardiner wrote up for the first time his ideas about how to interpret the material which was brought from the Marquesans.

When Kardiner delivered his paper at the New York Society, I had already heard the material; I had read Edward Westermarck's three-volume study way back, so I knew there was such a thing as a polyandric society. Nobody else there showed that they understood; they knew there was polygamy, by which they meant one man and a harem. When Kardiner presented the material, Lewin was president, for that was after Brill had been edged out. And Lewin began to criticize Kardiner's paper in an almost obscene manner—poked fun at it, to indicate he thought how ridiculous it was: "So what? Go to Park Avenue, and find out how many women have I do not know how many lovers." Lewin had given no sign of grasping that Kardiner was trying to compare a social order, including a marital system, to our own society with its concept of monogamy.

I got angry and got up and gave a speech for Kardiner and against Lewin. I said that while this might be a source for a good many jokes, there was serious scientific material here which I would like to call attention to. So Kardiner was happy that I did that, and we had naturally grown closer to each other because I knew him already from Berlin.

The trouble with Kardiner was his lack of judgment and his impulsivity. He was capable, from one day to the next, of saying the exact opposite, not only scientifically but about people and everything. Despite the allies that I had at the time, I told them that nobody knew how this new Columbia Institute came about. Most people have accepted Nolan Lewis's story that he persuaded the dean. But I know that Lewis could sometimes not get an appointment with the dean, who could not stand Lewis and hated psychiatry. He had brought in Lewis, who was a neurologist who suddenly had come up with psychoanalysis.

In the first year of the Columbia Clinic we had five or six people; once the war was over we were mobbed. Some were attracted by my name; others came because they heard there was such an opportunity, even though they did not know anything about psychoanalysis. I brought in a group from the New York Psychoanalytic Society who taught in a rather orthodox fashion at Columbia. I had invited, for instance, Hartmann and Waelder, who turned me down. Raymond de Saussure came from Europe, for I had asked him. Others offered their services. As director I could kick people out; for example, one analyst sent a student he had analyzed for supervision to two members of the New York Society without having cleared it first with the Columbia school. Everybody was supposed to be sent for supervised sessions by the faculty, not to someone outside the school; so I discharged him.

In 1955 I retired, and Lawrence Kolb, Lewis's successor as professor of psychiatry, did not know who should succeed me. He appointed Kardiner, who started out his activity with an attack on me. After two years Kardiner was out, succeeded finally by George Daniels. In the end we managed to train a number of people who are now in important positions.

In my ten years at the Columbia Clinic I had tried from the first day to break down the barricades around psychoanalysis. From the initial semester on I forced psychoanalytic students to learn psychiatry. I brought someone in to teach genetics, brain pathology, and brain physiology. At the time it seemed outlandish. Even though genetics is the foundation of all medicine, they did not appreciate what that could have to do with psychoanalysis. From the beginning we aimed to bring psychoanalysis out of its isolation and into contact with medicine, as well as to teach doctors the connection with psychoanalysis. I could not have accomplished what

I did at Columbia if I had not been dreaming for years that this had to be done.

After I left Columbia, I re-established the whole set-up, many times larger, at the New York School of Psychiatry. I believe that the mutative genes of schizophrenia will one day be on the laboratory table.

The Columbia Clinic had itself caused panic within the psychoanalytic world. I had had to make some concessions to George Daniels, who was a conscientious, devoted, rational person but physically weak. He pressured that we should accept recognition from the American Psychoanalytic Society, and I finally said yes. Had I said no and got support for this, the subsequent development of psychoanalysis in this country would have been different. The Columbia Clinic was the first at a university to give training in psychoanalysis. Everywhere else they learned nothing from what we had done here and tried everything to destroy that which was really worth attempting to do.

13

WORLD WAR II AND ADOLF MEYER

The insights I learned about war neuroses during World War I made it possible for me to know what to expect here during the Second World War, except that the clinical picture had changed. I hardly saw here war neurotics with the same type of earlier symptoms. Instead they came with psychosomatic problems, but the underlying substance of the story was the same. When the war started in 1941, I had just passed my fiftieth birthday, and 50 was the limit for military service, so I could not get into uniform.

But at the Psychoanalytic Institute of the New York Society I stopped my weekly conferences and said, "Now we will study traumatic neuroses," or war neurotics. That was right after Pearl Harbor. I did not want to continue studying the usual cases. A member of the class, whom I was supervising, came to say that he knew socially one of the Scandinavian consuls; I think it was a Swede. It turned out that he had been complaining that they were carrying war materiel in their merchant marine and had any number of what appeared to be war neurotics who were put ashore in New York and turned over to the consul, who did not know what to do with them. My student asked this man to let us take a few of these war neurotics in the evening hours.

So he began to bring these men to the Psychoanalytic Institute. I remember one fellow who went through the whole bombardment of Coventry; it was either at the end of 1941 or early in 1942. In the presence of the whole group I examined these people, as they told their whole story—what they did when the bombs hit, how many died, and who did what. From then on, and for many months, this seminar of mine, which to the best of my knowledge was the first one in World War II, took place. An institution was organized by the government to take care of these people, and my student made the seminar I had run the basis of that unit.

After the war I became a consultant to the Secretary of War and went down every 2 weeks to the Walter Reed Medical Center in Washington, D.C., and taught psychiatry to the residents. That went on for five years, every second Saturday; I enjoyed my work there, where I would spend the whole morning. That was successful and pleasant for me in the training of army psychiatrists.

By the outbreak of the Second World War Kardiner's book *The Traumatic Neuroses of War* was already out. That work was based on his experiences at a veterans hospital after World War I. There was difficulty with that book, however, because he postulated an actually existing difference between the peacetime neurosis and this one. He did not realize that he had applied two different methods; he analyzed the one neurosis in the ego framework, and the peace neurosis in terms of libido theory. They looked different not because of their true dissimilarities, which Freud meanwhile correctly described, but because he was talking about them in a completely different terminology. I read Kardiner's initial work in the 1920s in Berlin, or here on my arrival, at any rate long before World War II.

Sometime after 1942 an organization was established for the care of merchant marine people, British and others. In the beginning we saw only British cases because the ones in Hawaii did not come to New York. During those years my interest in war neuroses diminished. Then came the atomic bomb and the end of the Second World War, and I said to myself that this must be the end of such traumatic neuroses because there would be no more war.

In my observation one of the most powerful motives that had unconsciously driven soldiers into finding refuge in war neurosis was the envious idea that there were those at home sleeping with their wives. This strong emotion was the feeling, "Why am I on the battlefield and not at home with my wife?"

I remember conversations with Kardiner, Adolf Meyer, and a number of other people back in 1942. We felt that there was no way of telling how many war neurotic cases would be produced in London, in particular due to the Nazi bombing. And during the Blitz, we had phenomenal radio reporting by Edward R. Murrow, who invented and masterfully practiced the almost hourly reporting of what was going on. He even flew in some of the airplanes that defended London. He wondered what would happen to the civilian population with regard to the number of neurotics.

Then came in short order the surprise that within London, which had become a theater of war operations, there were no war neurotics to speak of. Perhaps in an ordinary, peaceful period more Londoners developed this kind of neurosis. That was the point which made it clear to me how powerful a motive was the idea "I am singled out." In London there was a wholesale, indiscriminate bombing which transformed a civilized city into a war zone; nobody could develop an envy that he was discriminated against. British national talent also played a part in the absence of war neuroses; in those days we had no comparable records from the Soviet Union.

I had patients who went into the war with high military ranks because they were important people in civilian life. One came to talk to me a few times during a furlough. Such people became so careless that they did not even bother to go into bomb shelters. As the siren sounded, indicating the approach of an airplane attack, the men were lying in a hotel bed with their girlfriends, and they were supposed to get up and go down to safety. More and more people began to ignore this recommendation. If there were a straight hit, it would be the end, so why bother? The whole population took the crisis without nervous tension or excitement. And my patient assured me that he had not invented this, but that friends and people who were in the service with him all did the same thing. Churchill, too, paid little attention to the raids.

I was reminded what I learned when I examined the first survivors of the Coventry attack; many died and some escaped, which came out in my Psychoanalytic Institute seminar. So people in London ignored the Blitz; it was already clear by January 1942. Going into a shelter protected you against flying debris, but if your house were hit you were finished. So it did not make sense to run – these were the old TNT bombs. If a building were struck it collapsed, and people in the so-called shelters were the first to be annihilated unless only part of the building was bombed.

So far, in all I have reminisced about, I have somehow not discussed an American psychiatrist with whom I had the closest and warmest personal relationship in the early days: Adolf Meyer. He was then the dean of American psychiatry and he had actually introduced scientific psychiatry to the United States. His history and biography seem to me sufficiently well known. He started out at the Cornell Medical School, came to New York at the Manhattan State Hospital, then around 1910 he created the Phipps Clinic at Johns Hopkins University.

On my arrival I became acquainted with Meyer in short order. I do not remember when I first met him; probably it was when I arrived here as a visitor to the first International Congress for Mental Hygiene in May 1930. Official dinners and receptions were arranged for us then. Meyer knew my name well, because he had seen the German-language psychoanalytic journals, and I was pleased to talk to him because he knew all about Europe; our friendship started right away.

When I was director of the Psychoanalytic Institute in the 1930s, he came frequently to New York for meetings at the Academy of Medicine. I remember a series of lectures he gave, and we met relatively often. He lived in Baltimore, but I saw him more frequently than any number of psychiatrists who lived in New York City. On the occasion of one of the annual academy meetings, he met my wife, Emmy, and discovered that she was, like himself, Swiss. That opened up a new relationship; he talked with her for hours about issues that had nothing to do with psychoanalysis or psychiatry; they were two people who came from the same little country.

At one point in the 1930s he sent me an invitation to come down every second Saturday to Baltimore and take over his clinical conference. In his teaching, the Saturday morning rounds were very important; everybody on his staff had to be there, from the next professor under him to the youngest resident. They sent me the case history of the particular patient at the Phipps Clinic. In the morning, 8:30 or 9, we all assembled in this sizeable room, and whoever happened to be the doctor of the patient in the hospital (they were all inpatients) gave a case history. Then the patient came in to be interviewed. I do not remember who examined the patient, but I think sometimes it was Meyer. Afterwards he said to me, "Well, this is what we have. What are the psychoanalytic comments?"

I usually had to arrive Friday night; in those days there were no flights. I kept my usual schedule and took a train around 7 or 8, arriving late in the evening at Baltimore. Meyer insisted every time that I should be his houseguest; this was an honor. If I came early, I was served dinner; and if I arrived later, there was still some food. Mrs. Meyer retired in no time and we settled down early in his library, which is difficult to describe. It was half again as wide and longer than my own consulting room, everywhere there were books, and I do not know how many tables with stacks of magazines and journals. And we carried on conversing until I gave out. Meyer suffered from sleeplessness, so if I had been a party to it he would have talked until 3 A.M. Usually by 12 or 1, I just got up and excused myself. Next morning I had to get up at 7 or 7:30. Usually we talked about Europe – what was going on, people whom we both knew or whose work we were interested in. I am reasonably sure he was able to discuss with me people about whom he had not talked since he had arrived in the United States.

It was all pleasant except for his pathological sleeplessness. He slept until 5:30 or 6, he told me, and then he was up. He lived on 3½ or 4 hours of sleep daily and, according to what I heard from him and his wife, this was normal for him. It was not enough for me. On the first visit I stayed over Saturday; there was a dinner Saturday night to which he invited the people from the hospital. Sunday I asked permission to get up late, then I had a bite and they drove me to the train. This schedule went on for many months, I do not remember how long or in what year. I was there after Paul Schilder had arrived at Johns Hopkins from Vienna; I started sometime in October and kept it up until the next spring.

Meyer was by education and medical training a so-called organicist. He was, though, interested in learning about psychoanalysis and, when he discovered my own critical attitude, he was particularly interested. I will explain what the difficulty with him was. He was basically not even a physiologist; he was an anatomist. For him science was completed when you discovered a formation and gave it a name. Dynamic thinking, that is, motivational understanding, was foreign to these kinds of psychiatrists. They had no experience or interest in it. So, when he came to the description of psychological factors, he intuitively tried to talk about them the same way as he dealt with parts of the brain. It was clear to me that the emotions – love, hate, and so forth – were matters he had read about in books. His heart was not in it, and I never was sure how much he understood of what I was trying to say. He had an absence of motivational interest and understanding which I began to see fully only in retrospect.

For instance, he introduced the terminology of aphasia; that gave him a splendid opportunity to indulge in descriptive name-calling. Everything had an aphasic name. And he thought that if you knew the name of something, you knew everything about it, just like the ancients in earliest times.

A paper of mine was published in 1939; that must have been after I stopped going to Johns Hopkins, though Meyer may have heard the talk when I first gave it. I had been describing the typical errors as well as the new developments in therapy. One of his residents, who also was a European and with whom Meyer had a special relationship, confided in me. (Meyer's Mayflower was Europe.) Meyer had read the paper, and under the seal of secrecy he made a comment: he said to this resident that he did not quite know what I was talking about.

I was at first surprised. Then it turned out that just as I first took it for granted, because of my mother, that every woman was intelligent, so I assumed that each psychiatrist had to be concerned with motivation. But Meyer had no inkling of what motivation is, beyond looking for the obvious like what reason a man has to kill someone. This was a crucial experience for me, one which eventually forced me to analyze Meyer and make it clear to myself that he was an anatomist and not a psychologist, that he did not know what dynamics are. It was a shock to me. From anatomy for him the next step was philosophy – not psychodynamics but empty abstractions. So either he described and named material which you can touch or he appealed to abstractions which, to him, looked like something real except that they had no substance to them. They were equally remote from psychodynamics.

Yet Meyer's scientific curiosity, his interests, and his desire to contribute were at the highest level, right up to the end of his life. But he had no understanding of human relationships. Therefore, he could not understand the concept of transference in psychoanalysis.

But in a sense he saved psychoanalysis in the United States. They wanted to throw analysis out of the American psychiatric profession, and it was under Meyer's influence that this did not happen. If they had passed such a resolution, it would easily have taken ten or twenty years to remove it.

He had an encyclopedic knowledge. I do not say that he read all the books – that would have been impossible – but he had an enormous knowledge from reading, and this was by no means limited to neurological psychiatry. And he was a man of impeccable integrity, goodwill, and fairness. He knew all the machinations and manipulations that went on, but I never heard even a thought that he should be party to any cabal. Compared to the others he was a saint. Everybody knew that and respected him, and also was afraid of him. He could not write at all though, and people poked fun about nobody being able to understand him. For he lacked a guiding point of view that clear theory provides.

14

AN APPROACH TO FEMININITY

I have had to wonder, in addition to everything else of an introspective nature, specifically what light my relationship to my mother shed on my later life. Abraham was the first to point out to me that I had always been searching for a mother. At the time my analyst said that, it was a revelation. It took me about three decades before I got a real picture of the intellectuality of women. I lived happily in my teens and in my second decade somehow with the expectation that women are just as bright, well trained, and well educated as men. That was my original approach to everyone, except to women who had never been to school or did not know how to write. I was so oriented in this direction that my own observations took place in terms of my anticipations.

I believe a woman has an entirely different emotional life chiefly because the biological function of the female is to continue the species by reproducing the offspring. The production of children is the result of a pair, but over 90 percent of it all is on the shoulders of the woman. I must have been in my thirties when this sort of conviction gradually began to dawn on me. I had had a thoroughly masculine view of the universe, which was fairly easy to maintain, because another man who thought, felt, and acted exactly the same way was Freud.

In consequence when, through practice, it gradually began to dawn on him that a female is a female, and a male is a male, and that this difference goes down to every cell of the body and each component of the mind, by that time it was too late for him. It was not so for me because I was many years younger than he.

It was spectacular that Freud wrote that sentence of his about women being mysterious. She had to be so as long as you looked at her with the expectation that she is a man. I was still in Berlin when I began to see that point. It was only here in the United States that I finally came to a general characterization of Freud's early theories, the sociological system that he actually completed sometime in the '20s, that if I am trying to place Freudian psychoanalytic theory in proper context, it is a phallocentric anthropology. Penis envy, and the whole line of thinking associated with that concept, is a result of viewing humanity from the point of view that the male possesses the phallus. And that tendency went to such extremities that Freud stated in one of his papers that maternal love receives a massive component from the sublimation of penis envy. Supposedly the arrival of the baby satisfies a woman because the child is the substitute for the penis. In the first years of the New York Psychoanalytic Institute, I did not dare to criticize Freud. And the moment I started, tragedy broke loose.

As I have mentioned, Jeanne Lampl-de Groot actually said that the birth of a baby was the most active, masculine thing a woman could do. There was this disastrous confusion, which Freud tried to retract, that identified maleness with activity and femaleness with passivity. In Freud's view, sexual intercourse was a passive submission of the woman. The male function is an output of sperm; the female function is an intake. But to take anything in is an activity! This confusion within Freud's thinking rendered any scientific discussion of the different psychologies of the sexes impossible.

I am talking about Freud now because this tendency, which in my case derived from my relationship with my mother, was then reinforced by hearing from him the same thing in much greater detail. And it took so long before I came to wonder, "How is that in reality?" Then I started to listen to my patients. Waiting for a sign of penis envy and related theoretical concepts, I began to discover that the emotional life has entirely different rules and has little if anything to do with logic. The female is more emotional than the male—even the female mathematician. Those were deplorably late discoveries on my part.

My full systematic elaboration of these ideas came only finally when the Columbia Clinic was established. And by then the situation was bewildering, both in my professional life as well as in social contacts. The idea that if a woman were to be thinking like a man, she would have a reduced emotional life, like the man has, because of the pressure of reality, that sort of thinking was a late conclusion of mine. If women were more like men, then who could shower affection on the baby for years and years? I think men are incapable of that. Any ordinary man in working life would be a great exception if he knew how to handle babies emotionally without being taught. Women learn it; they know it from their mother and they have an inclination to it. The mere fact that the women are in charge of bringing up babies because the men are away and working, and that this can go on easily for ten years, has to be taken into account. For women live with their babies in another world. They have to understand the baby, converse with the baby, answer the baby. It would be a biological absurdity if it were different than it actually is.

Not only did I get oriented erroneously because my mother was a uniquely brilliant woman, with an unemployed intelligence; but then, when I came to psychoanalysis, Freud was also curiously attached to his own mother. And to his dying day he never understood women. That was also possible because when he was a medical student, biology did not exist. It was chiefly a histological orientation. One learned anatomy, and then came histology, and that occupied all the interest. The penetration of medicine with physiological thinking happened in this century. By that time Freud was a practicing doctor. What he learned in medical school was not calculated to open his eyes, and by that time he was completely oriented to his culture in the sense of its fiction and poetry. Freud died without having really to think about what is the difference between male and female.

In the Berlin years, when I was the editor and Freud the publisher of the German-language psychoanalytic papers, I made frequent visits to Vienna, not only to transact business, because that was not of real interest to me. In all these years, he perhaps once wrote me a letter to watch out for this or that or to be nice to a certain person. He expected me, when I was visiting, to spend every minute of that time on what is news in the psychoanalytic movement—not what is fresh in the development of psychoanalysis, because no such thing existed, and he knew it. If any question ever came up, he often asked, "What is most misunderstood?" He was interested in how much, and in what way, his propositions were misapprehended. But who did what or who contributed anything—this· area literally did not exist.

I was young and daring then, and his implicit approach was not 100 percent clear to me at the time. But by and large the truth was already evident. Then occasionally I brought him books and magazines to read. For instance, I took him a summary article about the development of sexual physiology written by a man at the Kaiser Wilhelm Institute. That was like the Rockefeller Institute is here. They were beginning to isolate what goes on in the male and what happens in the female. I read it naturally with tremendous interest.

And once I spent at least five minutes trying to tell him the gist of what had happened. His answer was noteworthy: "This is all very nice, but you know that we get along fine having postulated just one libido. We do not have two kinds of libido." In other words, when I made this joking remark about phallocentric anthropology, it was not my invention. I supplied only the words to characterize the nature of his thinking. When he said to me, "We have found it convenient to describe mental life with just one libido," he was stating that the female must be understood in terms of the male, especially female sexuality. This can and did lead only to a blind alley; that is obvious. So I have evidence, because I heard it from his own mouth, that this was, indeed, his whole conception of sex.

Decades later, rereading some of his passages, I rubbed my head. I could not believe that the greatest psychologist, the only genius psychology ever produced, should have gotten stuck in this serious error.

As a child I could observe that if it were a proposition of accepting an abstract idea or a long-range plan, and the task was to win my parents over to that, I had gradually to work on my mother and explain everything to her. My father would awaken and express his views, my mother would convince him, and he then easily consented to anything. She was the intellectual leader and he the inferior.

But while I was confidently looking for women with brains, my attitude was also reversed. In my feeling and not-clearly-formulated judgment, a woman was bright when she understood and accepted what I had to say. And when she did not do so, then I would say that she was almost smart. That went on for a long time. And then came the period in the late 1940s when I discovered that I also implicitly thought of the woman as a sort of doll.

I was looking for a bright woman, not only in marriage but in social life and among friends. My search was not limited to matrimony but was an overall quest. Naturally and accordingly, it was late and difficult for me at that time, being guided by an erroneous standard and textbook, to discover the tremendous value of female emotionality. A woman has a healthy, desirable, and variable emotional organization. If you cannot keep your eyes open, how can you see it?

The truth could even be an irritation. First of all there was an understanding on my part which was either flatly zero or just a bit above zero. Accordingly, I was always attracted by the theater; I was a passionate theater-goer. In my birthtown there was a stock theater; the larger town where I lived later had a permanent theater, and the stock business lasted half a year, not in July or August. The pride of the city was the *gymnasium*, and everybody went on vacation over the summer. So the theater came sometime in the late fall and departed in the spring.

Students at the *gymnasium* had a special prize; standing room was not reserved. The first one there got the best place, like here. I hardly missed one play; I was at the theater almost every night, except when they did plays I had already seen two or three times. I went to the theater more often than any of my friends. And no one else was admitted to the standing room, which had an exceptional entrance, but only students. The professors had set up this arrangement. There was a center part of the balcony and two sides; there was a space in between on each of the sides, and that is where we stood. The king was the one who got the place right at the front row.

I adored the theater. Later, in Budapest, I went to most of the opening nights. When I came to the United States I tried to keep up with that, but in a few weeks I discovered that an opening night in America bears no resemblance to the same occasion in Europe; here it is a social event, where there it was a cultural issue because all the theaters were repertory companies. We did not have companies formed for one play and, if it is good, goes on for years. This kind of commercialized theater was unknown in Germany, Austria, or Hungary. Our theaters had a standing director and lifelong membership if the theater was maintained by the state. Otherwise it was run by a corporation, but still the arrangements were the same. Here it was an admittedly plain business matter, with financial "angels"; most of the people present at openings were relatives of the actors and actresses, friends of the relatives, the angels and their acquaintances. It was a selected audience engaged in the pursuit of theater as a business; so I gradually gave that up.

Emotional life could be found in the theater. Before World War I, for the first time the famous Russian Ballet Theater decided to go abroad. Under the supervision and direction of Sergei Diaghilev, they arrived first at Budapest. Gilbert Miller came from America for opening nights, and in those days there were no flights. I was there and had an experience such as I have never had before or since. Vaslav Nijinsky came floating onto the stage in a manner that no one could imagine. That was not in the building of the Royal Opera; it was in the second opera house. Budapest had at that time not quite 800,000 people, and there were three operas. When this performance ended, which nobody had dreamt of before, the audience applauded for a solid hour—a standing ovation for every dancer.

It was easy for me to appreciate figures on the stage, because we had serious plays. But I did not understand the women; what were they doing on the stage? I laugh now, too. But if one had the idea that men fight each other for power, that could be confirmed by Shakespeare. I learned it first in the Greek tragedies. But then I arrived at the conclusion that in Shakespeare the women play almost always a secondary role, except in comedies; I was helpless. Decades later I had to re-examine his plays, because by that time I almost knew the psychology of women better than that of men, which is so simple—shrewdness, dishonesty, the list of male characteristics can be put down on a piece of paper. But with women it is a more complicated matter.

Look up Freud's writings on the Shakespearean characters. It is all about the men. I am happy to say that I have been able to get out of this Victorian prejudice in Freud. The whole society was organized in that pattern then; it was not a pathological phenomenon in Freud to be attached to this patriarchal view and to consider it self-evident. It was part of the society in which he grew up. Besides, he missed what he could have learned from his wife and daughters; that was my point of departure. My grandmother was naturally a Victorian woman. I had this same bias and then came under the domination of a great man who had the same viewpoint, only more so. And it had been fortified by my mother, even though she was unusual.

But she was herself a completely Victorian woman. Years later such problems came as women cigarette smokers, or my sister dreaming of using lipstick or powder. Every one of these changes was viewed by my mother as a tragedy. She was once sitting on a train, and a young woman suddenly pulled out a little compact from her pocket and began to fix her face. Mother came home and talked about it for I do not know how long. It was inconceivable to her that a woman who had a decent home and up-bringing should invent such an idea. The practice was unknown and fantastic; this is part of the Victorian culture that people are apt to ignore in talking about the past.

15

PSYCHOANALYTIC THERAPY AND ITS FUTURE

I believe that the influence of genetics, especially biochemical genetics, is going to be so enormous that it would be bootless to try to outline it. The educational task of psychoanalysis remains great; old-fashioned therapeutic practice will disappear for lack of money. We will have any number of neurotics who can pay minimal fees and go for years to psychoanalysts, as they have been going for years to therapies of whatever kind, but the heydays of analysis are over. Analysts are beginning now to talk ordinary language in their meetings, without using *libido* or *superego*, but they are making these changes quietly; they have nothing to offer, either therapeutically or in terms of research, which has never been done on a serious basis.

Therapy itself, as it stands today, remains dependent on the individual qualifications of an individual doctor. When we teach a theory of therapy, it is based on the life of the patient which the therapist observes. This is actually an educational course for the patient, or rather re-educational. But how can you re-educate a patient if you spend three months on analyzing a dream that patient allegedly had when he was age 5? For research, though, I am in favor of doing almost anything. Therefore, I do not mean to say that classical psychoanalysis will disappear completely. But all the pretenses and the ballyhoo, along with the fraudulent distinguishing between first- and second-class psychiatrists, will have to change.

We should be teaching what therapy is and that which is not true therapy—how and what the therapist should do. And when I say it is a re-educational process, I am quoting Freud's own position. The individual in training should be enabled to get the education which he needs. The re-education offered to patients should be an emotional process that nobody else can give him but someone who is well versed in psychodynamics.

My basic theoretical framework involves each person being self-reliant. In keeping with this conviction of mine, I think that the whole development of dependent transferences has to be prevented, because that means that the patient is encouraged to go back into the nursery. The analyst should not be deified. And the patient ought not to escape the responsibility of self-reliance; the desire to take care of oneself should be encouraged. Instead, the patient is apt to hope that his analyst will perform some magic. Nothing can come of this sort of treatment because in its terms nobody has any interest in offering therapy. Analysts should not have either therapeutic ambition or overambition. There are today I do not know how many different schools of psychotherapy. Who can tell who does what? The field is in utter chaos, but it will gradually clear up by people being forced to rediscover the commonsense task of therapy.

Proper re-education cannot be done with any drugs. *Ego strength* is another concept for self-reliance. The word *self-reliance* is self-explanatory. You must rely on yourself. On the other hand, what is *ego* and what is *ego strength*? As far as I am concerned, these terms are already in the clouds.

To my mind, the only way you can understand other human beings is through a motivational approach. Without that neither psychiatry nor the humanities can exist. Motivational dynamics is the basis of everything, beginning with comprehending the man who cleans the streets right up to the president. If organized psychoanalysis is set up for the purposes of research, and for better understanding of the organism as a guide to physiological studies, then it is part of the coming era. If not, all these people will get kicked out, as the romantic speculations will go.

It might continue as it has because of the vested interests and the weight of organizational machinery; that is a power question. As long as they can perpetuate themselves, they will succeed. Ultimately it will be impossible to do this, and the medical profession will sit aside and watch it end. What you see here is limited to the United States, and it has not happened anywhere else.

In America the influence of psychoanalysis on the general culture has been enormous. It has enriched the language and become part of literature. And the basic idea that through analysis a human being can find out more about himself than he ordinarily does is pure gold. But I wonder how many people whose language includes references to psychoanalysis would ever come to a proper conclusion about what psychoanalysis actually is.

Interesting new developments are taking place within psychoanalysis. The orthodox partisans appear to me, watching from the outside, to realize that they cannot forever come only with the libido theory and that sort of thinking. But they have bad luck in that the recent orthodox psychoanalytic writers proceed in English that is much more abstract and unintelligible than what Freud ever wrote. For example, Hartmann did not provide the language for the description of anything; whatever its merits or weaknesses in clarifying theory, Hartmann's work is not such as to have helped to do clinical studies.

The future of psychoanalysis is primarily the future of psychodynamic theory and the description of psychodynamic processes that can be communicated only as the result of deep introspection which is a developed form of free association. I have complained that the difficulty is that Freud discovered a phenomenal method which is unique, and I failed to see who could discover something else which could do the job of the psychoanalytic investigative method. In addition, Freud had a genius for describing his findings. He reintroduced into science the motivational point of view, which has a 5,000-year history. Under whatever name people always wanted to know what others do, why they do it, and what can be done to influence them. These are all urgent practical needs.

We cannot in fairness say that the motivational study of human behavior started with Freud. Only systematic psychological studies began with him, because he discovered the free association of ideas. Without this method, ordinary life observation, based on high degrees of self-awareness, of which so many outstanding people proved to have been capable throughout history, is as old as could be. Take such a man as Thucydides; when you read him, you find pages which could have been printed yesterday in *The New York Times*.

So it went throughout history, and these ancients had actually started the development of a psychological language, which, however, was not yet science. But it was an expression of the understanding of the inner life. The climax was reached by the great dramatists of the so-called Golden Age of Greece: 600 B.C. to approximately 300 B.C.

What Freud did was to make the exploration of the subjective experience of other people more reliable because he undertook such examination in a situation where it became the foremost interest of the patient. In any case, Freud paid no attention to methodological consider- ations and therefore lost sight of his own original goal: to correlate in one way or another the psychological findings with the physiologically observ- able activities of the brain. He went further and further away from elementary methodological requirements; he loved to coin broad and practically undefinable terms. And since those concepts became popular, at least among his pupils, a situation has developed in which one and the same word came to mean almost everything; it could have one meaning and the opposite. Only by virtue of the context could the reader have some idea in what sense that same word got used in one place or another.

During my whole stays in both Budapest and Berlin, and on my visits to Vienna, later when I participated in meetings of the Psychoana- lytic Society there, nobody ever came anywhere into the neighborhood of inquiring into methodological questions. Everybody was satisfied that the man who invented psychoanalysis knew best how to use it. This was not the result of a considered judgment but the self-evident, natural assump- tion on the part of everybody in the movement.

To all this is to be added the hostile reception to Freud in the environment. There are any number of books in which the history of this attitude is recounted. If you examine carefully the actual facts, you will see that while there were occasionally rather hostile responses to Freud's work, his own reaction to that was, from the beginning, exaggerated. Right from the first reception in Vienna upon his return from the visit to Charcot in Paris, Freud was oversensitive to these reactions, possibly because he was overambitious.

Freud, in a half-sentence argument with Breuer, states in his auto- biography that Breuer naturally was an academic scientist. Freud com- plains that Breuer was talking about hypnoid states and everything possible in neurological terms. Freud said he had simplified all that and talked about tendencies and motives analogous to those used in everyday life. The same remark probably appears in several places in Freud's writings.

Then came the libido theory, and Freud had no interest in realizing that this was all motivational psychology he had been working with. He had made a methodological discovery by means of using free associations, and he rediscovered the only system in which you can describe material intelligently so that people will understand it. He did not know that this was motivation or did not think of it as such. If someone had asked him, he would have recognized that this was as old as mankind.

With this equipment he opened up an untouched field of exploration, and that is what he began to do. Everything went phenomenally until 1905, when he turned to the libido theory. The trouble with his use of libido thinking was that he "extended" the meaning of the term *sex*, which is a biological impossibility. Sex is a fact of biology, which prescribes that there is only the pair of two sexes – one male, one female. This is an evolutionary differentiation, and nothing can be called sexual which has no legitimate place in this definition.

This generalization of *sexual*, until it became equivalent to *pleasure*, eliminated the concept of any pleasure which is not sexual and led to the development of what I call a *romantic* theory, which is a relapse into prescientific times. He generalized from sexual feelings which were not directly connected with the sexual organs and called this the *component instincts of sexuality*. You can find the correct attitude in the first introductory lectures of Freud, where he begins to argue, "Why should we not call this and that sexual?" But later he unquestionably adds other acts and perversions. Who is going to tell when something becomes sexual? Earlier in the same book he says "meaning depends on motivational context." Since there is no sexual interest in a child, only a desire for pleasure, it can simply be described as a pleasurable activity, and there is absolutely no earthly reason to call it sexual. When a child learns to kiss a mother whom he loves and the mother kisses him, and gradually, in our civilization, the mouth becomes an important executive organ, in these cases it is always sexual. A human being has a pleasure organization, and all the pleasure-producing mechanisms can be used for a large variety of purposes. So that was an arbitrary business that made any contact with the biologist impossible because he did not know what this man was talking about: is one to believe that defecation is a sexual act, or that the baby sucking at his mother's breast is a sexual act?

And then came these hypothetical so-called structural theories of the superego, ego, and id, which are all beautiful dramatizations. Nobody can invent any better ones, but they have no possible application in clinical phenomena. Better that you talk about conscience, which everybody knows the meaning of; I question whether there is anything to be gained by calling it *superego* instead of *conscience*.

All that you achieve in accomplishing is the creation of a lot of misleading problems. How does the superego emerge? Freud proposes a false description of conscience. He thought it was the internalization of the father, which it was more or less in patriarchal society. But in the United States the middle-class child scarcely sees its father, and all the early discipline and upbringing of the child is handled by the mother.

The great tragedy followed that psychoanalysis developed a terminology composed of a few dozen words, every one of them referring to a huge amount of clinical data. For instance, hypochondria was supposed to be a damming-up of libido in the organs. Nobody knew whether by *organ* was meant an organ itself or the mental representation of the organ. And megalomania as well as inferiority are both considered *narcissistic* phenomena, even though they would appear to be the opposite of each other.

It became impossible to build up a scientifically oriented theory, and the orthodox school went on with this way of proceeding. In cases of helplessness and insecurity people fall back on the old magical type of thinking. It was Bronislaw Malinowski who discovered this. Freud had agreed with earlier thinkers that the classification of human development falls into three periods: first magic, then religion, and finally science. I read this first outside of psychoanalysis but later said to myself, "This is nonsense. If mythological thinking had been in force for millennia, during that time the whole human species would have died out." You must have the means of finding out what reality is, or you die.

Malinowski's answer was that as much as it was possible to accumulate practical knowledge, that has been done; but to the extent that people desired it and could not have it, they turned to magic. Magic was always a compensatory system. And the same thing happens in science. It goes so far; and people are insecure, because the means of reality testing are not available. First of all there were not proper definitions in psychoanalysis, but even so you could not have tested anything because nobody could tell for sure what anything meant.

Freud started out to devise a system under the organic aegis. But it was impossible because there was no such science as brain physiology at that time; there were half a dozen speculative principles but no facts. Brain physiology was actually created by Sir Charles Sherrington in the first decade of this century. So Freud gave that up and turned his back on brain physiology.

Now in the last ten years brain physiology has come completely under the influence of the computer. Computers can do fabulous things but still can only carry out mathematical operations which you put into the program; the computer cannot invent or check whether the invention has any value or not. But neurophysiology is in the process of being swallowed up by these images of computers. I was present when Norbert Weiner first talked about cybernetics; it was clear, although he did not put it that way, that he considered the human brain a poor replica of a computer.

So that now is our despair. It is also why I said that psychoanalysis has a great future, by *psychoanalysis* meaning the investigative method and original ideas which have to be brought closer to brain physiology. But the problem remains: how can you correlate an animistic, romantic description of the mind with the mechanistic account of the brain?

Too often that which is most important in psychology and human life, namely, the emotions, fell by the wayside. Everybody always talks about libido and nobody speaks about the emotions; but the driving force in people's lives are these feelings. And therefore the exploration of the emotions is the number-one job of psychodynamics, once a language is created with which you can describe them. You cannot explain things in terms of a poor explanatory hypothesis because chaos results. This confusion has dominated orthodox psychoanalysis for at least the last forty years or more.

Let me read from myself; I am talking about my theory of *adaptational* psychoanalysis:

> In our revised theoretical structure of psychoanalysis, the emphasis was on the exploration of man's emotional life. But the truly scientific exploration of this aspect of man's life has hardly begun. Also, the pre-eminence of the task has become obvious. Man's fear of studying his emotions is seen to be spectacular. We are afraid of exploring our emotions. Freud's theory turned from biology to what my late friend, Siegfried Bernfeld, accurately called . . . the romanticisms of instinct.
>
> On the other hand, the brain physiology of our times becomes completely overwhelmed by the computer. Man is an emotional animal who is capable of adapting his emotions to the environment under the guidance of reason. In my opinion, the road to man's understanding includes his emotional life, and this road starts with the emotional self-understanding of the individual. There is absolutely no conceivable alternative to these obvious facts.
>
> Thus our future will have to take us between the Scylla of romanticism and the Charybdis of the computer.

And that is the future of psychoanalysis, much more clearly stated. Let me close with the prediction that psychoanalysis has a still undreamt-of future.

PART III

FREUD'S LETTERS
TO RADO

Edited by Paul Roazen

Jan. 13, 1925

Dear Doctor:

I thank you for your first editorial report of the fifth of this month. I hope that in this way I shall be able to participate in all of your work and your little worries. On the other hand, I am being instructed by Storfer,[1] who recently spent an evening with me. I can only approve of your decision regarding the projected Swiss special issue. But I made to Storfer the concession, which will likely lead to the same result, that you should address yourself to Oberholzer[2] to inquire whether he can provide you

1. Albert Josef Storfer (1888–1944). In 1924, Storfer replaced Otto Rank as managing editor of the *Internationaler Psychoanalytischer Verlag*, a post he held until 1932.

2. Emil Oberholzer (1883–1958). In 1919 Oberholzer, a physician and psychiatrist, founded, with Oscar Pfister, the Swiss Society for Psychoanalysis. Oberholzer's wife, Mira Gincburg (1887–1949), was also an analyst. Oberholzer created a second Swiss psychoanalytic society, the Swiss Medical Society for Psychoanalysis, because of the issue of lay analysis; it never became affiliated with the International Psychoanalytic Association. The Oberholzers emigrated to New York City in 1938.

with a sufficient number of Swiss articles by the due date. The answer, I expect, will be negative, but the editors have been kind in any case. Each of the last five issues of the *Zeitschrift* has contained a contribution of mine. So do not be surprised if I now leave it alone for awhile. I must devote myself to the reworking of *The Interpretation of Dreams*.[3]

With cordial greeting,

Your

Freud

Typed

March 15, 1925

Dear Doctor,

I thank you for the report of March 11 and will reply to the individual points in the following.

I have received and thoroughly approved Sachs's[4] report on Rank's *Trauma of Birth*. On Tuesday evening Storfer is coming to see me and will take it with him.

It is completely in accordance with my wishes that you intend to bring in the second issue of the *Zeitschrift* the Salzburg Congress addresses of Jones,[5] Sachs, and Alexander,[6] which had been marked to appear in brochure form. I have always been of the opinion that our periodicals ought not to be robbed of their best materials for the sake of separate publications. Of course Storfer's contention that circulation and sales need to be considered is also justified. We will have to do some maneuvering.

---

3. An enlarged and revised edition appeared later in 1925.

4. Hanns Sachs (1881–1947) was, although trained as a Viennese lawyer, one of the first to function as a training analyst at the Berlin Institute. Among other books he wrote *Freud: Master and Friend*. Sachs died in Boston, where he had helped set up a training institute.

5. Ernest Jones (1879–1958), originally from Wales, trained as a neurologist in London. After practicing in Toronto before World War I, he returned to London to found the British Psychoanalytic Society. Jones is perhaps best known for his having written his three-volume life of Freud.

6. Franz Alexander (1891–1964) came from an educated Hungarian family, graduated from the Berlin Psychoanalytic Institute, and then was the formative influence in setting up the Chicago Psychoanalytic Society. He was a prolific writer and specialized in psychosomatic medicine.

I know of no objection to the articles which you announce, mainly of a clinical nature.

I have been informed by the Progres Medical of the Charcot celebration. They asked me for some contribution, and I decided to point out to them the eulogy in the first issue of my Shorter Writings,[7] which surely has remained unknown in Paris. I suggested to them to have Laforgue[8] prepare translations of an extract or portions of this essay. For that is where, under the fresh impression of the news of his death, I said all that there was for me to say about my impressions of Charcot and my relations with him. Today, forty years later, I wouldn't know of anything better to write out of my faded memories. No reply has yet come from Progres Medical. You are right that our *Zeitschrift* ought also to take notice of the celebration. But it would be better for someone else to take up this task, someone whose perspective has been altered by the events in the meantime. If Ferenczi[9] decides to do this, it would surely be excellent.

I am not surprised to hear that nothing can be accomplished with Oberholzer. It is very regrettable, but he will have to be let go.

Your remarks about the mystic writing pad of course aroused my special interest. I can't very well picture the apparatus which you describe, since this piece of technology is completely unknown to me. But I think it would be very nice of you and increase the value of my notice, if you would inform the public of the analogy you have found, in a little written piece of your own. It would not have to take up more pages than my notice[10] about the mystic writing pad, and I hope it would not add noticeably to your burden of work.

With cordial greetings,

Your,

Freud

Typed

---

7. Cf. "Charcot," in *The Standard Edition of the Complete Psychological Works of Sigmund Freud*, ed. James Strachey. London, The Hogarth Press, 1953–1974), vol. 3, pp. 11–23.

8. Rene Laforgue (1894–1962), an early French analyst, became president of the Paris Psychoanalytic Society when it was formed in 1926. He corresponded with Freud. Laforgue was accused of being a collaborator with the Nazis at the beginning of World War II, but the case against him was ultimately dismissed.

9. Sandor Ferenczi (1873–1933) was the founder of the Hungarian Psychoanalytic Society and a great personal friend of Freud's.

10. Cf. "A Note Upon the 'Mystic Writing Pad,' " *Standard Edition*, vol. 19, pp. 227–232. 1232.

n.d.

Dear Doctor,

I have read Alexander's excellent report and am sending it on to the publisher.

For myself, I am in agreement with the change concerning the description of the editorship on the jacket of the *Zeitschrift*. But you must get Ferenczi's and Eitingon's[11] consent.

I know that I am in general on complete agreement with your intentions concerning the small and the large aspects of the Z. [*Zeitschrift*]. Storfer is a competent and good man, but he has a fondness for continual little innovations in which his restless head seeks expression. Such little satisfactions of lust must be withdrawn from him gently.

I was very glad of your promise to hold back with your notice about the mystic writing pad.

The delay in the appearance of both periodicals – an expression of Rank's absence – ought really to be evened out.

With cordial greetings and thanks for your efforts,

Your,

Freud

Handwritten

April 26, 1925

Dear Doctor,

Just a few lines to ask you to give your full attention to the prompt appearance of our *Zeitschrift*. It is very disadvantageous that today, the end of April, the first issue of the new year has not yet come out. Of course I know that these are the initial difficulties of your job, and I hope that we will have brought out both the issues that are due on June 30.

With cordial greetings,

Your,

Freud

Typed

_____

11. Max Eitingon (1881–1943) was a Russian physician of great wealth who for years functioned behind the scenes in forwarding the psychoanalytic movement.

May 3, 1925

Dear Doctor,

I have read your report *with understanding* and hope that we are both of one mind concerning it. I, too, value Storfer and know his peculiar inclinations, against which I sometimes have to be on my guard during the preparation of the complete edition.[12] My letter to you was not in the slightest intended to put any restraint on you if you have to confront him in maintaining the deadline.

I am completely in agreement with the editorial page for the second volume.

Cordial greetings,

your

Freud

Typed

Sept. 30, 1925

Dear Doctor,

Many thanks for your detailed report. I have nothing to say concerning the editorial page for the fourth issue. The intention of moving the date forward for the issue's appearance will surely make a favorable impression. The number of issues from the previous year that have appeared so far has remained respectably high. I hope all goes as well again. The submissions that you enumerate don't all seem to be first-rate. But among them there are the excellent Congress pieces.

I have read Burrow's[13] manuscript, and I fully endorse your criticism as well as that of Dr. Eitingon. Burrow seems to be a confused blatherer. Recently I had correspondence with him about a submission in which he wanted to introduce the Theory of Relativity into psychoanalysis. I don't think that reproaches in a letter will change his ways at all. But a notice such as the one devised by you would not be out of place. It could sound even more forceful, perhaps: "Because of the abstract style of the author's

---

12. Storfer was in charge of preparing that edition of Freud's works.

13. Trigant Burrow (1875–1950) was an American physician who developed original ideas, for example, about group psychotherapy.

indefinite formulation. . . ." Of course he will have to be informed of the editor's intention of adding a note worded thus to his essay. I doubt that he will be highly offended, for he is probably invulnerable in his self-overestimation. At any rate, we can risk it. It is simply too nonsensical, and the consideration for the gentlemen from America need not go too far. His election to the presidency this year is no sign of particularly high esteem. The Americans transfer the democratic principle from politics into science. Everyone has to be president once, no one may remain president, no one may distinguish himself from the others, and thus they all learn and produce nothing, one and all.

I am wishing you the best for the further flourishing of your work.

Your,

Freud

Typed

Dec. 4, 1925

Dear Doctor,

I thank you for your messages. I ask you still to wait awhile for my comments concerning your essay. I was sick again in November, but not in connection with my earlier illness: I had a serious dental operation, which brought me down quite a bit, so that I have got quite far behind in my work. I have just now begun chewing again, and hope I will soon be able to take in heavy intellectual food. But I would not like to see the printing of your work delayed on this account.

We are all weighed down under the impression of our Abraham's prolonged illness, about which we are insufficiently informed. What I know I learn basically from you by way of Dr. Deutsch.[14] Dr. Sachs, who is generally a very conscientious reporter, does not seem to know much himself. I have the impression that even those closest to Abraham don't know very much. Let's hope for a good outcome!

Cordial greetings,

your,

Freud

Typed

14. Felix Deutsch (1884–1964), a Viennese physician who for a time functioned as Freud's own doctor, was married to Helene Deutsch, a leading psychoanalyst; they both moved to Boston where they became prominent in American medicine.

Jan. 28, 1926

Dear Doctor,

I was not pleased with your intention of delaying the Abraham issue to December, and I did not find your motivation transparent. I then demanded an accounting from Storfer and got from him the solution, which I had not guessed myself: that the editors of both periodicals intend to celebrate my round-numbered birthday, each with a volume of collected articles. In principle, my attitude towards all kinds of celebrations is negative; however I can't oppose this plan, and I only hope that your tact will watch over seeing that the articles of congratulation are kept as short and modest as possible, so that the world is not treated to the spectacle of the publisher's having himself celebrated in his own organs. I am sure I need not worry on this score.

But now it seems to me all the more urgent that the homage to Abraham should not be delayed any longer, if I myself should be the hindrance to carrying it out. One cannot celebrate festivals before the duty of mourning is accomplished. It seems to me unavoidable to have Abraham's eulogies appear before the congratulatory issues, and to this end I have worked out the following solution with Storfer. Since the date of the congratulatory issues is determined, the second issue of the *Zeitschrift* is to appear as soon as possible after the first one, at any rate a few weeks before the May issue. It need contain nothing more than the protocols of the memorial sessions and the eulogies—with Jones's placed first as the official one. According to Storfer's estimate this volume should contain about three sheets; the excess can be distributed between the following volumes, i.e., the third and the fourth. It also does not seem advisable to me to commission articles from the late Abraham's circle of pupils for a special issue, since these are not conditions favorable to scientific work, and as we know they cannot call forth accomplishment such as would cause the late lamented to feel himself honored. Of course this applies to articles which are destined for my issues. But in the case of these there is no restriction to particular given themes, and the periodicals will bring just what they have and would have used to fill up their space in any case.

I hope you will be amenable to these requests of mine. If my having already become so old is really the occasion for a celebration, then let us not for a moment have our celebration disturbed by the thought that we have on this account postponed the urgent duty of honoring him who has departed this life early.

With cordial greetings,

Your,

Freud

Typed

Feb. 5, 1926

Dear Doctor,

Dr. Jones has sent me the copy of his last letter to you, from which I see what difficulties my influence on the Abraham memorial issue is causing you. I am sure you will find the right way out, but would not like to neglect to clarify my standpoint one more time, perhaps to your relief.

I must hold to my demand that Abraham's issue must appear before the one dedicated to me. No festivals before the mourning is completed. Mourning cannot be postponed. Now, I see two possibilities for this issue. Either you let it contain nothing but what relates to Abraham, to the extent to which it is available, or you make it into an ordinary issue, in which the picture and the articles about Abraham form the first part. No one will raise the demand that the scientific articles in his honor must appear now. For everyone knows that such work takes time, and one can't prepare for a bereavement as one can for a birthday whose date is known in advance. Hence the need for a separation in time between the memorial announcements and the scientific articles. It may then take a year or more for your idea of an Abraham-issue, filled with pieces by his pupils, to take shape. This idea does not at all have to be dropped.

It is different with the issue dedicated to me. I think that even if it appears in order to mark May 6th, yet it needn't appear *on* May 6th. Scientific work has its own necessities that should not be sacrificed to personal considerations. In this connection, there occurs to me a comparison, inappropriate in many other respects, but which I will set before you anyway: the memory of conquered Belgrade, which absolutely had to be laid at the feet of the old Kaiser exactly on August 18th. Now, fortunately, I am not that old, and our efforts are not the same. I think no one will be offended if the issue dedicated to me comes out sometime in the summer as No. 3, and posterity will never notice the discrepancy in the date. It was different with the issues that had to be ready for a Congress. In that case, the concern was to show to a great many people, including guests and outsiders, what work is going on in the Society, and to suggest new ideas to the Society itself, and even to entice outsiders to subscribe. All of these considerations fall away in the case of an intimate celebration.

I may have made your difficult task somewhat easier by these remarks.

Cordial greetings,

Your,

Freud

Typed

Feb. 11, 1926

Dear Doctor,

Thanks for your letter. I am glad to hear that the collision has been avoided.

The rest of what I have to say may surprise you. While I am at pains to keep the festivities low-profile, yet I am suddenly appearing to put such a matter on stage. A few days ago I accepted an invitation from Prof. Schmutzer to have my etching made. You probably know that Schmutzer is the leading practitioner of this art in Vienna. I have already visited him, been photographed several times, and the actual work will be done on the coming Sundays. Schmutzer knows of my birthday, and makes no demand for his work. I have now thought that he could be assured of a certain sales potential if we acquired the picture, which I hope will not be a complete failure. If you approve this project, you can write to him, Address: Vienna XVIII, Sternwartestrasse 62, to ask him to supply it to you by your deadline. My changed behavior is thus explained by the fact that it is a matter of the *Zeitschrift*, against which I do not show resistance, but which on the contrary I willingly accept.

With cordial greetings,

Your

Freud

Typed

April 30, 1926

Dear Doctor,

I received the Abraham memorial number today and find it so successful and worthy that I can't help congratulating the revered editors for this achievement. By the way, I am also very pleased that I got my way concerning the appearance of this issue before my celebration.

With cordial greetings,

Your

Freud

Typed

May 14, 1926

Dear Doctor,

Please don't be too sensitive to the fact that my thanks for your many-sided efforts for my birthday don't reach you until today. I have a big job of saying thanks ahead of me, and I reach into the basket at random and answer whatever my fingers touch first. Suddenly I must interrupt myself and say to myself that I can no longer leave to chance my appreciation for your extraordinary accomplishment in editing the two Festschriften. It is of course the most valuable present that I received. It will probably have cost you considerable toil. I know that your willing fondness for the task lightened the toil.

No chance of my reading the articles right now. But on June 15 we are moving to Semmering. There I will have time to plunge into them.

Your cordially devoted

Freud

Typed

June 3, 1926

Dear Doctor,

A few months ago, when I received the large two-volume work *La Psicoanalisi* by Morselli[15] in Genoa, I asked our Ed. Weiss[16] in Trieste to write a detailed and unsparing criticism of it. Morselli is regarded as a great

---

15. Enrico Morselli (1852–1929) was a professor of neurology at the University of Turin.

16. Edoardo Weiss (1889–1970) was the founder of the Italian Psychoanalytic Society. For his review of Morselli's work, and Freud's differing letters to both Morselli and Weiss, cf. Paul Roazen, *Freud and His Followers*. (New York Da Capo, 1992b), pp. 501–502.

psychiatric authority, and this book of his is in every respect a miserable, shoddy effort. Dr. Weiss has now sent me the very detailed report, and I have asked Storfer to fetch it for me. I ask you to let him know whether to send the manuscript to Berlin or directly for typesetting. It will need a few corrections, small cuts, perhaps a too-harsh word struck out – changes with which the author has already declared himself in agreement.

With cordial greetings,

Your

Freud

Typed

Semmering, Sept. 14, 1926

Dear Doctor,

I thank you for your editorial report which arrived today, and regret that at the moment I am not meeting your need. I have nothing to communicate to the public,[17] and I think they would do well to prepare for the drying up of my production. If contrary to expectation I should come upon some idea, I will immediately place it at your disposal.

On the *Imago* question I share your point of view in two points. I would like to preserve the organ and not offend Storfer. Your entry into the editorial team as a conciliatory middle person between Storfer and Sachs seems quite expedient. Dr. Eitingon wants to visit us on the 25th of this month; I hope that while he is here we will reach agreement on the matter.

I am awaiting with suspense Ferenczi's criticism; such an expression of opinion has unfortunately become unavoidable.

I am also glad to take advantage of the occasion to thank you for all your so successful accomplishments.

Your

Freud

Handwritten

Dec. 4, 1926

Dear Doctor,

A big surprise for me! But a pleasant one, and I am glad to share your hope that this step will bring you full and lasting happiness in life. Your

---

17. The phrase "at the moment" is scratched out.

work will not have to change from what it has been, and the worker may feel himself happier. Please accept my hearty congratulations, and convey my best regards to your new wife, whom I do not yet know.[18]

Your

Freud

Handwritten

March 22, 1927

Dear doctor,

Enclosed are two talks of Ferenczi's, which the *Zeitschrift* will surely not want to do without. One is in German and English, the latter already destined for Clark's Archives. I don't know whether we can also offer it to Jones, but I think not. The other essay is to be translated at your place and the original sent to Jones.

I have been very glad to hear my daughter's[19] reports about Berlin, and I send my hearty greetings

Your

Freud

Handwritten

May 11, 1927

Dear Doctor,

I find it particularly pleasant that you, who are perhaps the one among us who does the most work for the common good, celebrate my birthday by a report on the present status of this work. Any other form of celebration or congratulation or presentation would not suit me, and I have asked all my friends to refrain from observations of this date in the coming years.

I am glad to hear that you are satisfied with the material for *Imago*. The article about the healing of a case of war neurosis came from Dr. med. C. Staudacher in Saarbrücken.

18. Freud had analyzed Rado's second wife toward the end of World War I; she died in January 1923.

19. Anna Freud (1895–1982) was already practicing as a child analyst.

With cordial greetings and warm wishes for the further success of
your productive work

Your

Freud

Typed

May 30, 1927

Dear doctor,

You will probably approve of my judgment that the two enclosed
contributions of Prof. H. Gomperz[20] deserve the *Zeitschrift* readers' attention. Gomperz doesn't wish to sign them himself, and leaves it up to you
to edit them.

One of them I would entitle "From the Childhood of a Philosopher,"
and add ("Communicated by Prof. H. G."); the other, "An Anticipation of
the Psychoanalytical Sublimation Theory," and introduce it as follows:
Prof. G. writes to us: By chance. 2nd line, instead of "your," of course "of
the psychoanalytical."

With cordial greetings,

Your

Freud

Handwritten

Semmering
Villa Schüler
June 20, 1927

Dear Doctor,

What I intend to write is rather a postscript[21] to my book than a final
word to the discussion. But first I want to try out the effect on me of all the

---

20. Heinrich Gomperz (1873–1943) was a professor of philosophy at the
University of Vienna; his mother was treated by Freud, and Gomperz's father
arranged for Freud to be a translator of J. S. Mill's.

21. "Postcript," *Standard Edition*, vol. 20, pp. 251–258.

statements. I will ask Storfer when he is going to need the manuscript. It will not be long.

Cordial greetings,

Your

Freud

Handwritten

Semmering
Aug. 8, 1927

Dear Doctor,

Dr. Eitingon said to me on his last visit that you wanted an essay from me for the first 1928 issue of the *Zeitschrift*. I couldn't promise it since I did not at all feel like working. In the meantime things have picked up and I am sending you forthwith my opus,[22] which however is not very extensive. At least it brings a very simple solution to a problem that has seemed far more complicated.

With cordial greeting,

Your

Freud

Handwritten

October 16, 1927

Dear doctor,

I have read your excellent piece of work, and sent it on to Storfer. In it, you make come true the hunch that I once spoke about, that we would come into a position of being able to find the processes which we studied between ego and object repeated between ego and superego. This then would be the secret of the narcissistic neuroses.[23] In two points your account doesn't seem quite clear to me. One of these is the derivation of guilt feeling.

---

22. "Fetishism," *Standard Edition*, vol. 21, pp. 152–157.
23. *Narcissistic neurosis* was an early term of Freud's for describing psychosis.

My new piece of work[24] is going to appear this year. Its analytic content and its value otherwise are slight; that doesn't need to disturb its distribution.

I greet you cordially, and wish your activities, so important to us, the same success as up until now.

Your

Freud

Handwritten

Feb. 23, 1928

Dear doctor,

How else should I react to the enclosed letter than to send it in to you and ask you kindly to take care of it? I can add the request that you *not* submit the essay in question to me, since I am swamped with duties and feel ever more disinclined to work.

With cordial greeting,

Your

Freud

Handwritten

Feb. 28, 1928

Dear doctor,

I think you will willingly follow the order of Dr. Galant, who is an unpleasant fool.

Cordially,

Your

Freud

Handwritten

Nov. 15, 1928

Dear Doctor,

Enclosed is an article by Dr. Schultz for the *Zeitschrift*, which I recommend that you accept. I once saw Schultz for an (unavoidable)

---

24. "The Future of an Illusion," *Standard Edition*, vol. 21, pp. 5–56.

consultation in Tegel, and was pleasantly surprised by his behavior. He spoke very candidly, almost like in a confession, and earnestly assured me of his need to come close to our circles. I do not fail to recognize his opportunism and his diplomatic skill, but he may nevertheless find the way.

I hear that at last you may be congratulated, which I am herewith very glad to do.

Your

Freud

Handwritten

Dec. 28, 1928

Dear doctor,

Your letter has really brought me great distress and embarrassment. Replying to it will not be easy. Above all, let us exclude the solution of your relinquishing the editorship. I am, like everyone else, convinced of the excellence of your work as well as of the irreplaceability of your person. Nor do I for a moment waver in deciding on which side to look for the mental instability, which has led to such incompatibility. But if I summon Storfer to me, to tell him what I think, I am in a very disadvantageous situation. I seem to have taken the one side without having listened to the other, and because I am not informed, I am defenseless against an account which will probably incriminate you. The outcome of such a conversation would be none other than Storfer's immediate resignation, with the facade of having suffered an injustice, and this could be just what he is trying to accomplish. I imagine that in his exaggerated ambition, he cannot tolerate the poor financial position of the publishing house, and is looking for a way out. But his departure will also put the publishing house in a bad position. It is possible that your rude letter had a bad effect—Storfer has not yet asked to speak to me. I think I should do nothing so long as nothing happens. I am not yet giving up the hope that he will yet stop and think things over, and that you will not insist on pursuing further this regrettable conflict. In the interest of such a difficult matter to manage, we must all resolve ourselves to far-reaching tolerance.

I do not understand what Wälder[25] has to do with this. His entry

---

25. Robert Waelder (1900–1967) received a Ph.D. In physics from the

into the publishing house took place over Storfer's express wish – Let me close with a word of satisfaction that your wife is doing so well, finally, after so many ups and downs.

Cordially,

Freud

Handwritten

Jan. 6, 1929

Dear doctor,

I really couldn't say how my conception of the Storfer affair still differs from yours. I also imagine a similar solution. Storfer, whose ambition is very strong, will probably want to complete the editions [illegible] before he leaves. That he makes it impossible for us to thank him for this accomplishment is part of the tragedy of his existence.

I was very glad to have confirmed by you what I had been told about your wife's satisfactory condition. Let's hope it will soon only be a memory.

Cordially,

Your

Freud

Handwritten

Berchtesgaden
Hans Schneewinkl
June 27, 1929

Dear doctor

In an article by Ella Sharpe,[26] entitled "Hamlet's Impatience," intended for the Jones issue, the explanation of the Hamlet problem is

University of Vienna and became an analyst in the mid-1920s. He was an outspoken critic of Melanie Klein, and a leading orthodox theoretician. He was a Professor of Psychiatry at Jefferson Medical College in Philadelphia.

26. Ella Sharpe (1875–1947) was a British analyst with a flair for understanding literary issues; her article "The Impatience of Hamlet" (1929) appeared in *The International Journal of Psycho-Analysis* vol. 10, pp. 270–279.

attributed without reservation to the man being celebrated, whereas, as is known, it actually comes from me, and is found in a "Note" to the first edition of The Interpretation of Dreams (Standard Edition 4: 264–266). I am not usually a stickler about questions of priority, but this particular idea I would not like to let anyone else have, not even Jones, who took it up in the well-known essay and developed it.

I believe the editors should inform the authoress of this matter, or, if you think it better, emphasize it in an independent footnote.

Cordial greetings

Your

Freud

Handwritten

Schneewinkl
July 8, 1929

Dear doctor,

I thank you for your influence upon Sharpe's essay, and I am pleased to affirm that I share your opinion in every point upon which your letter touches. We are going to put an end quietly to the jubilee issues. This could not be done before Jones's turn.

I fully approve of your intention of celebrating the Policlinic (a year too early, unfortunately) instead of Dr. Eitingon. I will be glad to write the introductory sentences in Eitingon's honor, if at that time I am still able to wield a pen. He has earned this honor well. I too believe that this brochure cannot be prepared without his knowledge and his help. But it could be kept hidden from him that with this publication are connected thanks to him, which I have taken upon myself. Do you not think this possible? A further suggestion would be the actual postponement of this brochure until the year 1931, so that it appears for Eitingon's birthday, if the latter doesn't occur too late in the year, which I don't know. Eitingon would not have to notice the motive for this postponement, and there is nothing remarkable about not adhering strictly to the date for celebrating an Institute. Please think these possibilities over.

As for Dr. Zilboorg's[27] plans, I would like to draw the appropriate-

---

27. Gregory Zilboorg (1890–1959) was born in Russia, and received his M.D.

conclusions from our skepticism. Z. is an enthusiast with no influence at all in America, and the repeated failure of all our efforts at getting money from America for Analysis should deter us from any further attempts. Official as well as private America sees in Analysis an enemy of its specific culture — and rightly so. My daughter also thinks this way, and refuses to take steps in Z's direction in Oxford.[28] I think we will lose nothing by this omission.

I regret that you do not intend to go to the Congress. I hope that you and yours are well.

Cordially,

Your Freud

P.S. I almost forgot to mention that our publishing house will publish the brochure — so much do I take this for granted.

Handwritten

November 7, 1929

Dear doctor,

Enclosed is the first draft of the preface for Eitingon. Let me know if you wish any changes in it, and if so, what. I also ask you to insert the chronology in two places, if it seems necessary to you (how many years Eitingon will have been in charge of the Institute, when he turns fifty).

I am, to be sure, in agreement with your wish that Eitingon should take over the chairmanship in Berlin, but the present moment, which finds him preoccupied with his mother's severe illness, is not a suitable time for trying to influence him in that direction.

With cordial greeting

Your

Freud

Handwritten

---

in 1926 from Columbia University. He was trained in Berlin, and wrote many books, among them *A History of Medical Psychology* (1941).

28. The reference is to the Oxford Congress of Psychoanalysts, July 27–31, 1929.

November 17, 1929

Dear doctor,

I am very sorry that I misunderstood your intentions regarding my preface. If it is now the case that no reference is to be made to Eitingon's 50th birthday, and that the accent should not at all be on his person, then my preface really seems to me to be superfluous. With the dedication to E and the detailed description of the foundation and the achievements of the Institute, all needs have been met. It would perhaps not even be very artful for me to anticipate in an introduction the reader's value judgment of the Institute, which he ought to make for himself on the basis of the material presented. And since I do not at all like writing for the public, I am glad to spare myself for once. The task of a personal appreciation of Eitingon would have placed me under a compulsion that I would have had to yield to.

With cordial greeting

Your

Freud

Handwritten

Nov. 22, 1929

Dear doctor,

Since you insist upon it, and really only for your sake, I place at your disposal the following "preface," which in reality says nothing.

"The following pages depict the establishment and accomplishment of the Berlin Psychoanalytic Institute, to which have fallen three important functions within the psychoanalytic movement. First, to have made our therapy accessible to great numbers of people who suffer from neuroses no less than the rich, but are not able to pay the cost of their treatment. Second, to have created a place where Analysis can be taught theoretically and the experience of older analysts can be transmitted to pupils eager to learn, and, finally, to perfect our knowledge of neurotic illnesses and our therapeutic technique through application and testing under new conditions.

Such an Institute was indispensable, but we had waited in vain for help from the state, and also for interest on the part of the University, for its foundation. In this situation, it was the energy and willingness to make sacrifices of one individual among the analysts that intervened. Dr. Max Eitingon, at present president of the International Psychoanalytical Association, created such an Institute out of his own means, ten years ago now. He has since maintained it, and directed it with his own labor. The report of the Berlin Institute's first decade is a homage to its creator and director, and an attempt to say a public thanks to him. Everyone who has any part in psychoanalysis, in any way, will join in these thanks."[29]

It is rather wooden, but I can't do any better with made-to-order verses.

Cordially,

Your

Freud

Handwritten

March 2, 1930

Dear doctor,

I hope that you received Spielrein's[30] manuscript about a month ago (Pushkinkaya 96, Rostov on Don). Enclosed, as an appendix to that, a self-report. For personal reasons, because the article is dedicated to her sick father, she would like to be informed as soon as possible as to whether it is intended to print it in the *Zeitschrift*. I ask you to reply to her.

Greeting you cordially

Your

Freud

Handwritten

---

29. Cf. "Preface to *Ten Years of the Berlin Psychoanalytic Institute*," *Standard Edition*, vol. 21, p. 257.

30. Sabina Spielrein (1885–1941) was a Russian-born physician with whom Jung had an affair while she was his patient; she practiced in Geneva and was Piaget's analyst. Later she returned to the Soviet Union, where she died during World War II.

Grundlsee
Sept. 26, 1930

Dear Doctor,

I am replying, not to your congratulations for the Goethe Prize, which has receded deep into the past, but to your friendly admonishment that I should write something for the *Zeitschrift*.

Gladly, and if I have anything, it will only go to the *Zeitschrift*, but I have nothing, and since I have not been allowed to smoke at all, I find it very hard to work. I have begun something, which is not moving forward, and its completion awaits better health.

Cordially, your

Freud

Handwritten

March 20, 1931

Dear Doctor,

We are all looking forward very much to your speech — naturally, I may add — and it is equally to be taken for granted that we will have a leisurely chat about your trip to America.

Cordially

Your

Freud

Handwritten

May 5, 1932

Dear Doctor,

Thank-you for your greetings from your new place of work! I have no doubt that you will be very successful there and exercise a lasting influence.

Of course we have missed you bitterly here. What I am about to tell you, you may take as a consequence of your absence. I could not be satisfied with Fenichel,[31] who took your place, and taking into consideration the savings and the advantages of concentration, I have decided to move the editorial offices of both periodicals to Vienna. Federn and Hartmann are to take on the editorship of the International; two nondoctors, Kris[32] and Wälder, are to take on *Imago*. Of course, it is counted on that you will resume the editorship if you return, and if you wish. As well, I am occupied, as you know, with concerns about the publishing house, the management of which my son Martin has taken on. Storfer's disastrous management could go on no longer.

I greet you cordially

Your

Freud

Handwritten

November 22, 1932

Dear Doctor,

Thank you for your very happy news. I am convinced that you are exercising a strong and beneficial influence, and I don't know whether you are more necessary in U.S.A. or in Berlin. The old phalanx is shrinking more and more; now even Ferenczi can hardly be counted on any more. It is to be hoped that new people will step into the gaps.

I am having a hard time recovering from a bout with the flu, with an ear infection. The lectures[33] should be available in about two weeks.

Cordially greeting you,

Your

Freud

Handwritten

––––––––––––––

31. Otto Fenichel (1898–1946) became well known as the author of *The Psychoanalytic Theory of Neurosis* (1945), and died in Los Angeles.

32. Ernst Kris (1900–1957) was originally an art historian, and he was married to Dr. Marianne Kris, a daughter of Freud's friend Oskar Rie; both Ernst and Marianne Kris became famous as analysts in America.

33. "New Introductory Lectures on Psychoanalysis," *Standard Edition*, vol. 22, pp. 5–182.

PART IV

EPILOGUE

by Bluma Swerdloff, D.S.W.

A BRIEF SKETCH
OF RADO'S
PERSONAL LIFE

The ideology inherent in Columbia's collection of oral history memoirs emphasizes the relationship of personality to significant life events. During the series of interviews with Rado many questions about his personal life were asked, but he managed to avoid answering them quite successfully.

In an effort to fill in some of the gaps I interviewed Rado's two sons, George and Peter, in 1992 and 1993. With their permission, I have included some of the material in this section. I include some data from articles about Rado, an excerpt from Helene Deutsch's biography by Roazen, and recollections of my own off-tape discussions with Rado that took place during our long personal association extending from 1947 until his illness in the early 1970s.

On rereading Rado's memoir with the focus on his personal life, I constructed a clinical developmental history in my mind. This helped me understand Rado's personality more clearly. The most startling revelation was that the early childhood character traits so well described by Rado had never undergone significant changes throughout his life. He was keenly aware of the detrimental aspects of some of his behavior but could not change their pervasiveness.

Rado's natural gifts—his brilliance, his unusual photographic memory, his vitality and wit, and his avid search for knowledge—served him well. His stubbornness, quick temper, grandiosity, and inability to sustain close emotional relationships remained unsolved problems. Rado's two-year analysis with Abraham helped him become aware of the detrimental effects of some of his behavior but it made few inroads in helping him modify or control them.

Abraham was the most clinically oriented psychoanalyst in the first generation of Freud's followers. But like the other first-generation Freudians, his main concern was to test and explore Freud's new way of studying human behavior and to maintain congruence with Freud's evolving conceptual principles. The development of therapeutic processes was of later concern. Abraham therefore concentrated on Rado's oedipal attachment to his mother. Abraham told Rado that in his adult life, Rado was still searching for a mother. This was a perceptive interpretation and Rado's mother was the model for his relationships with women. What Abraham did not recognize was that cultural and environmental factors made for severe limitations to the development of early emotional bonding, so important for future relationships. Rado admired his mother's untutored intelligence. He described at length the devouring of novels and magazines that preoccupied most of her spare time. Because of the family's affluence, the supervision of the daily activities of her son was relegated to a changing array of governesses and servants. The main goal of the family was to secure him the best education so that he would be financially successful. At age 9½, his relationship to his mother and the rest of his family was essentially terminated. He was sent to the best gymnasium where he lived with a series of different families and only came home on holidays and vacations. At 17, he moved to Budapest and began his life as an independent adult. His future career was determined when he found Freud's writings. From then on, and for the rest of his life, psychoanalysis became his major preoccupation.

In Chapter 14 of this volume, "An Approach to Femininity," Rado suddenly shifts from discussing women to a discourse on his love of the theater. Throughout his life he was an avid theatergoer. At first it seemed irrelevant, but upon further consideration it is clear that this free association served to illustrate two points. The first was that Shakespeare's plays and some of the Greek tragedies contributed to a phallocentric view of women, which Rado shared with Freud. Rado believed that in most of the dramas women play a subsidiary role. His discussion of theatrical performances also seemed to reveal his enjoyment of emotional displays on the stage – at a safe distance from his own life.

During his early years, Rado was fully aware that he was looking for a woman with intelligence, but at the same time he "implicitly thought of the woman as a sort of doll," (p. 138, this volume). Although Rado was not particularly attractive physically, he had no trouble enchanting bright, good-looking women. His brief affair with Helene Deutsch, discussed in her biography, describes Rado's assets and "technique."

Rado and Deutsch were both in Berlin without their respective spouses. They were both experiencing difficulties in their marriages. (This occurred during Rado's second marriage to Elizabeth Révész.) Deutsch described their relationship as "a companionship in suffering" (Roazen 1992a, p. 204). which developed into a brief sexual affair. Roazen stated that "at that time Rado was not just one of the most learned and intelligent of the post–World War I generation . . . , but he was also, as Helene later put it a 'seducer' of women" (p. 204). She explained that his appeal to women was the "intensity of his desire" which "mobilized their sexuality" (p. 205). Rado and Deutsch remained lifelong friends, but she always resented how little their affair meant to him emotionally.

It is interesting that Rado's break with Freud occurred at least in part because of Rado's growing dissatisfaction with Freud's conceptualization of female development. The final break with Freud is based on Jeanne Lampl-de Groot's review of Rado's 1933 paper, "Fear of Castration in Women." In his paper Rado found inconsistencies in applying the same causes for fear of castration in both sexes. He retained the phallocentric view of penis envy, but suggested a different, more biological origin for the fear of castration in women. This started a veritable storm among the classicists, who did not wish to alter any of Freud's concepts. It was the starting point for Rado's reconsideration of female psychological development. However, it was not until the mid-1940s that his radical reformulation of women's different development from men took shape. He admitted that it was late in his life when he finally freed himself of the phallocentric anthropology that was central to Freud's theories about women.

Rado's later reformulations abandoned castration fear, penis envy (except as a cultural phenomenon), and the concept of bisexuality. He found his previous beliefs to have been incompatible with evolutionary theory and biology. He now contended that "a woman has a healthy, desirable, and variable emotional organization" (p. 138, this volume) which differs from that of men. His explanation for her richer emotional capacity was her biological role as childbearer and rearer.

In lectures at Columbia Clinic, Rado used to state that psychoanalytic theories of female sexuality were a disservice to women because they differentiated clitoral from vaginal orgasms, the former being considered less desirable. He would jokingly add that "God gave them both."

Although Rado freed himself from a Freudian phallocentricity, his personal relationships with women continued to reflect his early influences. Rado was married three times, always to bright and attractive women. His first wife, Ilona Krasso, was a fellow medical student in Budapest who later became the first woman surgeon in Hungary. She was the mother of Rado's first son, George. Elizabeth Révész, his second wife, was a psychoanalyst and an analysand of Freud's. This marriage was unhappy and short-lived, ending with her unexpected death from pernicious anemia. His third marriage to Emmy Chrisler, the mother of his second son, Peter, lasted many years, though they lived separate lives. Emmy Rado was active in civil rights and she worked for the Office of Strategic Services during World War II. She died of cancer in 1961.

Rado, as would be expected, was intent on securing the best educations for his sons. After his divorce from Ilona Krasso, Rado secured custody of George. George, whose childhood was spent in Budapest and Berlin, was sent, like his father, to boarding schools at an early age. He only saw his father on vacations. And though Rado never denied his Judaism, in the face of growing anti-Semitism he had his family baptized to facilitate George's education. As an adult George brought his mother to the United States where she practiced medicine. She died at age 92.

Peter was brought to the States at age 3, accompanied by their Berliner housekeeper/governess. She stayed with the family until her death two weeks before Rado's. She was a consistent figure in the home who created a more stable environment for Peter. For a number of years during his mother's illness while she lived in Mexico, Peter remained with his father. He accompanied Rado on vacations to Cape Cod, where Rado was a popular figure surrounded by vacationing psychoanalysts and acquaintances. Peter has described himself as being an old man during his childhood and adolescence. He spent much time with his father in the role of observer. Peter's education was typical of an American upper-middle-class boy's—private schools and an Ivy League college. Peter devoted much of his adult life to living with Rado and taking care for him during his illness, and stayed on until Rado's death. Peter once said, "My father had no close friends, only acolytes." He admired and felt compassion for his father, despite Rado's complex and contradictory personality that left in its wake certainly acolytes, enemies, and a few friends.

Surprisingly, neither George nor Peter related any unusual outbursts of anger on the part of their father, nor are they aware of ever being used by him as middle men in whatever difficulties Rado had in his marriages or affairs. They were also not privy to any of the vicissitudes of their father's psychoanalytic career.

Like their father, both sons developed a strong commitment to their respective careers. It was of some pride to Rado that George became a successful physicist, particularly because of Rado's own interest in physics and the fact that physics is a scientific discipline. Peter followed in the footsteps of his father's aborted path: he became an accomplished estate lawyer. Both sons, from what I could gather, had long-term, satisfying marriages. Peter married at age 48 after the death of his father.

In assessing Rado's developmental history, it seems inevitable that his preoccupation with, and dedication to, his career remained his main priority — at the expense of a better focus on his close personal relationships. Although Rado was aware of some of his personality difficulties, he nonetheless enjoyed an exciting and productive life.

NOTE

It would have been of considerable significance if we were able to find Rado's extensive correspondence and the transcripts of his lectures. So far, we have had no clues as to where they are. Peter thinks that when Rado moved from his office to an office in his apartment, he may have left many papers there. The search continues.

Rado was very discreet about revealing anything about his patients, particularly if they were eminent. Peter, aware of the confidential aspect of his father's work, shredded Rado's appointment books and discarded them. Unfortunately, he also discarded Rado's office furniture which was designed by Ernst Freud. Rado had brought the pieces over from Berlin and was very proud of his analytic couch and chairs. After Rado's death and Peter's marriage, Peter and his wife thought the furniture seemed shabby and it was discarded, much to Peter's later regret.

THE FUTURE OF
PSYCHOANALYSIS

Rado ends his memoir on a positive note: that psychoanalysis has an "undreamt-of future." His optimism was contingent on his conviction that psychoanalysis would move away from classical theory toward his adaptational psychodynamics. He hoped that continued research efforts would validate what he considered Freud's enduring presuppositions as specified in his brief article included in Appendix 1. To fortify this hope, Rado usually added jokingly, "When it comes to research, I'll take anything." Research, in his mind, would ensure the future survival of psychoanalysis.

This epilogue has been added in order to contrast Rado's predictions for the future of psychoanalysis with the current and extensive dialogues on the subject. For many, psychoanalysis is undergoing a serious crisis, which echoes Rado's concerns of 1963. Numerous articles and conferences address this very issue thirty years after Rado voiced his assessment. But now, divergent theories of and amendments to Freud's work are not deemed heretical, nor are they the catalysts for schisms that were prevalent in Rado's day.

Psychoanalytic theoreticians are currently divided into two major groups: those who believe that psychoanalysis should maintain a scientific basis and incorporate knowledge from other related sciences, and those who believe that psychoanalysis should be considered a humanistic discipline. The latter group's efforts revolve around clarifying Freud's theories and discarding obvious contradictions, the goal being to produce a more coherent, logical framework and include new ideas from the social sciences and communications theory. The humanist camp is not concerned with transforming psychoanalytic theory so that it can be correlated with new brain research. They envision psychoanalysis as a unique, independent theoretical entity that does not need to be subjected to rigorous research methods. Rado would have agreed with the former group.

Rado thought that the changes crucial to the future of psychoanalysis were the use of more pertinent language and a motivational rather than an instinctual approach. He also thought that a greater emphasis on the individual's emotional life was crucial to the understanding of human behavior. He stressed the importance of a closer correlation of the introspective findings of psychoanalysis with brain physiology and related scientific knowledge He believed that this would not entail losing sight of the cognitive and unconscious traumas suffered by patients throughout their life cycles.

In the 1960s, Rado predicted that old-fashioned therapeutic practice would disappear for lack of money, adding that the future of classical psychoanalysis would sustain itself only through power and politics, and might continue as an elite therapy for the rich. Rado's fear was that medicine and psychiatry would ultimately ignore the potentially valuable data that can come only from the introspective method of psychoanalysis.

In the 1990s many of Rado's ideas are accepted by a number of psychoanalysts, though the ideas are not necessarily attributed to him. Psychoanalysts concur with Eric Kandel's (1979) statement that "psychology and psychiatry can illuminate and define for biology the mental functions that need to be studied if we are to have a meaningful and sophisticated understanding of the biology of the human mind" (p. 1037).

In 1982, Arnold Cooper, a student of Rado, recommended in his final address as president of the American Psychoanalytic Association that "the barriers which were required to help regulate the early phases of our maturation may no longer be applicable for our potential and talents" (p. 115). He now believes that psychoanalysis has the opportunity to make serious efforts "to find the way to combine the basic science of psychodynamics with the basic science of psychobiology" (p. 29).

Currently, there is interest in the field of neuropsychology. In an article published in 1993, Laurence Miller reviews efforts by neurologists to combine neurology and the brain sciences with personality theory to create a unified "model of personality" (p. 188). He states that previously, most of the data related only to cognitive psychology such as "language, memory, spatial relations and other aspects of active, conscious cognition"

(p. 186). He adds that in "most cases, it is more difficult to design an experiment that will study an unconscious motive, rather than conscious intention" (p. 188).[1] He cautions that the results that come from combining introspective data with organic findings are still provisional.

Most brain researchers, like Kandel and others, do not question that the important contributions derived from psychoanalysis, such as unconscious motivations and introspective data, are crucial to the understanding of human behavior. Some believe that it may be premature to expect to combine the nuances of psychoanalysis with current knowledge of brain function, which they believe is still in its very beginning, even in relation to cognitive functions (Personal communication with Dr. David U'Prichard, a neuropharmacologist). That does not mean that research should not be attempted in at least the following areas: carefully designed clinical studies, clarification of diagnostic categories to include descriptions that take into consideration the nuances of psychoanalytic treatment, and reformulation of psychoanalytic concepts into testable, clearly defined, and generally agreed-upon hypotheses.

It is interesting to recall that in the last chapter of his oral history, Rado discerned the potential future developments of computer sciences. His concern was that overenthusiastic computer scientists would decide that the computer functions could surpass the activities of the brain. His fears would have been assuaged by a statement by Oliver Sacks, a neurologist and psychiatrist who stated in a television series on consciousness entitled "Glorious Accident," aired on public television in June 1994, that "[t]he brain is not a library. It's not a granary. It's not a computer. I think that what happens comes into the mind always with a different context. I think memory is close to imagination. Memories are constructions and not Xeroxes, not facsimiles, not reproductions." Rado did not recognize that the use of the computer to collect large amounts of data could be utilized to sort out successes or failures in the treatment of specific diagnostic entities and thus eliminate those patients with such disturbances who do not respond to the psychoanalytic techniques as currently practiced.

---

1. See also Laurence Miller, "Brain and Self: Toward a Neuropsychodynamic Model of Ego Autonomy and Personality," *Journal of the American Academy of Psychoanalysis*, 1991, 19(2): 213–234, "The Primitive Personality and the Organic Personality: A Neuropsychodynamic Model for Evaluation and Treatment," *Psychoanalytic Psychology*, 1992, 9(1):93–109, and "On Aphasia at 100: The Neuropsychodynamic Legacy of Sigmund Freud," *Psychoanalytic Review*, 1991, 78(3):365–378.

In the *Journal of the American Psychoanalytic Association*, 1993, Otto F. Kernberg reviews a series of articles entitled "The Future of Psychoanalysis" written by nine distinguished psychoanalysts from the United States. In his article "The Current Status of Psychoanalysis," Kernberg discusses the current challenges and controversies regarding psychoanalysis as a science. Kernberg states, "While the papers evince significant differences in their approach and conclusions, they all point to some serious and apparently growing problems in our field. Jointly, they provide a lively illustration of the sense of crisis experienced by the psychoanalytic community in this country in this time" (p. 45).

Kernberg belongs to the group that believes that psychoanalysis should be part of science, but, unlike Rado, he has maintained basic classical Freudian theories that Rado claimed impeded the very possibility of psychoanalysis' becoming more scientific. Kernberg stresses the need for research, and suggests some innovative ways to teach psychoanalysis. Yet his juxtaposition of contradictory points is difficult to assess.

In 1993, I began a series of interviews with Roger A. MacKinnon, the director since 1991 of the Columbia University Psychoanalytic Center. I wanted to investigate how much of Rado's contributions and assessments still prevailed in the institute he founded.

MacKinnon includes Rado's contributions in his capacity as a teacher and supervisor. He shares many of what were Rado's concerns for psychoanalysis, and believes that psychoanalysis should have remained under a medical aegis. He believes the acceptance of nonmedical trainees was based on the expectation that it would compensate for the reduced number of psychiatrically trained applicants. Currently, the number of nonmedical applicants has also diminished. In MacKinnon's mind, psychoanalysis is in a state of crisis.

MacKinnon stated that current residents, particularly those at the Psychiatric Institute, where he supervises and teaches, are now well versed in scientific methodology. Those who have decided to continue their training at the Center are eager to subject some psychoanalytic concepts to acceptable research methods. MacKinnon disagrees with Rado about his effort to use an organismic language. He believes that there should be "a language of the mind. The language will necessarily differ from the language of the brain. This will differentiate the brain events from mind events, which occur simultaneously. The mechanisms of action are different. To comprehend the mind, a depth psychology will always be necessary to understand human motives, aims, and goals." MacKinnon's efforts as director of the Center are to stimulate and augment interest in research.

A current research project is already in process at the Columbia University Psychoanalytic Center entitled "Current Psychotherapy Research Methodology Applied to Psychoanalysis: A Feasibility Study." The initial objective is to design a one-year feasibility study as a first step in devising an open, and later controlled, clinical trial to examine the efficacy of psychoanalysis. The study will assess the feasibility of applying current research methodology developed for controlled clinical trials of psychotherapy to the psychoanalytic setting.

The Columbia Center is not the only place where research in psychoanalysis has begun. At the 1993 winter meeting of the American Psychoanalytic Association, Howard Shevrin, a psychologist from the University of Michigan, was invited to give the plenary address. He delivered a presentation intriguing in its format and content, entitled "Psychoanalysis: One Science, Two Sciences, or No Science At All: A Discourse among Friendly Antagonists." In this imaginary discourse, he described, as one of the participants, his view of science and included some examples of research under his aegis. His approach differs from that of others, but they all reaffirm the need for developing research methodologies capable of being applied to psychoanalytic concepts and therapeutic results.

MacKinnon's frame of reference is not necessarily shared by most of the faculty of the Columbia Center. I have carefully examined the 1993–1994 curriculum and the reading lists appended to each course. There is no evidence of authoritarianism or dogmatic control over the material assigned. A variety of theoretical points of view is being taught. Reading assignments range from classical Freudian theories to ego psychology; object relations theory; self psychology; the contributions of the British Middle School, such as Farbairn, Guntrip, and Winnicott; Melanie Klein and the papers of her followers; and some of Lacan's ideas. Scattered among the readings are papers by some of the first-generation Freudians, like Karl Abraham, Sandor Ferenczi, Ernest Jones, and others. There are also papers by many of Rado's contemporaries from the Berlin Institute, some of whom he analyzed or taught. There are papers assigned that were written by psychoanalysts among the most eminent of the Vienna school.

The curriculum could be described as ecumenical. Classical papers are combined with new ideas (or old ideas in a new form). In the early years, the papers of Rank, Ferenczi, and Melanie Klein were not given much attention because of Freud's sharp disagreement with their contributions, or their changes in the psychoanalytic metapsychology. Now they are included in the new, expanded curriculum. The objective seems to be to acquaint the candidates with the historical development of psychoanalysis, and, concurrently, to present options to them for selecting a variety of therapeutic procedures. Perhaps this type of curriculum reflects the present status of psychoanalysis in its transitional phase. In the absence of acceptable outcome studies or research to validate the numerous concepts, a plethora of metapsychologies are being offered. Candidates are then free to choose treatment modalities that they believe will be useful in their analytic work.

There is, however, a striking omission. There are almost no papers or research projects done by the founders, or the early graduates, designed to acquaint the current candidates with the history of their own analytic institute. Rado's early papers on melancholia and drug addiction are mentioned, and his book appears on one reading list only. Are the founders and the early graduates still considered heretical, anti-Freudian, or simply inconsequential by the curriculum committee? When did this omission occur, and why? With the fiftieth anniversary of the Columbia Center to be celebrated in 1995, it would be of interest to trace the evolution of analytic thought at the Center from its inception to its present disregard, and to discern the rationale for this absence.

Perhaps the most obvious reason is that it was understandably difficult for the early graduates to be so severely deprived of participating in the mainstream of the psychoanalytic community in the United States during the early period of the Center's existence. Glover's contention that the Radovian psychodynamics precluded him and his followers and the Center's graduates from being considered psychoanalysts was hard to ignore. As a number of Rado's followers achieved maturity and stature in their own institute, they began to expand their interests and develop their own ideas. Their papers and research efforts were ignored by the analytic mainstream—publications and conferences.

Some validation of this supposition appears in reading *The Developments in Psychoanalysis at Columbia University*, a book published in 1966. It contained the proceedings of the twentieth anniversary conference of the Columbia University Psychoanalytic Clinic for Training and Research (its original name) held in 1965, ten years after Rado's retirement. Under the title of "Theoretical Considerations" is Aaron Karush's paper "An Adaptational Approach to Psychic Representations, Perception and Psychic Apparatus." Before quoting from this paper, it is important to recall that in July 1959, a series of four papers written by Karush, in collaboration with Abram Kardiner and Lionel Ovesey, was published in the *Journal of*

Nervous and Mental Diseases, in consecutive issues. The papers were a critique of Freudian theory called "A Methodological Study of Freudian Theory." The second paper in particular was a critical disavowal of the libido theory, and the last paper took issue with the structural hypothesis. The papers expand Rado's critique of Freudian metapsychology and, in addition, included their own carefully thought-out ideas. In 1959, and perhaps even today, it was a brave, though risky, deviation from classical theory still dominating the ideas of the major theoreticians of that time.

In 1965, Karush's conflicting feelings began to be evident. After praising adaptational psychoanalysis and some of the papers of his colleagues, Karush writes, "Adaptational theory has so far been no more successful than have other psychoanalytic frames of reference in solving the riddle of choice of neurosis or defining the factors in self-object relationships that lead to arrests or distortions in the development of particular ego functions. Nor has it dealt satisfactorily with the genetic and psychodynamic origins of the positive coping aspects of personality" (p. 3). In the body of this paper, the vocabulary shifts away from adaptational psychodynamics, and words like "cathexis" and "nuclei in the ego" appear. He further states that "much that is being presented today as new had its beginning in the writings of Freud, Ferenczi, Abraham, Reich and others about characterological traits and types" (p. 4). Karush's article is quoted here as an example of the early conflictual reactions felt by some of Rado's followers. In 1971, Karush was the first graduate of the Columbia Clinic selected to become director. It should be added that it was particularly difficult for some of the early candidates to divest themselves of the strong influence of their analysts, who were classically oriented, since Rado's innovations were hardly known by them. It was also difficult to reject totally Rado's brilliant expositions. It was after his departure and his authoritarian control that shifts in ideology began to occur. Simultaneously, the orthodoxy and the authority of the classicists also diminished, as new leaders became less threatened by emerging modifications of Freudian theory. With the general agreement and the proliferation of new institutes and new frames of reference, some psychoanalysts are wondering, "whither psychoanalysis?"

In order to broaden my inquiry as to the present state of psychoanalysis, I am including material from interviews with Jacob Arlow conducted in 1990 and 1991.

Arlow, like Rado, had a reputation for being one of the most lucid and effective teachers of classical Freudian theory. Belonging to a generation younger than that of Rado, he was able to introduce with impunity new ideas to supplement Freudian theory. When I interviewed him, I noted that Arlow had reevaluated his earlier classical theoretical and therapeutic views with courage and candor. He evolved a new way of working analytically and rejected the use of psychoanalytic language, formulating his theoretical and therapeutic innovations in understandable English. Like Rado, he no longer found libido theory and structural theory compatible with new medical knowledge, related sciences, and communications theory. According to Arlow, theory should be influenced not by preconceived ideology, but by trained listening to the patient's communications during the therapeutic sessions. The disparate introspective disclosures acquired a coherence directing the analyst from session to session. One aspect of his listening was to discern the patient's unconscious fantasies. As to the future of psychoanalysis, Arlow agrees that it is in a state of crisis. He believes that some of the changes he has suggested might help clarify the definitions of psychoanalysis, and elucidate the psychoanalytic strategies that will influence its tasks and goals. Arlow is not without hope; he believes that out of the present seeming chaos, new beginnings will emerge.

Arlow's hope is not unfounded. The impetus for change comes from a variety of sources: (1) the current political reassessment of medical and mental health coverage, (2) the proliferation of new drugs that bring about quick relief of patients' symptoms, (3) the increased attacks on Freudian theories, and (4) the growing awareness of psychoanalysts and therapists that some of their unverified presuppositions may lead to the undermining of their professional and economic status.

At a meeting of the Association for Psychoanalytic Medicine in June 1994, a panel was presented entitled "What Does Analytic Process Mean?: Research, Clinical and Educational Perspectives." It was introduced in the program as follows:

> Analytic process has no agreed upon clinical or research definition. Many analysts are left with the feeling that "I may not be able to define it, but I know it when I see it." Without clear definitions, even a fundamental concept like analytic process can suffer deterioration in its usefulness. However, there appears to be a consensus that essential components of analytic process include free association, resistance, interpretation, and working through. This panel will review the definition, meaning, and utility of analytic process from research, clinical, and educational perspectives.

At the end of the meeting, Steven P. Roose, a graduate of the Columbia University Psychoanalytic Center and now an associate professor of clinical psychiatry at Columbia University, stated that psychoanalysts can no longer use the excuse that it is too difficult to subject the nuances and complexities of psychoanalysis to acceptable research methods.

After more than fifty years, Rado's plea that efforts must be made to steer psychoanalysis on a scientific course is finally being taken seriously. Rado, who so ardently believed that his own ideas would help preserve Freud's incomparable contributions to twentieth-century knowledge, said in the last sentence of his oral history as previously mentioned, that psychoanalysis has "an undreamt-of future." My hope is that this prophecy may becone reality.

PART V

APPENDICES

APPENDIX 1: OBSERVATIONS ON THE DEVELOPMENT OF PSYCHOANALYTIC THEORY

by Sandor Rado*

No, science is no illusion. But it would be an illusion to suppose that we could get anywhere else what it cannot give us.

Sigmund Freud

Science feeds and grows on fruitful ideas, new techniques of observation, the discovery of significant facts and the construction of improved conceptual schemes. While writings of great philosophers, poets and novelists may be preserved forever by their artistic integrity, the greatness of a scientist is evidenced, beyond his lasting achievements, by the fresh inquiries to which his contribution has given rise.

*Article excerpted from *Current Approaches to Psychoanalysis*, Paul H. Hoch and Joseph Zubin, eds. (New York and London, Grune & Stratton, 1960), pp. 3–12.

Applying these obvious truths to Sigmund Freud, I shall here attempt to sum up those aspects of his work which promise to be of lasting value, point out others which have called for re-examination. . . .

MEDICAL STUDY OF BEHAVIOR

Freud received his training and started his career in a medical era that derived its scientific inspiration from the philosophy of Descartes enhanced by the success of Newtonian physics. The organism was viewed as a physicochemical machine; the scientific method was identified with procedures based on inspection, culminating in measurement by yardstick and clock. The concept of "physiologic organism" neatly disposed of the subject matter of mind; but it could not change the embarrassing fact that the organism is largely controlled by mechanisms of consciousness. Freud demonstrated that these mechanisms can be scientifically explored by the psychoanalytic method based on communicated introspection. Building on the patient's need for help and hope for recovery, Freud persuaded the patient that with his physician he must voice his feelings and thoughts freely by relinquishing those precautionary restraints which he had been trained to observe in daily life. At the same time, by organizing his own introspection, Freud prepared himself to understand the communicated introspection of the patient. He thus created a process of interaction in which the patient's introspection could be observed, interpreted and to some extent controlled by a participant-observer, namely the physician himself. In this arrangement, introspection became a scientific method, potentially capable of restoring medicine to its ancient scope. To free medicine from its nineteenth century limitations and to make biology human in fact as well as in name is the ultimate goal of psychoanalytic inquiry. To make this goal possible was Freud's epochal feat.

The reliability of inspective investigation depends, aside from other factors, on sound methodology and the possibility of measurement; that of introspective inquiry, on sound methodology and the workers' integrity and emotional health.

Freud's first psychoanalytic period, from the early 1890s until 1905, included his masterpiece, *The Interpretation of Dreams*. In my opinion, it was during this period that he laid the foundation for a science of psychodynamics. He constructed a groundwork of six superbly chosen elements: (1) motivation, (2) pleasure-seeking and pain avoidance, (3) repression, (4) mental mechanisms, (5) mental apparatus and (6) evolutionary and individual history. We shall comment briefly on each of these ideas.

1. For centuries, men have used the point of view of motivation to understand, predict and control human behavior. As Freud mentioned, he absorbed this point of view from the psychology of daily life. Motivation became the basis of his dynamic theory of mental activity.

2. The regulatory function of pleasure and pain has been known at least since Aristotle. Freud made the "pleasure-pain principle" a pillar of his dynamic theory.

3. The repression of memories beyond voluntary recall and the undoing of such repressions by the technique of free association are theories based on observational evidence discovered by Freud himself. It was through these theories that psychoanalysis became a unique method for the disclosure of motivation that is hidden from, and rejected by, the patient's consciousness. The interpretation of dreams is the "royal road" to such disclosures.

4. The concept of "mental mechanisms" was introduced into psychiatry by Freud's teacher Theodor Meynert. It was Freud who extended it to the mental description of certain processes of which the patient is wholly unaware. He interpreted the process of repression as a mental mechanism which is both automatic and fundamental.

5. The idea of a "mental apparatus" visualized as a spatial and temporal arrangement of functions based on cerebral physiology was altogether Freud's own creation. Its significance for the development of a dynamic theory of mental activity can hardly be overstated. In its early version (published in *The Interpretation of Dreams*), Freud postulated that the mental apparatus includes an "unconscious system" separated from a "conscious system" by the dynamics of repression. It is on this distinction that the edifice of psychoanalytic theory rests.

6. Darwin's influence on Freud's thinking is evidenced by the fact that psychoanalytic theory aimed at a developmental system of dynamics from the outset. It attributed due significance to phylogenic as well as to individual history, climaxing in the recognition of the part played by the formative period of childhood in the shaping of the human individual.

It would be indeed hard to conceive of a dynamic theory of mental activity based on communicated introspection that could dispense with any one of these six constituents.

DEVELOPMENT OF FREUD'S THEORIES

1905 was a turning point in the development of Freud's theories. While heretofore his scientific thinking was mechanistic, it now became more and more vitalistic, or, rather, animistic. By stages, he came to interpret almost all motivation in terms of instincts, and, from 1923 on, he transformed the mechanistic concept of a mental apparatus into an animistic triad of superego, id and ego. At the same time, he continued to speak of mental mechanisms, and upheld his earlier view of the relationship between psychoanalytic theory and human biology:

> It should be borne in mind that all our tentative psychological formulations (psychologische Vorlaufigheiten) will have ultimately to be grounded in the organic. [Freud 1914][1]
>
> The edifice of psychoanalytic doctrine which we have erected is in reality but a superstructure which will have to be set on its organic foundation at some time or other, but this foundation is still unknown to us. [Freud 1917]
>
> The shortcomings of our description would probably disappear if for the psychological terms we could already substitute physiological or chemical ones. [Freud 1920]
>
> The future may teach us how to exercise a direct influence, by means of particular chemical substances, upon the amounts of energy and their distribution in the apparatus of the mind. [Freud 1940]

Biologist W. M. Wheeler (1939), expressed his dissatisfaction with animistic thinking as follows: "We at all times . . . feel a dim mental affinity with the animistic savage. And what is instinct as employed in most biological and psychological literature, but camouflaged animism?"

While Freud was apparently unaware of the animistic nature of instincts, certain shortcomings of his theorizing did not escape his attention. In reviewing the development of his theory of instincts, he wrote: "The theory of instincts is, as it were, our mythology. The instincts are mythical beings, *superb in their indefiniteness*. In our work we cannot for a moment overlook them, and yet we *are never certain that we are seeing them clearly*" (italics Rado's, 1933).

This is precisely the point. Animistic notions may at first be serviceable, for instance, by stressing a new point of view, but in short order they inescapably prove to be unpenetrable and shadowy wholes.

---

1. Translation revised by Rado.

One cannot dissect them into component relations, cannot reach those details on whose disclosures progress in an observational science depends. Instincts are miniature personages, veritable homunculi. Such notions always have a magical touch of grandeur, are bound to fascinate and engender illusions, obscuring the true causal problems which sound mechanistic concepts might better help to disclose. It is hard to conceive how such notions could be correlated with mechanistic physiology. No wonder that after an initial success Freud's theory of instincts proved to be unfruitful.

The same is true of superego, id and ego. These notions are personifications of conscience, passion and common sense; while scientifically useless, they have profound cultural depth, reflecting divine commandments, satanic temptations and the adaptive task [Rado 1958]. Obviously, Freud was a superbly dramatic writer (winner of the Goethe prize) as well as a scientist.

After 1905, his bent for dramatization soon pervaded all his theories. But the dramatist can put only a limited number of characters on the stage. This explains Freud's preference for a few personified or otherwise attractive terms, packing into them more and more and often completely contradictory connotations. Freud did not call his creations dramatis personae; he referred to them as the shibboleths of psychoanalysis. Every one of these pet terms stems from fundamental clinical observations; most of them are "superbly indefinite"; hence, from a logical point of view, superbly inconsequential. In Freud's psychoanalytic work the artist eventually defeated the scientist.

Aside from these great shortcomings, the libido theory was hopelessly at variance with the basic biological conventions on which it was supposed to rest. Freud considered his separation of "ego instincts" from "sexual instincts" a "psychological concomitant" of the "biological fact that the living individual serves two purposes, self-preservation and the preservation of the species" [Freud 1933]. When sucking at the mother's breast, urinating or defecating, the baby's organism obviously serves the purpose of self-preservation but not of reproduction. Nevertheless, it was a postulate of the libido theory that these activities are sexual (libidinal, erotic). Freud never offered a valid reason for this language usage. In one of his last papers he wrote:

> The baby's obstinate persistence in sucking gives evidence at an early stage of a need for satisfaction which, although it originates from and is

stimulated by the taking of nourishment, nevertheless seeks to obtain *pleasure* independently of nourishment, and *for that reason* may and should be described as "sexual." [italics Rado's, 1949]

The extension of the concept of "sexual" to include all pleasurable activity brought the motivational analysis of human behavior into a regrettable state of confusion.

As is generally known, the final version of the libido theory — expanded over the vast domains of evolutionary, cultural and individual history — explained all life as the "titanic struggle" between the "divine Eros" and the "instinct to die." The attempted application of these abstractions to the facts of clinical observation did not and could not produce any result. . . .

APPENDIX 2:
BOOK REVIEW OF
PSYCHOANALYSIS
OF BEHAVIOR:
COLLECTED PAPERS,
BY SANDOR RADO

by Edward Glover

Book review of *Psychoanalysis of Behavior: Collected Papers*, by Sandor
Rado, M.D., D.P.Sc. New York: Grune & Stratton, 1956, 387 pp. Book
review originally published in *Psychoanalytic Quarterly*, vol. 26, no. 2, 1957,
pp. 251–258.

It is now almost a habit among the one-time leaders of the second freudian
generation to celebrate their seniority by the production of volumes of
Collected Papers. These fall roughly into three categories: expository,
clinical, and testamentary. The present volume, by Sandor Rado, although in part expository, in part clinical, is in main testamentary, in the
sense that it describes the development of his own theoretical and
therapeutic ideas regarding clinical psychology, or as he would doubtless
prefer to say, regarding 'adaptational psychodynamics.' This is immediately apparent from the Table of Contents which displays three sectional
headings; viz., Contributions to Clinical Psychodynamics (or in more

familiar terminology, contributions to classical psychoanalysis); second, Quest for a Basic Conceptual Scheme (which proves to be a calendar of the basic shortcomings of classical psychoanalysis); and third, Development of Adaptational Psychodynamics (or, as one might say, the Radovian system of pure and applied psychology).

Having gathered that classical psychoanalysis is *sub judice* of Rado, the reviewer naturally casts back to the title page, where yet other issues confront him. Do the 'new' ideas justify, as the title takes for granted, the use of the term 'psychoanalysis' as a synonym for 'psychodynamics'; and in what sense does the author employ the term 'behavior'? Putting the first of these questions aside for the moment, we may note that whereas Rado's connotation of ordered 'behavior' is not correlated or contrasted with standard psychological definitions of the term, it is clearly regarded as an adaptation process running in cycles 'from desire to fulfillment and back.' This, incidentally, is a standard psychoanalytic view which regards the end-products of instinctual stress as adaptations, whether or not they are autoplastic or alloplastic and whether or not they are adequate or inhibiting. By including psychic autoplastic reactions, the author avoids the Watsonian limitations of 'behaviorism.' Yet in his consideration of 'disordered behavior', Rado has clearly been influenced, wittingly or unwittingly by Watson, wittingly by Cannon and other neurologists, and indeed produces a neuropsychiatric classification of disordered behavior which runs through the whole gamut of abnormal psychology. Whether his classification is a good one or not – and heuristically there is more to be said against it than for it – it is in this wide sense of the term 'behavior' that Rado's 'psychodynamics' must be examined and evaluated.

Leaving these terminological issues aside, we may now examine the development of Rado's 'psychodynamics', pausing however to appraise his contributions to classical psychoanalysis, which comprise six articles written or published in the decade 1922–1932, a period characterized in psychoanalytic literature by exposition, rather timid expansion (excepting always in Freud's own work), clinical support of freudian theory (including the then most recent formulations regarding the ego, superego, and id), and a few outstanding essays which, as in the case of Ferenczi and Rank, heralded subsequent defection sometimes from the principles, sometimes from the practices of psychoanalysis.

Of these six articles the best known are those dealing with the psychic effects of intoxicants or pharmacothymia, and with the problem of melancholia. In the first of these papers Rado introduced his conceptions of 'pharmacotoxic orgasm' and 'metaerotism' (by which, Rado held, the peripheral sexual apparatus can be by-passed) and a psychophysical primary function, which he described as 'alimentary orgasm' and regarded as the fixation point disposing the subject to morbid craving. The pregenital erotisms, he believed, were the 'psychic garb' of this alimentary orgasm: the erotogenic zones 'take shelter under the metaerotic regime.' Had Rado linked this theory of alimentary orgasm with the intestinal and urinary expulsion associated with oral activity, rather than with the phenomena of oral repletion and diffused well being, it might have been more plausible. But that is perhaps no great matter since what in effect he postulates is a constitutional factor which, both in theory and practice, leaves the psychoanalyst to determine for himself the relative importance in drug addiction of later pregenital and genital phases of libido development. It is perhaps not surprising to find that in Rado's view 'no specific role in the etiology of morbid cravings can be ascribed to the unconscious tension of consciences (sense of guilt)'; a factor which, in the reviewer's opinion is decisive, certainly in the obsessive and depressed types of alcoholism. But perhaps Rado at that time (1926) was operating with the more limited concept then current of a (genital-libido-determined) superego.

This paper on melancholia is a remarkable achievement. Rado is a fluent and sometimes a persuasive writer and has manifestly a genius for the word-spinning of etiological webs. I know of no paper in which, using throughout a theoretical idiom, the author can combine, as Rado does here, the reduction of complexity to simplicity with a complementary elaboration of simplicity into complexity. From the theoretical point of view Rado's main contention is that the fixation point of the melancholic lies in the hunger situation of the infant. At this point the author again introduces the concept of "alimentary orgasm" which the child *later* works over to form the connection—"guilt, atonement, forgiveness."

Turning now to the second section, viz., the quest for a basic conceptual scheme: this consists of seven papers written between 1933 and 1942. The series starts with a monograph on Fear of Castration in Woman which, by and large, reflects the classical views and classical differences of opinion on a subject which continues to tantalize analysts, driving them often to risk their reputations for objectivity by joining too patently in the psychoanalytic battle of the sexes. From the theoretical point of view the main point of Rado's dissertation is the emphasis laid on the factor of genital masochism arising from the girl's discovery of the absence of a penis; this gives rise to a narcissistic defense reaction of the ego and leads to the fantasy of possessing a penis which however can only flourish in the unconscious. Following this there develops a fear of castration in the ego. From this theory Rado proceeds to consider modifications of castration fear and the part they play in giving rise to a number of clinical manifestations which he subsumes under the heading of the woman's 'neurosis', surely a very selective use of the term. Perhaps this is the beginning of Rado's new orientation.

However that may be, the author soon settles down to his quest. In 'Developments in the Psychoanalytic Conception and Treatment of the Neuroses,' Rado states roundly that our understanding of the etiology and treatment of the neuroses has been hindered rather than aided by Freud's theory of instincts itself, which, he says, has outlived its usefulness. Neuroses are disorders of integrative ego functioning which should be described in terms of ego pathology. This purely structural approach to mental function comes strangely from the author of a book on psychodynamics. To be sure, Rado then embarks on a consideration of the behavior motivating forces of fear, anxiety, rage, etc., introducing the neurological concept of 'emergency control,' the 'riddance principle,' etc. Neurotic fantasies are 'illusory operations acting vicariously for inhibited normal operations.' *Ergo*, says Rado, restore normal functions by removing the obstacle of anxiety from their range.

And so at last to 'adaptational psychodynamics.' Fifteen papers (dating from 1946 to 1956) are devoted to this subject. These are extremely repetitious: indeed the gist of his thesis is given in the first and the last two, viz., Psychodynamics as a Basic Science, Adaptational Psychodynamics and Adaptational Development of Psychoanalytic Therapy. The motive forces of behavior 'are to be viewed in the context of the operating organism in relation to its parts, environment and history'. Adaptation and survival are to be the cornerstone of the new science, Cannon's concept of emergency function its main pillar. The unconscious is only a nonreporting organization of causative links between processes of which we are aware, − a definition which would correspond to Freud's 'descriptive unconscious', not his 'dynamic unconscious'. Yet Rado retains the concept of repression in his description of 'nonreporting' levels. It is incidentally practically the only psychoanalytic term he does retain. The 'psychodynamic cerebral system' is an integrative apparatus having four hierarchic levels: the hedonic, the level of brute emotions, of emotional thought, and of unemotional thought. Its supreme unit is the 'action-self'. The mainspring of man's culture is not the oedipus complex but man's primordial craving for omnipotence. The psychodynamic apparatus is regulated in the first instance by mechanisms of 'emergency control'.

Overproduction of emergency emotions (fear, rage, guilty fear, and guilty rage) produces 'emergency dyscontrol', at which point Rado introduces his classification of the phenomena of 'dyscontrol' which, as has already been indicated, comprises the whole abnormal psychology. These abnormal products constitute *inter alia* manifestations of the 'riddance principle' which includes not only organic reflexes, but ego efforts to control mental pain, e.g., fear (a term which Rado now uses to replace anxiety). Repression is, for instance, an automatized form of riddance impulse operating at nonreporting levels. And so on.

It is impossible within the scope even of a lengthy review to summarize the various ideological systems of which Rado's adaptational psychology is comprised or to give detailed definitions of the plethora of terms he employs to extend it. On the other hand, it is not difficult to see what has happened to psychoanalytic concepts under Rado's ministrations or indeed to see what has happened to Rado himself. Apparently fascinated by the attempts of neurologists to explain cerebral functions with the help of a special set of analogies, metaphorical expressions, terms, concepts, and working hypotheses; equally apparently fired with the ambition to create a new psychobiological functional science of behavior the terms of which will be, as far as he can make them, congruent with those of neurology or for that matter biochemistry or any other branch of biology, he has entered the field of freudian metapsychology armed with the latest psychobiological model of Occam's safety razor. With this instrument he scythes down lustily the basic concepts and many of the central tenets of psychoanalysis. One ransacks his presentation for the familiar terminology to find merely a modified definition of repression and an odd reference or two to identification and projection. The rest of psychoanalytic terminology has either disappeared or is clad in paraphrase. Naturally, with the abandonment of instinct theory the concept of the id vanishes; and with the disappearance of this boundary concept goes one of the main bulwarks of psychoanalysis. For, whatever the clinical misconceptions to which the id concept may give rise in the minds of overenthusiastic or underoriented disciples, it does afford the analyst an escape from the confusions that are prone to arise when neurological concepts are merged with those of psychic function. The concept of the id provides a boundary wall behind the shelter of which the psychologist may proceed to mind his own business, viz., the study of mental functions, energies, structures, and mechanisms, in a word, metapsychology.

I have described Rado's use of Occam's razor as a safety device. Because when one comes to ask whether 'psychodynamics' can be regarded as a purified extension of psychoanalysis or indeed as psychoanalysis at all, one is baffled by the author's orgies of paraphrase. True he does uncompromisingly dismiss the libido theory, he discounts the pathodynamic significance of the oedipus complex, he discards the freudian scheme of mental organization and function, and he sets aside Freud's theory of symptom-formation. (For if 'disorders of adaptation' are emotional and essentially reactive responses of the individual to the demands of society, and if again emotional dyscontrol is determined by purely environmental factors during childhood, there is no room in Rado's scheme for the unique factor in symptom-formation, viz., 'unconscious compromise-formation'.) Added to which Rado, in effect, reduces the concept of the unconscious to its more popular descriptive level. All this would of itself be sufficient to justify the view that Rado has abandoned psychoanalysis, or at least mutilated it beyond recognition. On the other hand, if one is at pains to restate some of his 'adaptational' propositions in analytic language, they seem to contain no more than has already been current in psychoanalytic thinking during the past forty-odd years, e.g., that mental disorders are essentially maladaptations due ultimately to a conflict between internal forces and external conditions. Rado apparently likes to have it both ways.

Faced with this dilemma in evaluation, there is no alternative but to examine Rado's therapeutic notions to see how far they preserve psychoanalytic values. Here we find that the aim of psychodynamic therapy is 'total reconstruction': any methods sighted below this aim are merely 'reparative'. In order of development, there are four levels of cooperation on the part of the patient, magic-craving, parentifying, self-reliant, and aspiring; and treatment must be adjusted accordingly. During treatment organized sequences of events are encountered which are either 'miscarried prevention" or miscarried repair', due to faulty 'emergency responses' of childhood, which in turn are signs of 'emergency dyscontrol'. These emergency reactions Rado seeks to bring under control. Emergency inhibitions are removed, so that there is generated in the patient an 'emotional matrix' dominated by 'welfare emotions' and controlled by 'adaptive insight'. This change is achieved by 'priming' and 'modifying'. Priming is simply 'holding' the patient at adult levels. But the patient must himself make an effort, must learn to understand himself better and practice new modes of performance based on new emotional skills. He is also prevented from repeating child reactions to the therapist by 'interceptive interpretation', during which process his self-confidence is deliberately bolstered up. Actual rage-provoking scenes, for example, must be reproduced in memory with the 'original cast', i.e., not displaced to the analyst. Interpretation however begins and ends with the patient's present day 'life-performance', involving a 'penetrating analysis of his life situation'. Provided the patient will practice the new modes, emotion will be adjusted to reason; and so we are left to presume that if he does, all will be well, or, in clinical terminology, that the patient will either be cured or have cured himself of his psychodynamic disorders.

It is to Rado's credit that he himself distinguishes between those methods and the teachings of psychoanalysis; first, when he maintains that he has developed a 'new' technique, and again when he admits that in treating 'parentifying treatment behavior' (a concept which seems to have some resemblance to the 'transference neurosis' of Freud) by means of priming, interceptive interpretation, exhortation and bolstering up, he is effecting a 'radical departure from the clinical technique'. To which it is perhaps sufficient to add that the effect of radical changes of this sort cannot be limited to their proximate action – they alter radically the rationale and course of psychoanalytic therapy, reducing it ultimately to the status of transference exploitation on an authoritarian level. The therapeutist may interpret to his heart's content in the most exemplary freudian fashion, but the moment he assumes the role of life mentor, he has forfeited his claim to be a freudian analyst. By comparison, the abstinence rules imposed by Freud in the case of certain neuroses and the more draconic 'activities' practiced in certain refractory cases by Ferenczi at one stage of his career are timid and tentative innovations. Priming and exhortations to the patient to practice new modes in his adult life may have on occasion excellent therapeutic effect (what psychotherapeutic device has not?) but by no stretch of the imagination do they qualify for the designation of 'psychoanalytic therapy'. For the matter of that it is open to any follower of Jung to maintain that, however freudian are some of his interpretations, Rado is still a good Jungian, differing in his psychotherapeutic ideology only by the use of the term 'life-performance' instead of the expression 'life-task' favored by Jung.

And this brings us to Rado's claim that his methods are 'new'. As far as can be judged from the details given in this volume, there is nothing new either in his psychodynamic theories or his psychotherapeutic methods. They have been held and practiced by eclectic psychiatrists and psychotherapeutists ever since it became the habit to mix a little bit of Freud with little bits of Jung and Adler (there is indeed more than a reminiscence of Adler in Rado's power psychology) together with anything else they fancy in a compost of theoretical views and psychotherapeutic practices. What is really new in Rado's psychology is the terminology he coins; and even that derives in part from neurological to say nothing of Jungian sources. As has been suggested, a good deal of this terminology consists of paraphrases of freudian concepts in terms of Rado's central assumptions which, as has also been suggested, are nothing if not commonplaces. However that may be, it is clearly no service to psychoanalytic psychology to confuse it with 'adaptational psychodynamics'. No doubt psychoanalysis has its share of omissions and inadequacies in theory; its psychotherapeutic virtues may be much slighter than is generally held or maintained by psychoanalysts themselves. (Rado was apparently encouraged to seek new pastures through dissatisfaction with the therapeutic results of pure psychoanalysis.) But all this notwithstanding, psychoanalysis does maintain certain basic principles and practices which are fundamentally different from the principles and practices held and adopted in other psychological fields of enquiry. There is therefore some consolation in the thought that by adopting the term 'adaptational psychodynamics', Rado has afforded both general reader and psychoanalytic student a simple means of distinguishing it finally and irrevocably from psychoanalysis.

References

Alexander, F. (1966). Sandor Rado: the adaptational theory. In *Psychoanalytic Pioneers*, ed. F. Alexander, S. Eisenstein, and M. Grotjahn, pp. 240–248. New York: Basic Books.

Arlow, J. (1991). *Being a candidate at the New York Psychoanalytic Institute in the forties*. Paper presented at the New York Psychoanalytic Society in honor of the 80th anniversary of the Society, November 1.

Burnham, J. (1983). *Jelliffe: American Psychoanalyst and Physician*. Chicago and London: University of Chicago Press.

Cooper, A. (1982). *Psychoanalysis at 100: beginning of maturity*. Presidential address delivered at the meeting of the American Psychoanalytic Association, New York, December.

Daniels, G. (1971). The history of the Association for Psychoanalytic Medicine and the Columbia Psychoanalytic Clinic. *Bulletin of the Association for Psychoanalytic Medicine*, October, December, May issues.

Daniels, G., and Rado, S. (1956). *Changing Concepts of Psychoanalytic Medicine*. New York: Grune & Stratton.

Davidman, H. (1964). The contributions of Sandor Rado to psychodynamic science. In *Science and Psychoanalysis*, ed. J. H. Masserman, pp. 17–38. New York: Grune & Stratton.

Eckhardt, M. H. (1978). Organizational schisms in American psychoanalysis. In *American Psychoanalysis: Origins and Development*, ed. J. Quen and E. Carlson, pp. 141–161. New York: Brunner/Mazel.

Ferenczi, S., and Rank, O. (1986). *The Development of Psychoanalysis*. Madison, CT: International Universities Press.

Fine, R. (1973). *The Development of Freud's Thought*. New York: Jason Aronson.

Freud, S. (1914). Narcissism: an introduction. In *Collected Papers*. New York: Basic Books, 1958.

_____ (1917). *A General Introduction to Psychoanalysis*. New York: Horace Liveright, 1935.

_____ (1920). *Beyond the Pleasure Principle*. London: International Psychoanalytic Press, 1922.

_____ (1933). *New Introductory Lectures*. New York: W. W. Norton.

_____ (1940). *An Outline of Psychoanalysis*. New York: W. W. Norton, 1949.

Frosch, J. (1991). The New York Psychoanalytic civil war. *Journal of the American Psychoanalytic Association* 39(4):1037–1064.

Gay, P. (1988). *Freud: A Life for Our Time*. New York: W. W. Norton.

Gaylin, W. (1973). Rado the teacher. *Bulletin of the Association for Psychoanalytic Medicine* 12: 10, 19.

Gero, G. (1973). The years in Berlin. *Bulletin of the Association for Psychoanalytic Medicine* 12:4. Special issue.

Glover, E. (1957). Book review of Rado's *Collected Papers*. *Psychoanalytic Quarterly* 26(2):251–258.

Goldman, G. S., and Shapiro, D., eds. (1966). *Developments in Psychoanalysis at Columbia University: Based on Proceedings of the 20th Anniversary Conference of the Columbia University Clinic for Training and Research*, pp. 89–275. New York: Hofner.

Grosskurth, P. (1991). *The Secret Ring: Freud's Inner Circle and the Politics of Psychoanalysis*. Reading, MA: Addison-Wesley.

Hale, N. G., Jr. (1971). *Freud amid the Americans*. New York: Oxford University Press.

Kandel, E. R. (1979). Psychotherapy and the single synapse: the impact of psychiatric thought on neurobiological research. *The New England Journal of Medicine* 301(19):1037.

Kardiner, A., Karush, A., and Ovesey, L. (1959a). A methodological study of Freudian theory. 1. Basic concepts. 2. The libido theory. *The Journal of Nervous and Mental Diseases* 129:133–143.

_____ (1959b). Narcissism, bisexuality and the dual instinct theory. *The Journal of Nervous and Mental Diseases* 129:207–221.

_____ (1959c). The structural hypothesis, the problem of anxiety, and post-Freudian ego psychology. *The Journal of Nervous and Mental Diseases* 129:341–356.

Karush, A. (1966). An adaptational approach to psychic representations, perception and psychic apparatus. In *Developments in Psychoanalysis at Columbia University: Based on Proceedings of the 20th Anniversary Conference of the Columbia University Clinic for Training and Research*, ed. G. S. Goldman and D. Shapiro, pp. 3–22.

Kernberg, O. (1993). The current status of psychoanalysis. *Journal of the American Psychoanalytic Association* 41(1):45–62.

Klein, G. (1973). Two theories or one? *Bulletin of the Menninger Clinic* 13(2):102–132.

Kurzweil, E. (1989). *The Freudians: A Contemporary Perspective*. New Haven: Yale University Press.

Miller, L. (1991a). Brain and self: toward a neuropsychodynamic model of ego autonomy and personality. *Journal of the American Academy of Psychoanalysis* 19(2):213–234.

———— (1991b). On aphasia at 100: the neuropsychodynamic legacy of Sigmund Freud. *Psychoanalytic Review* 78(3):365–378.

———— (1992). The primitive personality and the organic personality: a neuropsychodynamic model for evaluation and treatment. *Psychoanalytic Psychology* 9(1):93–109.

———— (1993). Freud's brain: towards a unified neuropsychodynamic model of personality and psychotherapy. *Journal of the American Academy of Psychoanalysis* 21(2): 183–188.

Rado, S. (1956). *Psychoanalysis and Behavior: The Collected Papers of Sandor Rado*. New York and London: Grune & Stratton, two vols.

———— (1958). From the metapsychological ego to the bio-cultural action-self. *Journal of Psychology* 46:279–285.

———— (1960). Observations on the development of psychoanalytic theory. In *Current Approaches to Psychoanalysis*, ed. P. H. Hoch and J. Zubin, pp. 3–12. New York: Grune & Stratton.

———— (1969). *Adaptational Psychodynamics: Motivation and Control*, ed. J. Jameson and H. Klein. New York: Science House.

Roazen, P. (1992a). *Helene Deutsch: A Psychoanalyst's Life*. New Brunswick, NJ: Transaction.

———— (1992b). *Freud and His Followers*. New York: Da Capo.

Roose, S. P., Vaughan, S. C., Marshall, R. D., and MacKinnon, R. A. (in manuscript). *Current Psychotherapy Research Methodology Applied to Psychoanalysis*. New York: Columbia Psychoanalytic Center.

Roose, S. P., Vaughan, S. C., Marshall, R. D., and MacKinnon, R. A. (1994). *Current Psychotherapy Research Methodology Applied to Psychoanalysis: Feasibility Study*. Unpublished Study.

Swerdloff, B. (1980). Oral history among psychoanalysts: a personal experience. *Bulletin of the Association for Psychoanalytic Medicine* 19:44–49.

———— (1986). A historical portrait of Sandor Rado. *Bulletin of the Association for Psychoanalytic Medicine* 25 (¾):118–126.

Wheeler, W. M. (1939). *Essays in Philosophical Biology*. Cambridge, MA: Harvard University Press.

Young-Bruehl, E. (1988). *Anna Freud: A Biography*. New York: Summit.

Credits

The authors gratefully acknowledge permission to reprint material from the following sources:

Text from the statement of philosophy of the Columbia University Oral History Research Office; used by permission.

Text from the oral history record of Dr. Jacob A. Arlow at the Columbia University Oral History Research Office, used by permission of Dr. Arlow.

Text from the oral history record of Dr. Sandor Rado at the Columbia University Oral History Research Office; used by permission of Peter T. Rado.

"Observations on the Development of Psychoanalytic Theory," by Sandor Rado, in *Current Approaches to Psychoanalysis*, edited by Paul H. Hoch and Joseph Zubin. Copyright © 1960 by Grune & Stratton, Inc,. and used by permission.

"Book Review of Sandor Rado's *Psychoanalysis of Behavior: Collected Papers*," in *The Psychoanalytic Quarterly*, 1957, vol. 26, no. 2, pp. 251–258. Copyright © 1958 by *The Psychoanalytic Quarterly* and used by permission.

Freud's letters to Rado. Copyright © 1995 A. W. Freud et al., by arrangement with Mark Paterson & Associates.

Index